KU-186-710

Volume 1
THE ENVIRONMENT
◆ Prof. Dato' Dr Sham Sani
Universiti Kebangsaan Malaysia

Volume 2
PLANTS
◆ Dr E. Soepadmo
Forest Research Institute of Malaysia (FRIM)

Volume 3
ANIMALS
◆ Prof. Dr Yong Hoi Sen
Universiti Malaya

Volume 4
EARLY HISTORY
◆ Prof. Dato' Dr Nik Hassan Shuhaimi Nik Abdul Rahman
Universiti Kebangsaan Malaysia

Volume 5
ARCHITECTURE
◆ Chen Voon Fee
Architectural Consulting Services

Volume 6
THE SEAS
◆ Prof. Dr Ong Jin Eong and Prof. Dr Gong Wooi Khoon
Universiti Sains Malaysia

Volume 7
EARLY MODERN HISTORY
[1800–1940]
◆ Dr Cheah Boon Kheng
Universiti Sains Malaysia (retired)

Volume 8
PERFORMING ARTS
◆ Prof. Dr Ghulam-Sarwar Yousof
Universiti Malaya

Volume 9
LANGUAGES AND LITERATURE
◆ Prof. Dato' Dr Asmah Haji Omar
Universiti Pendidikan Sultan Idris

Volume 10
GOVERNMENT AND POLITICS
[1940–THE PRESENT]
◆ Prof. Dr Zakaria Haji Ahmad
Universiti Kebangsaan Malaysia

Volume 11
RELIGIONS AND BELIEFS
◆ Prof. Dr M. Kamal Hassan and Dr Ghazali bin Basri
International Islamic University Malaysia and Institute for the Study of Islamic Sciences

Volume 12
CRAFTS AND THE VISUAL ARTS
◆ Datuk Syed Ahmad Jamal
Artist

Volume 13
THE ECONOMY
◆ Prof. Dr Osman Rani Hassan
Universiti Pendidikan Sultan Idris

Volume 14
PEOPLES AND TRADITIONS
◆ Prof. Dato' Dr Hood Salleh
Universiti Kebangsaan Malaysia

Volume 15
THE MALAY SULTANATES
◆ Datuk Prof. Emeritus Dr Mohd Taib Osman and Prof. Emeritus Dato' Dr Khoo Kay Kim
Universiti Malaya

THE ENCYCLOPEDIA OF MALAYSIA

PERFORMING ARTS

PATRON

TUN DR MAHATHIR MOHAMAD

EDITORIAL ADVISORY BOARD

The Encyclopedia of Malaysia was first conceived by Editions Didier Millet and Datin Paduka Marina Mahathir. The Editorial Advisory Board, made up of distinguished figures drawn from academic and public life, was constituted in March 1994. The project was publicly announced in October that year, and eight months later the first sponsors were in place. In 1996, the structure of the content was agreed; later that year the appointment of Volume Editors and the commissioning of authors were substantially complete, and materials for the work were beginning to flow in. By early 2004, nine volumes were completed for publication. Upon completion, the series will consist of 15 volumes.

The Publishers wish to thank the following people for their contribution to the first seven volumes:

Dato' Seri Anwar Ibrahim,
who acted as Chairman of the Editorial Advisory Board;
and
Tan Sri Dato' Dr Noordin Sopiee
Tan Sri Datuk Augustine S. H. Ong
the late Tan Sri Zain Azraai
Datuk Datin Paduka Zakiah Hanum bt Abdul Hamid
Datin Noor Azlina Yunus

EDITORIAL TEAM

Series Editorial Team

PUBLISHER
Didier Millet

GENERAL MANAGER
Charles Orwin

PROJECT COORDINATOR
Marina Mahathir

EDITORIAL DIRECTOR
Timothy Auger

PROJECT MANAGER
Martin Cross

PUBLISHING MANAGER
Dianne Buerger

PRODUCTION MANAGER
Sin Kam Cheong

DESIGN DIRECTOR
Tan Seok Lui

EDITORS
Ameena Siddiqi
Stephen Chin
Shoba Devan
E. Ravinderen a/l Kandiappan
Fong Peng Khuan
Tanja Jonid
Yvonne Lee
Ridzwan Othman

DESIGNERS
Kevin SJ Francis
Lawrence Kok
Yusri bin Din

Volume Editorial Team

EDITOR
Shoba Devan
Sumitra Visvanathan

DESIGNER
Kevin SJ Francis

ILLUSTRATORS
A. Kasim Abas
Anuar bin Abdul Rahim
Chai Kah Yune
Chong Kah Leong
Lee Sin Bee
Lim Joo
Tan Hong Yew
Yap Eng Huat
Yeap Kok Chien

SPONSORS

The Encyclopedia of Malaysia was made possible thanks to the generous and enlightened support of the following organizations:

- DRB-HICOM BERHAD
- MAHKOTA TECHNOLOGIES SDN BHD
- MALAYAN UNITED INDUSTRIES BERHAD
- MALAYSIA NATIONAL INSURANCE BERHAD
- MINISTRY OF EDUCATION MALAYSIA
- NEW STRAITS TIMES PRESS (MALAYSIA) BERHAD
- TRADEWINDS CORPORATION BERHAD
- PETRONAS BERHAD
- UEM WORLD BERHAD
- STAR PUBLICATIONS (MALAYSIA) BERHAD
- SUNWAY GROUP
- TENAGA NASIONAL BERHAD
- UNITED OVERSEAS BANK GROUP
- YAYASAN ALBUKHARY
- YTL CORPORATION BERHAD

PNB GROUP OF COMPANIES
- PERMODALAN NASIONAL BERHAD
- NCB HOLDINGS BERHAD
- GOLDEN HOPE PLANTATIONS BERHAD
- SIME DARBY BERHAD
- MALAYAN BANKING BERHAD
- MNI HOLDINGS BERHAD
- PERNEC CORPORATION BERHAD

Published by Archipelago Press *an imprint of* Editions Didier Millet Pte Ltd
121, Telok Ayer Street, #03-01, Singapore 068590
Tel: 65-6324 9260 Fax. 65-6324 9261 E-mail: edm@edmbooks.com.sg

First published 2004
Reprinted 2005

Editions Didier Millet, Kuala Lumpur Office:
25, Jalan Pudu Lama, 50200 Kuala Lumpur, Malaysia
Tel: 03-2031 3805 Fax: 03-2031 6298 E-mail: edmbooks@edmbooks.com.my

Colour separation by Singapore Sang Choy Colour Separation Pte Ltd
Printed by Star Standard Industries (Pte) Ltd
ISBN 981-3018-56-9

Note for Readers
Some dates in this book are followed by the letters CE or BCE, which mean 'Common Era' and 'Before Common Era', respectively. These terms are synonymous with AD Anno Domini (in the year of our Lord) and BC, which means 'Before Christ'.
Translations of titles are provided where applicable.

CONTRIBUTORS

Ahmad Sarji
Badan Warisan Malaysia

Ang Bee Saik
Drama director

Assoc. Prof. Dr Ariff Ahmad
Universiti Malaya

Prof. Dr Ghulam-Sarwar Yousof
Universiti Malaya

Joseph Gonzales
Akademi Seni Kebangsaan

Roselina Khir
Universiti Malaya

Adjunct Prof. Dr Patricia Matusky
Grand Valley State University/
Central Michingan University

Mew Chang Tsing
RiverGrass Dance Academy

Prof. Dr Mohd Anis Md Nor
Universiti Malaya

Assoc. Prof. Dr Jacqueline Pugh-Kitingan
Universiti Malaysia Sabah

Prof. Dr Clifford Sather
University of Helsinki

Soon Choon Mee
New Era College

Prof. Dr Tan Sooi Beng
Universiti Sains Malaysia

Teoh Ming Wah
Writer

Premalatha Thiagarajan
Dance teacher

Rina Tung Pooi Ching
Universiti Malaya

Raja Morgan Veerappan
Abinaya Shetra Dance Company

THE ENCYCLOPEDIA OF
MALAYSIA

Volume 8

PERFORMING ARTS

Volume Editor
Prof. Dr Ghulam-Sarwar Yousof
Universiti Malaya

ARCHIPELAGO PRESS

Contents

Bangsawan was a popular theatre form in the 19th and 20th centuries and laid the foundation for the Malay cinema industry.

FAR RIGHT: Dance movement from the highly elegant Mak Yong folk theatre.

PREVIOUS PAGE: The *pohon beringin* puppet symbolizes the tree of life and marks the beginning and end of a Wayang Kulit performance.

HALF TITLE PAGE: Awang Batil performers play the *serunai* during their storytelling performances.

Introduction

Aspects of Malaysia's performing arts are the result of adaptation of foreign cultures. Zapin, for instance, reflects Islamic influences.

Over the past two millennia or more, indigenous elements as well as foreign influences from both the East and the West have shaped and reshaped the culture of Malaysia. These influences reached the Malay Peninsula from various cultural regions—the Middle and Near East, South Asia, East Asia as well as from within Southeast Asia. Furthermore, they came from almost all major Asian religions—Hinduism, Buddhism, Chinese folk religions and Islam.

A mosaic of performing arts

The impact of these influences upon the Malaysian way of life, as well as, consequently, upon the performing arts, was manifested in the development of new religious and social frameworks, new mythologies, and the development of specific music, dance and theatre genres. The repertoire of traditional theatre saw a great expansion through new literary sources and in many ways the art forms began to manifest diverse cultural values and systems of aesthetics. As a result of this fusion of cultures, today there exists in Malaysia a highly complex mosaic of theatre, music, and dance forms.

Elementary performance genres

Elementary indigenous performances include Orang Asli music and dance, the performances of pre-modern communities of Sabah and Sarawak and the Malay storytelling genres—Awang Batil, Selampit, Tarik Selampit—in which plots inherited from the past are developed through improvisation and embellishment with or without musical accompaniment. Styles that are ritualistic in character, typified by Main Puteri and Bagih, tend to be shamanistic as well. These genres are believed to have developed before the 7th century. In the most elaborate of these, elements of dance and music are combined with drama and a state of trance is a vital feature. Despite the passage of time, such ritual forms of proto-theatre continue to be highly important in rural areas even if in some cases they appear to be contrary to Islam, Malaysia's official religion. Through the storyteller and the ritual practitioner, participants in performances remain in connection with their community's mythical or legendary past. Despite social changes resulting from modernization, the ancient examples of earliest cultural forms have survived, for they continue to serve an obvious need.

Some folk traditions such as the Wayang Kulit are being maintained, with adaptation to changing social circumstances.

Folk traditions are again manifested in diverse forms—several varieties of shadow play (Wayang Kulit), a wide range of dance, vocal and instrumental music, and dance theatre forms such as Mak Yong, Menora and Mek Mulung. Artistically, these are more developed than the elementary forms and are among the most complex and sophisticated of Malay performance genres. Again, the precise origins of these probably ancient forms are uncertain. But even if the original context no longer exists they continue to be maintained, if only by small numbers of troupes.

Western influences began arriving in Melaka with the coming of the Portuguese and Dutch, paving the way for the development of certain dance and music forms. A greater Western impact upon the performing arts, however, came in the 19th century following the spread of British and the more recent, seemingly all-pervasive, American influences particularly through the electronic media and the cinema. One result has been the introduction of purely Western visual and performing art forms such as Western drama, dance and music. Based on these forms, there has been a proliferation of locally developed contemporary art forms. Since the 1950s, parallel to developments in the West, new trends in drama, new ideologies such as absurdism, as well as new 'experimental' art forms have continued to make their appearance. The results of such influences have not always been positive. However, the trend to imitate the West goes on, and the process of change continues. Innovations will undoubtedly continue to come about, while the old struggle to survive, are re-fashioned, or participate in some sort of fusion with the new.

The old and the new

In physical terms the history of Malaysian performing arts is demonstrated in the shift from village performances to those now held in the Istana Budaya (National Theatre), the Dewan Filharmonic Petronas, cinema complexes and other plush performance spaces. Also strongly evident is the participation by institutions of higher learning, particularly in research and development, with an attempt to stimulate interest in the traditions of the past.

These developments reflect not just the changes the country has experienced over the past two millennia. More importantly, they are indicative of inherent cultural realities. The beginnings saw the fusion that came with the introduction, upon an animistic base, of foreign belief systems and the development of genres that became what is loosely defined as 'Malay'. This situation continued from around the 5th and 6th centuries to the arrival of Islam, for which there are two possible dates—evidenced by the Terengganu Stone, dated 1303 CE, and the introduction of Islam into the Melaka Sultanate in the 15th century. A new kind of fusion then began to take place, resulting in the development of what eventually came to be the 'Malay' tradition based upon Islam. This was to prevail until colonization and the introduction of Western models of performing arts, particularly following World War II.

The second wave of contact with foreign cultures came in the wake of the arrival of large communities of peoples from East Asia and South Asia into the Malay Peninsula from the time of the British arrival in the 19th century. In some instances these communities brought with them their own traditions of performance arts: the Chinese puppet theatre and opera in various dialects, indigenous Javanese and Javanese-Islamic performing arts, those of the Thais, Bharata Natyam, Carnatic music, Bhangra and the ubiquitous Hindustani cinema with its accompanying popular music forms. Following this phase, race or community-based performing traditions have also begun to evolve into, in some sense, a new tradition that may be described as truly 'Malaysian' in character both on stage and screen.

Above and Left: Traditions of other Asian cultures, such as Chinese opera and Indian classical dance, were brought by immigrants in the 19th and 20th centuries.

Traditional performing arts and diverse world-views

The traditional performing arts of the communities in Malaysia have always reflected the particular world-views of these communities. Following the integration of the communities there has been total absorption or localization of some of these genres. Wayang Kulit stands out as a good example. In other instances certain genres have seen adaptation to suit the new environment. The multiethnic character of performers is quite evident; for instance, Menora, originally based in animism and Thai-Buddhism, is now increasingly multiracial in character. In some locations the separate worlds—that of the village (*kampung*), the court (*istana*) and the new urban setting—have remained somewhat, though not altogether, cut off from each other despite the winds of change that have been felt for decades now. At other locations greater cultural fusion may be seen, with the shift of performances from villages to towns and from the palaces of the past to the cultural centres of the present. Modernization has introduced many changes both in style and content—the result of the inevitable impact of new arts forms, technologies and value systems. Where there is a clear breach with the past or where these distinctions have become blurred, no matter how

These Menora dancers from the 1970s illustrate that some genres of traditional arts have remained unchanged in content and style.

subtly, one senses a new urgency to revive artistic forms, if only as cultural symbols.

Renewal of tradition and creation of new forms

The old beliefs such as those connected with the cosmos on one level and with the spirit or soul on another continue to play a part in the performing arts. In these changing situations and new contexts the traditional roles assigned to the theatre have not been totally changed. Rather there has been renewal as the new traditions were planted on those of the ancient past. The earliest genres of ritual theatre, storytelling, dance, and music manifest these qualities strongly, whether these come from the Malay traditions, the indigenous communities of Sabah and Sarawak, the Chinese (as in the case of the puppet theatre style), and from the lesser communities in neighbouring territories including southern Thailand and Java, exemplified respectively by Menora, and Barongan and Kuda Kepang. These same beliefs are reflected in ritual theatre—Bagih, Main Puteri, Mak Yong and Wayang Kulit.

Top: A 1897 performance of Bangsawan theatre, which laid the foundation for the Malay film industry.

Bottom: One of the last Terinai dance masters of the 20th century.

Tarian Lilin (Candle Dance) is an example of new versions that have evolved from innovations to traditional Malay dance genres.

The imported traditions have been transplanted onto the rich Malaysian soil in interesting ways. The Asyik and Joget Gamelan dances, Kuda Kepang and Zapin as well as various forms of vocal and instrumental music reflect direct Islamic or Javanese influences. Nobat music continues to play a vital role in Malay court ceremonies, reflecting the functions of the *naubat* in Indo-Islamic courts. Similarly, the strong impact of South Asian Hindu and Buddhist elements, duly transformed, is widely evident in the several varieties of Wayang Kulit. In almost all instances, transformation and adaptation have, in fact, been important features in traditional Malay performing arts.

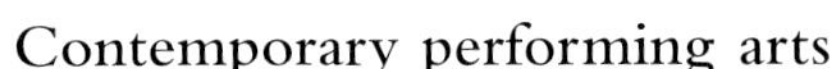

Contemporary performing arts

While tradition continues to be maintained there is a vibrant scene in the contemporary performing arts, developed in the early decades of the 20th century as a result of Western influence upon the education system and the way of life. A sizeable corpus of dramatic literature in all major Malaysian languages has developed, with parallel developments in music and dance. Today, not only is this sense of vibrancy and urgency reflected in the new physical facilities, it is also evident in the expanding of courses and offerings of academic programmes in local universities.

Malaysian musicians such as Ella (pictured), have initiated their own style by combining ethnic, Western and other elements.

Introduced during colonial times, modern drama has all but succeeded the once popular urban

A humorous view of traditional Malaysian theatre by popular cartoonist Lat.

Bangsawan theatre which in its own day was regarded as avant-garde. More importantly, Bangsawan gave way to the art of the Malay film. Indeed the Malay cinema industry, in its early days borrowing much from the Indian cinema, has developed its own identity, and continues to consolidate some of its gains while creating a niche for itself in regional and international terms, particularly with the kind of experimentation that is going on.

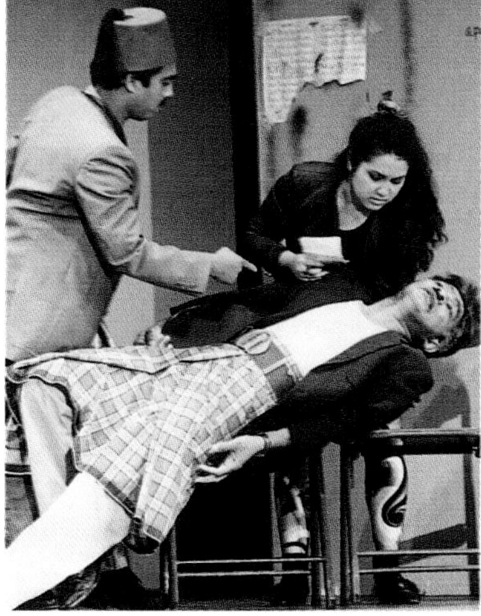

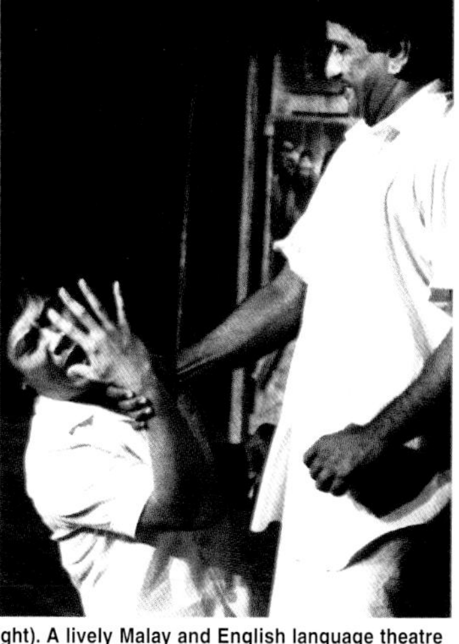

Scenes from the plays *Raja Lawak* (left) and *The Cord* (right). A lively Malay and English language theatre scene is enhanced by the offering of academic programmes in performing arts in Malaysian universities.

The music scene has changed much with the rise of new types of orchestral music, including Western and Chinese, contemporary art music and recorded popular music. Similarly, new directions have been developed in contemporary dance, with several choreographers making significant changes and dramatic innovations, inspired by indigenous as well as international traditions in an increasingly borderless world. Dance is also characterized by a new kind of fusion that could not even be imagined just half a century ago at the time of Malaysia's independence.

Recording labels from the early 20th century.

The zest for change, the search for identity and roots, the need to preserve heritage while also moving forward in creative ways, have been spearheaded by a new generation of performers as well as by local scholars. Research and documentation of traditional heritage in the performing arts have become focused. New opportunities have become increasingly available for the arts to develop in significant ways, and the performing arts forms—traditional as well as modern—are receiving unprecedented international attention. Locally, greater attention to the traditional arts forms, as well as new innovative productions, has brought the performing arts closer to the community than ever before.

Challenges

The overall picture is exciting and vibrant, with the new and old mixing in interesting ways, but there are issues to be addressed. One is the need for preservation, conservation, documentation and transmission of the older traditions to prevent their decline and ultimate demise. There is also the necessity to create ample employment opportunities in the arts, and problems connected with the assurance of quality, particularly in modern productions. Several factors—economic, religious and social—may be cited as possible agents of decline or loss of popularity in the performing arts. Government policies, including that of censorship, have undoubtedly led to the dampening of creativity and originality, as well as the acceptance of mediocrity. It is apparent that, compared with the activities in some of the neighbouring countries, more needs to be done for the arts. A more favourable environment needs to be created for the arts to flourish, while on their part, the artistes need to re-examine their own roles vis-à-vis the new realities. The potential in Malaysian performing arts has certainly not been fully exploited; there has not been the kind of blossoming, following independence, that is manifest in the fine arts or architecture, for instance. These issues need to be addressed so that while progress is made towards the future and the performing arts develop in important and creative ways, the heritage of the past does not vanish.

Contemporary dance in the 21st century is a manifestation of cultural fusion and creativity.

Chronology of Performing Arts in Malaysia

Pre-7th Century

- Bagih
- Main Puteri
- Ulik Mayang
- Gebiah
- Orang Asli dance, music and healing ceremonies
- Sabah and Sarawak dances
- Vocal music of Sabah and Sarawak

7/8th–14th Century

- Selampit
- Awang Batil
- Tarik Selampit
- Wayang Kulit Siam
- Mak Yong
- Mek Mulung
- Zapin

15th–19th Century

- Wayang Kulit Gedek
- Wayang Kulit Melayu
- Wayang Kulit Purwa
- Joget
- Inang
- Asli
- Keroncong
- Portuguese music
- Gamelan Pahang and Joget Gamelan
- Asyik dance and music
- Terinai
- Dikir Barat
- Dabus
- Kuda Kepang
- Hadrah
- Borea
- Nobat
- Bangsawan

20th Century

- Chinese puppets
- Randai
- Menora
- Bharata Natyam
- Odissi
- Kathakali
- Bhangra
- South Indian folk dances
- Jikey
- Chinese opera
- Dondang Sayang
- Ronggeng
- Malay drama
- English drama
- Chinese drama
- Tamil drama
- Chinese orchestra
- Contemporary art music
- Popular music
- Contemporary dance
- Malay films
- Malay television dramas

Origins and history of performing arts in Malaysia

A foundation of indigenous performing art forms in Malaysia has been enriched by other forms that have either been totally imported, or have developed locally through inspiration from foreign cultures. The various forms of traditional theatre—indigenous arts, puppet theatre, dance theatre and opera—are further influenced by the diverse dance and music styles in Malaysia.

Early Malay theatre developed out of animistic beliefs, and involved healing rituals to cure possession by malevolent spirits. This ritual pictured features a woman said to be possessed by the spirit of a tiger.

Purely local
One of Mak Yong's unique features is its almost totally indigenous repertoire. This is based entirely on myths, the origins of which cannot be traced beyond the Kelantanese heartland of Mak Yong. 'Dewa Muda', the original Mak Yong story, suggests the genre's origins.

Original forms

The diversity of Malaysian performing arts means that origins are not easily established. Some of the earliest forms of Malay music, dance and theatre have ancient origins. Bagih and Main Puteri, two styles of healing theatre, developed out of indigenous animistic beliefs and shamanism. They are rooted in the earliest layer of the Malay-Polynesian belief system, which is maintained by the Orang Asli. It explains disease as deriving from possession by malevolent spirits, or *semangat* (loss of soul) (see 'Belief systems of traditional theatre'), and may be cured by healing theatre conducted by a shaman.

Bagih, Main Puteri, Ulik Mayang, the Orang Asli's Belian ceremony (see 'Healing performances') and some native dances of Sabah and Sarawak share common beliefs and performance elements. Such connections make it all the more likely that they derive from an ancient common origin.

External influences on these indigenous performing traditions are so strong that they often obscure what is in fact local. Indian, Middle Eastern, Chinese and Western are the principal influences, which began arriving about 2000 years ago at the beginning of the Common Era. Existing indigenous elements served to alter these imported cultural features, or to bring about fusion. This is evident in the varieties of traditional performing art forms such as Wayang Kulit Siam (see 'Wayang Kulit Siam: The Kelantan shadow play'), Wayang Kulit Gedek (see 'Wayang Kulit Gedek, Melayu and Purwa') and Menora (see 'Menora').

Cultural fusion and adaptation

Religious and cultural influences from the Indian sub-continent brought into Southeast Asia new forms of theatre and major contributions in repertoire, music, dance and aesthetic concepts. They also included highly significant ritual elements. In this, the shadow play appears most prominent. Its theatre consecration (*buka panggung*) rituals, invocations and mythology feature animistic, Hindu and Buddhist elements. While the precise origins of the shadow play cannot be adequately established (see 'Malay shadow theatre in Southeast Asia'), regional similarities indicate that Malaysian styles of Wayang Kulit developed from Javanese and Thai forms.

Mythology in traditional theatre is principally Javanese, but also indigenous. Mak Yong, which is amongst the oldest traditional Malay theatre forms, shows the pervasiveness of indigenous elements in the face of external influences. Of the genre's 12

Animism

Animism forged the earliest theatre such as Main Puteri. It fuses shamanism with performance elements. Shadow play (Wayang Kulit, pictured, left) and the Mak Yong dance theatre (pictured, right) also have shamanistic elements.

Hindu/Buddhist

The shadow puppet theatre developed from multifarious cultural and religious influences.

Middle Eastern musical influences are seen in the use of such instruments as the *gambus* or *o'ud.*

'classical' stories, only one, 'Anak Raja Gondang', clearly derives from abroad. It is known in Cambodia, Tibet, as well as Thailand (there entitled 'Sang Thong'), and seems to have had an impact on the Kelantanese performance tradition.

Malay traditional dances and dance theatre styles feature complex Indian dance movements, but unlike the Cambodian, Thai and Indonesian styles, the original elements have been so diluted that even the meanings of gestures are no longer known. Dilution is also seen in music and make-up. Thus, Malaysian dance demonstrates a creative fusion of elements from the original folk culture and those that have been borrowed.

A striking resemblance to Middle Eastern dance styles is seen in the movements of Zapin (see 'Zapin'), Rodat, Hadrah and Borea (see 'Borea'). Middle Eastern musical influences are also seen in the use of the three-stringed lute (*rebab*) in Mak Yong, in Mak Yong singing styles, and in other performing arts such as *gambus* music. *Zikir* (religious) chanting, which exists in several styles, is Middle Eastern, and has remained distinguishably so, although in their present styles Malay zikir forms are no longer religious in character or function. Kuda Kepang (a hobbyhorse dance) and Dabus, a theatre form combining music, dance and martial art, came about as a result of Middle Eastern inspiration or Javanese origination. In all instances, while not having an altogether Malaysian origin, these genres have developed local characteristics as a result of cultural fusion and adaptation.

Recent connections

Nineteenth-century Javanese immigration into Johor introduced Javanese theatre styles such as Barongan, a dance theatre using animal masks, as well as styles of gamelan. The gamelan accompanies the Joget Gamelan dance (see 'Asyik and Joget Gamelan'), which is unique to Terengganu. The Randai theatre style and *taklempong* music (see 'Randai') reached Negeri Sembilan with the movement of Minangkabau communities into that state. By the end of the 19th century, Bangsawan theatre, an offshoot of the Hindustani Parsi theatre from India, was first performed in Penang (see 'Bangsawan and Jikey operatic theatre'). With it, the urban popular theatre came into being. Bangsawan gave rise to Sandiwara, which used complete scripts and realistic settings, and thence created modern Malay drama in the 1950s which was modelled after naturalistic Western drama. In the half century since then, Malay drama and theatre evolved in keeping with various styles, some direct imitations of Western drama, others fusing Western and indigenous elements.

Throughout history, Malaysian performing arts have been the vibrant products of dynamic syncretism, a process that is continually evolving.

Folk traditions
Most Malay performing arts have folk origins. Others, such as Terinai dance and music, Tari Asyik (above) and the Nobat orchestra, developed in the courts. In Malaysia, the folk tradition of performing arts—whether music, dance or theatre—is more significant than the court tradition because it is more pervasive and has a wider range.

LEFT: A long history of immigration has significantly enriched performing art forms in Malaysia. Barongan developed from 19th-century Javanese immigration into Johor.

Islamic/Middle Eastern

Middle Eastern influence in Malaysian performing arts is evident in Hadrah, a form of musical theatre.

Javanese

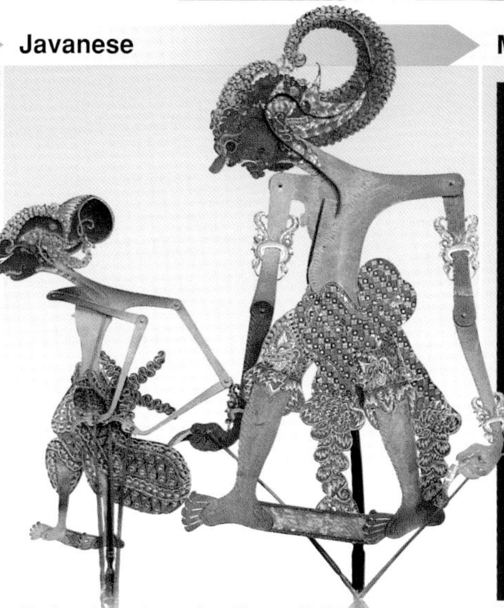

Shadow play styles such as Wayang Kulit Purwa were brought in by Javanese immigrants in the 19th century.

Modern

More recent performances feature efforts to blend Western elements into traditional Asian styles.

Belief systems of traditional theatre

Traditional Malay theatre is derived from a strong animistic base coloured with influences from religions and cultures which entered the Malay Peninsula from Asia and the Middle East at various times from about the 1st century CE. These genres not only provided entertainment, but also fulfilled a range of ritualistic purposes.

The origins of the Mak Yong dance theatre are linked to the spiritual realm, which renders it a mystical art form. Theories abound, but two main beliefs are that it originated through Semar, a Javanese god, and his two sons or from dance movements inspired by Mak Hiang the rice goddess.

A Semar Chronology

Javanese origination / Malaysian adaptation

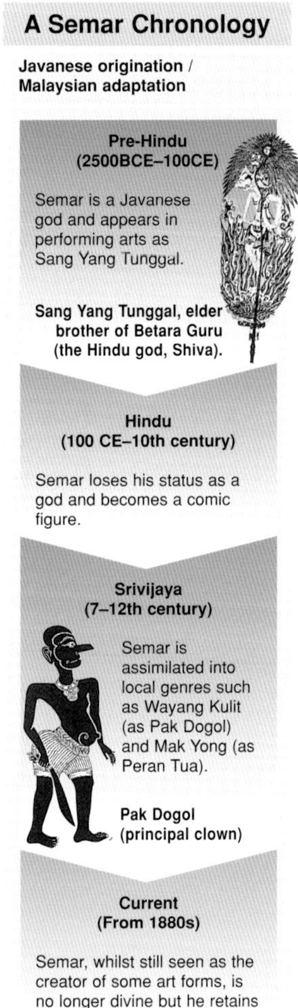

Pre-Hindu (2500BCE–100CE)

Semar is a Javanese god and appears in performing arts as Sang Yang Tunggal.

Sang Yang Tunggal, elder brother of Betara Guru (the Hindu god, Shiva).

Hindu (100 CE–10th century)

Semar loses his status as a god and becomes a comic figure.

Srivijaya (7–12th century)

Semar is assimilated into local genres such as Wayang Kulit (as Pak Dogol) and Mak Yong (as Peran Tua).

Pak Dogol (principal clown)

Current (From 1880s)

Semar, whilst still seen as the creator of some art forms, is no longer divine but he retains his performing arts roles.

Basic concepts

In traditional Malay performance culture, theatre is staged for a variety of ritualistic purposes, including *sembah guru* (the salutation of teachers), *semah angin* (adjustment of the 'wind') and the recall or strengthening of the soul (*semangat*). In this respect, three principal indigenous concepts have a direct bearing upon traditional theatre.

These are, firstly, the belief in a host of gods, spirits and other invisible beings—beneficent and malevolent including those responsible for causing diseases; secondly, the idea of an all-embracing vital substance, or anima, sometimes referred to as 'soul' and known among the Malays as semangat, which is believed to be present in all living things and in objects usually regarded as inanimate; and thirdly, the concept of *angin*, literally 'wind', but in the context of traditional theatre having a range of other meanings.

Gods, spirits and other invisible beings

Ancient myths and legends in Peninsular Malaysia trace the origins of traditional theatre directly to gods, spirits and other invisible beings. This imbues traditional theatre genres with an aura of mysticism, and renders the theatre a spiritual art. These beliefs are derived from a fusion of animism, Hinduism, Buddhism and Islam—influences which have been so closely interfused that it is almost impossible to extricate the individual strands.

The most important of these invisible beings is Semar, the ancient pre-Hindu Javanese deity. The role of Semar was brought with other Javanese cultural features to the Malay Peninsula, possibly around the time of the Srivijaya empire in the 10th century CE. Semar, in different guises, is no longer godly but continues to play an important role in Mak Yong dance theatre (see 'Mak Yong: Ancient folk theatre') and Wayang Kulit Siam shadow theatre (see 'Wayang Kulit Siam: The Kelantan shadow play'). In Wayang Kulit Siam, he is the principal clown, Pak Dogol, while in Mak Yong he appears as Peran Tua, the older and wiser of the pair of clowns.

In addition, Wayang Kulit puppeteers (*dalang*) usually point to Semar as the originator of this shadow play form. He is referred to as Sang Yang Tunggal, the elder brother of Betara Guru (the Hindu god, Shiva). In the genealogical tables of the puppeteers, Sang Yang Tunggal appears as the original dalang. Much of the symbolic meaning of the shadow play in Kelantan, as in Java and Bali, reiterates and legitimizes this relationship of the dalang with the god, often deeming the human puppeteer as a manifestation of the god.

Similarly, Mak Yong's origins are traced to Semar and two of his sons. An alternative theory links the

In this Mek Mulung theatre opening ritual, the masks are feted, indicating a belief that they possess *semangat*.

Semangat

Semangat may loosely be described as a soul's energy. Creatures at the lowest end of the life-spectrum possess only semangat, plants have semangat plus the vegetable soul; animals possess semangat in addition to the animal soul. Man, too, possesses semangat and the higher soul, *roh*, bequeathed by Allah.

An early view of semangat

Walter William Skeat in 1900 described semangat as 'a diminutive but exact reproduction of its bodily counterpart ... a vapoury, shadowy, filmy essence ... and is the cause of life and thought in the individual it animates. It is absent from the body in sleep, trance, disease, and is permanently absent after death. If you call the soul in the right way it will hear and obey you, and you will thus be able either to recall to its owner's body a soul which is escaping, or to abduct the soul of a person whom you wish to get into your power.'

The Malay *keris* (dagger) is ritually crafted to house its own soul.

Invocations

A traditional theatre performance usually begins with *buka panggung* (opening rituals). These rituals include the recitation of *mantera* (invocations) to gain the goodwill of the spirits. Its use shows the direct link between theatre and spiritualism. In the invocations, the officiating *bomoh* makes his appeals to Allah, the Prophet Muhammad, various Muslim saints, as well as to Hindu deities such as Shiva and Ganesha. Spirits associated with various sectors of the environment are also included in the invocations.

More recent theatre styles do not feature these mantera but normal Islamic supplications (*doa selamat*). This is done for the success of performances rather than for the protection of performers from spirits.

A shaman conducting theatre opening rituals.

genre's creation to the goddess of rice (semangat padi or Mak Hiang). According to this theory, Mak Yong dance movements were crafted in imitation of nature, a connection emphasized by the names given to specific dance movements, especially for the opening dance sequence called *menghadap rebab*. Mak Yong also has important links with the shamanistic dance theatre form, Main Puteri, which in turn is connected with various goddesses, spirits, and legendary and mythical Malay princesses such as Puteri Sa'adong of Kelantan.

Similar examples of myths and legends connected with other traditional theatre genres exist. The fact that theatre functions in various ways as a means of communicating with, and making use of, the invisible world probably ensured its continuous performance over the centuries, and sometimes, as in the case of Main Puteri, little has changed in style.

Spiritual causes of disease

According to the traditional world-view of the Malays, certain varieties of disease are caused by malevolent spirits and invisible beings, resulting in 'illnesses of the soul' that modern medicine would probably classify as psychoses. Illnesses may also be caused by the operation of negative magic on a person which is intended to weaken his soul. The theatre performance, with its mystical attributes, becomes the vehicle for curing such illnesses.

New Age thinking

There is documented evidence to indicate that, where in some instances modern medicine has failed to cure angin-related illnesses because it has not been able to reach the spirit, alternative therapies such as traditional theatre and music have succeeded. New Age medicine in the West is beginning to take similar approaches to disease with an increased cognizance that equal emphasis should be paid to the spiritual and physical aspects of healing.

The 'wind' phenomenon

Angin

Within the context of traditional healing rituals and theatre, the word *angin*, literally 'wind', refers to desires or urges, in particular those that may have remained unfulfilled or suppressed. Such situations result in illness which may be emotional or psychological. If left unattended, these illnesses have the tendency to manifest themselves physically. Cure is effected by allowing the patient to fulfil the suppressed desires, which sometimes leads to the enactment of theatre.

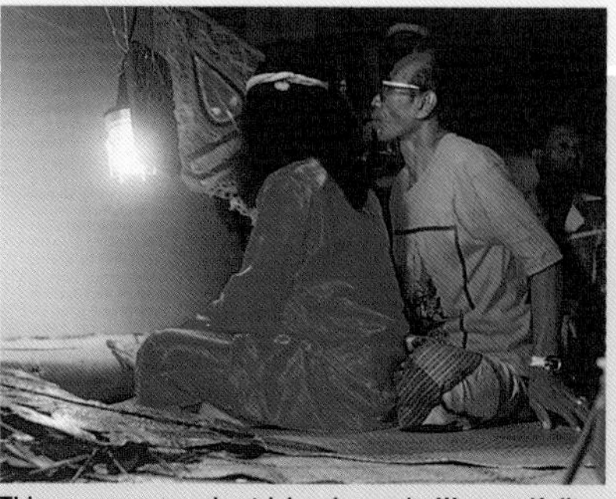

This young woman is stricken by angin *Wayang Kulit*. By giving vent to her suppressed desire to perform this shadow puppet play, a cure for her *angin* is achieved.

Inactive theatre practitioners may suffer from *angin* related illnesses due to non-fulfilment.

Types of angin

Several categories of angin are said to exist: those relating to royalty (*angin raja, angin puteri*); those related to specific types of activity or occupation (*angin bidan, angin pendekar*); and those connected with the arts (*angin Mak Yong, angin Joget*). Angin raja and angin puteri represent an intense desire to be a king or a princess. Angin bidan and angin pendekar are indicative of desires to become, respectively, a midwife or a warrior. This is, however, not an exhaustive list, and many others are known to exist.

The desire to remain young is a particularly prevalent form of angin, manifested in the form of *angin Dewa Muda*, the central character of the most important Mak Yong story called 'Dewa Muda'. Dewa Muda represents the young in search of the mysterious both within oneself and outside. Performances of this Mak Yong story are believed to lead to a feeling of wellbeing through emotional release.

Angin may be inherited, or may skip several generations before manifesting itself. For instance, a young woman from a family of midwives may suffer from *angin bidan* (midwife's wind) even if she is not engaged in midwifery. The angin, unknown to her, may exist within her and due to its non-fulfilment, she may suffer from severe depression, lassitude, lack of interest in life and so on. Similar phenomena may occur with practitioners of traditional theatre, such as Mak Yong or Wayang Kulit, either if the performers have been inactive for some time, or if someone amongst their ancestors was a practitioner of that particular art form.

Angin Dewa Muda derives from a Mak Yong story (pictured right), signifying a desire for eternal youth.

Cure

For all types of angin-related illness, cure is effected when the necessary desires are fulfilled. This leads to performances of specific theatre genres. The long inactive *dalang* can be cured of his *angin Wayang Kulit*, for instance, if he so much as attends a performance by another puppeteer. The sufferers of the various types of royal angin have to attend performances of Mak Yong in which royal characters play important roles, or perform a role themselves. Through such involvement in particular kinds of role-playing, emotional release and subsequent cure are achieved.

Cure may only be effected through the agency of a *bomoh* (shaman), and his objective of driving away offending spirits and strengthening the soul is often achieved through theatre performances such as Bagih and Main Puteri (see 'Healing performances'). The shaman contacts the offending spirit and utilizes mild coercion or conducts negotiations with it. He thus demonstrates his power over the spirit and expels it from a patient's body.

LEFT: The 'patient' pictured is afflicted by *angin Silat*. She performs this ancient art of self defence to effect a cure.
RIGHT: The *bomoh* (shaman) attends to the patient, and ensures that she is cured of her *angin*.

1. In Dondang Sayang performances, two or more singers exchange *pantun* (Malay quatrains) to the accompaniment of a musical ensemble.

2. Dikir Barat is a form of verse debate involving two groups who sing in a call-and-response pattern, each team led by a *tukang karut* or lyricist.

3. Ritual chants of some ethnic groups in Sabah and Sarawak recount, among other things, the creation of the world and journeys of the gods.

4. Storytelling in the longhouses of Sabah and Sarawak is an important part of the oral traditions of the indigenous peoples.

5. Awang Batil is an example of elementary theatre existing in Malaysia, involving a sole storyteller and minimal props and paraphernalia.

STORYTELLING AND ELEMENTARY THEATRE

Some of the most important forms of theatre in the Malay World evolved from storytelling or verse debates, simple performances that became more elaborate as they moved towards full-fledged theatre, incorporating costumes, masks and musical instruments. Yet, in certain communities in Malaysia, several storytelling, verse debates and elementary theatre styles continue to be active. While many of these are secular in character, some have retained their past connections with mysticism.

Among the various communities in Sabah and Sarawak, several genres of folk tales, myths, animal stories, tales of magic and romance, such as the well-known story of the meeting of a sky maiden and an earthly prince, are maintained. The theme of this story, for example, is in fact quite widespread through Southeast Asia and beyond, indicating the sharing of myths between communities spread far and wide, containing universal images, themes and messages.

While foreign epics, such as the *Ramayana*, found their way to Malaysia and became important, a repertoire of indigenous stories also developed. One such significant indigenous story is the epic of *Darangen*, which recounts the adventures and deeds of the mythical hero Bantogen. This story is shared by the Iranun of Sabah and communities in the southern Philippines, where it is an important source of stage presentations.

While epic recitation is a specialized activity, there are other lesser styles, involving the presentation of stories through the oral tradition. These include the *syair* of the Malays in Brunei, containing legendary stories or referring to actual events that may have taken place in the remote past, and the *tarsila* or *sarsila* genealogies—traditionally recited by skilled performers.

Pantun, less serious than the other genres, and highly flexible in the manner in which it is used, is essentially a series of quatrains which has developed in various communities in diverse styles. In the Malay communities, with the formalization of the pantun and its development as a literary genre, some of its original flexibility has been lost. Impromptu pantun, however, are still found in Bangsawan performances, and also continue to be popular in Sabah and Sarawak.

5

While these activities, in particular the lighter verse debates, provide the opportunity for social interaction, entertainment or preservation of tradition, the true importance of these genres, particularly of the more elaborate ones that incorporate ancient stories, lies in the preservation of legendary history—the recounting of the origins of the world or of a particular community, the remembrance of the deeds of a culture hero or the restating of the myth explaining the origins of rice, for instance. Through narration and repetition, and the use of performance as elementary theatre, such tales are kept alive, and connections with the past are maintained.

Storytelling and solo theatre

The earliest and simplest form of theatre in Malaysia involved a single performer—an itinerant storyteller who travelled from village to village, reciting stories memorized from legends and ancient epics. This form of solo theatre, known as Awang Batil and Selampit in Perlis and Kedah, and Tarik Selampit in Kelantan, demonstrates the beauty, essence and power of a tale told in the traditional way.

Storytelling forms of Awang Batil and Selampit are found in Perlis and Kedah, and Tarik Selampit occurs in Kelantan.

Malaysian solo theatre styles

The art of the storyteller is the most basic form of theatre. It requires talents such as rote memorization of stories and stylistic delivery for dramatic effect. The traditional storyteller strives to captivate the audience and command their attention principally through the power of his voice. Technical requirements, props and paraphernalia for solo theatre are minimal. This is essentially a matter of practicality, given that the itinerant performer has to literally carry the entire show with him on his travels.

In Peninsular Malaysia, storytelling forms occur as Awang Batil and Selampit in Perlis and Kedah, and Tarik Selampit in Kelantan, though performances are rare even in these states.

Awang Batil

In Awang Batil, the performer sits cross-legged upon a bare stage or platform to deliver his tale. He speaks in rhythmic prose mixed with verse to the accompaniment of music provided by striking the side of a brass bowl (*batil*) with his hand. Performances begin with a simple theatre opening ritual (*buka panggung*). Ritual offerings, consisting of betel leaves (*sirih*), betel-nuts (*pinang*) and money (*wang pengkeras*) are made to the spirits. The ceremony comprises invocations (*doa selamat*) and a salutation (*bertabik*) to thank the sponsor or host of a performance. The performer seeks forgiveness from the audience in advance for mistakes he may make during the performance, and to prevent any mishap from offending the attending supernatural beings.

The basic elements in a performance, apart from the extensive repertoire of stories, consist of the *batil*, a double-reed oboe (*serunai*), masks and a short dagger (*keris*). Costumes are optional. Some performers don formal Malay attire—*baju Melayu* complete with waistcloth (*sampin*) and headcloth (*tengkolok*). The batil, a brass bowl varying in size, is characteristic of this genre and is struck to create a distinctive hollow sound which provides the rhythm and tempo for a performance. To evoke a courtly atmosphere, the performer plays the *serunai*. It is intended to emulate the trumpet (*nefiri*) in the Nobat court orchestra. During a performance, the performer coordinates music with the story. Rhythm and tempo, crafted to create a hypnotic effect, are necessary for the smooth flow of the tales which are often linguistically and stylistically complex.

The stories are embellished with dialogue, narration, chanting, recitation and singing. The performer also engages in limited improvised acting. Costume and mask changes, which take place with those of characters, are accompanied by appropriate mime and vocal transformation by the performer. The keris also features in ceremonial situations to enhance the formality of an Awang Batil performance. The lengthy folk tales, legends or myths of gods or kings take several nights to

The Tarik Selampit performer accompanies his storytelling with the hypnotic music of his lute (*rebab*). His art is strongly linked to mysticism.

Awang Batil (top) and Selampit (above) performances take an hour or more each night, depending on the story, which may take a week or more to complete. They have lost favour with the village-based audience, who prefer more modern sources for their entertainment.

Masks in Awang Batil

The masks for Awang Batil storytelling are identical to those used in other genres such as Mek Mulung and Menora. Fashioned from wood and painted, their precise origins are unknown, and the craft has died out in Malaysia.

Varieties of clown masks used in Awang Batil storytelling: (1) Depicting a sad clown, (2) indicating chagrin, while (3) is the Tok Nujum mask donned when the storyteller is assuming the character of a magician or fortune teller.

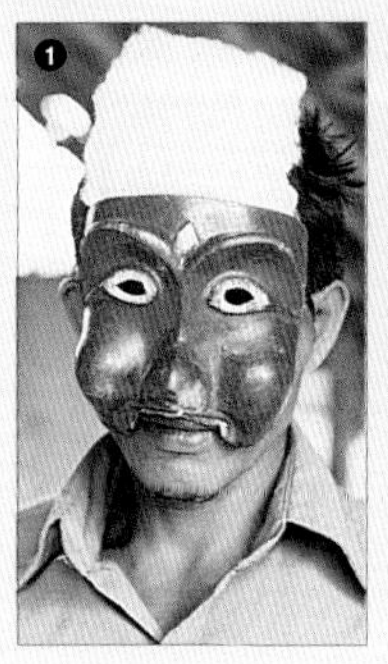

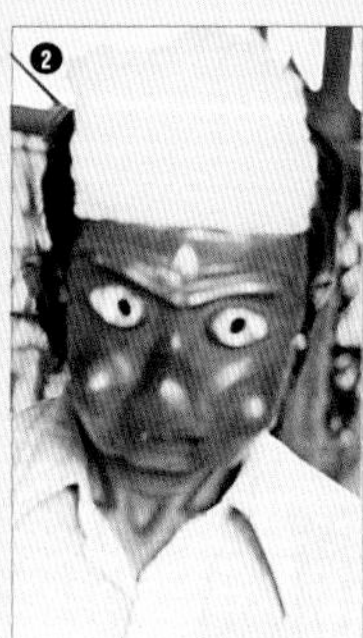

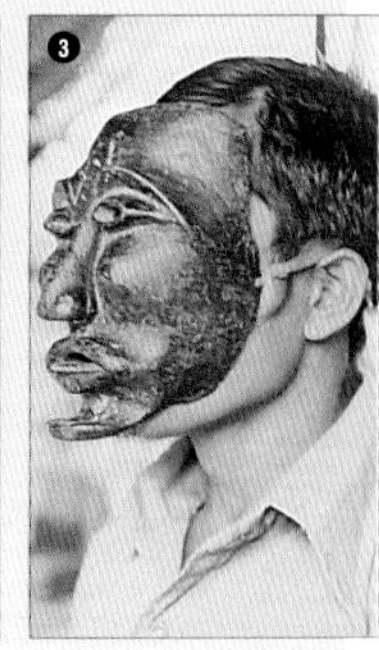

complete, with performances lasting an hour or more each night. Many of the traditional stories have yet to be documented.

Selampit

The art of Selampit is traditionally handed down from teacher to pupil. There are indications that in some instances there may be some form of supernatural summons, sometimes through a dream, to the calling of a Selampit performer.

The theatre opening ritual for performances involves the making of food offerings (*kenduri*) and the recitation of ritual formulae (*mantera*). The incense smoke (*kemenyan*), which the performer breathes in and uses to cleanse his face, produces a sense of ecstasy in him. It also serves as an aid to memory, ensures the prevalence of harmony, and prevents the intrusion of negative spiritual influences into the performance area. Occasionally, in addition to normal theatre opening rituals, a salutation song (*lagu bertabik*) is included. It is sung for the performer's teachers and ancestors, and to pacify the denizens of the spirit world.

Selampit is performed without any stage properties or musical instruments. Should it be necessary to indicate the use of an instrument within a given story, the effect is created by means of vocal sounds, or by using the body with associated gestures. An imaginary gong, for instance, would be struck with the elbows and the corresponding sound made vocally by the performer. Traditionally, a troupe of two or three performers appeared simultaneously in Selampit, providing, in addition to the music and narrative, the relief of some physical movement.

A Selampit performance incorporates the development of a plot through rhythmic narration, declamation, chanting or singing. Costume changes or masks do not feature in Selampit. The theatrical element is manifested in the constant transformation of the performer into a succession of characters, and spoken dramatic texts are used to herald such transformations. Thus, throughout an evening's performance which lasts several hours, the single performer assumes, by turn, the many roles that any selected episode requires.

Oral tradition

In Peninsular Malaysia, the solo theatrical art of storytelling is almost extinct. While there are unconfirmed reports of a single remaining Selampit performer in Pulau Langkawi, Kedah, the late Pak Mahmud bin Wahid of Kampung Chiung, Perlis, was the most famous of Awang Batil performers. He had also assisted researchers in documenting traditional stories that had hitherto existed purely in the oral tradition. Since his demise his son Romli Mahmud has taken over the art of Awang Batil in Perlis.

The repertoire of the storyteller is particularly vulnerable as its preservation depends entirely on the quality of the performer. Stories documented by researchers consist of tales such as 'Raja Dewa Lok', 'Awang ada duit semua jadi', 'Angan-angan', 'Anak Dang Pak Lang', 'Raja berdarah putih', 'Sultan Dewa', 'Awang Belanga', 'Awang Batil', 'Awang Malim', 'Awang Deman', and for children, 'Pak Kaduk' and 'Pak Pandir'. Many of the more famous stories such as 'Malim Deman' and 'Terung Pipit' have been published, and have evolved into classics of written Malay literature. Such efforts aid in preserving the oral tradition, albeit in a different form.

TOP: Tarik Selampit is traditionally performed by blind singers.

LEFT: Pak Mahmud was the quintessential Awang Batil performer, taking great pains to dress in traditional Malay costume.

Sometimes adorned with Qur'anic verses, the brass bowl (*batil*) is struck with the hand to provide music in Awang Batil storytelling.

Tarik Selampit

Tarik Selampit is probably the simplest form of solo theatre. It is associated with Kelantan and the Patani region of southern Thailand. Traditionally performed by blind singers using a fixed repertoire of stories, it also features chanting, recitation and the assumption of various roles by the single performer who is addressed as Tok Selampit. Tarik Selampit shares many elements with the other two genres, particularly the rituals marking the beginning and end of the performance. The performer accompanies himself on a three-stringed lute (*rebab*), the music being the sole ornamentation in the storytelling. In the absence of physical movement to emphasize dramatic shifts in presentation and plot, the Tok Selampit holds the audience's attention merely through the power of his voice and the hypnotic music of his rebab. Character changes are indicated purely by changes in voice.

Storytelling in Malaysia

Genre	Place	Storytellers	Music	Features	Existing stories
Awang Batil	Originally in Kedah and Perlis, still active in Perlis.	One itinerant performer.	A reed oboe (*serunai*) and a brass bowl (*batil*).	Masks, dialogue, narration, chanting, recitation, singing.	*Hikayat Malim Deman* and *Terung Pipit* have been published as written literature by Dewan Bahasa dan Pustaka. They are part of a collection of 11 stories documented and thus saved by researchers.
Selampit	Kedah and Perlis, reportedly surviving in Pulau Langkawi.	One itinerant performer, sometimes with assistants acting out the stories.	None.	Character changes are indicated by voice only.	
Tarik Selampit	Kelantan and Patani in Thailand, still existing in Kelantan.	One blind performer whose handicap is believed to enhance his ability to recall stories.	Three-string lute (*rebab*).	Strong vocalization and plaintive *rebab* music.	

Theatre opening rituals for the storyteller are a simple affair; he thanks the host of the performance, recites invocations and makes simple offerings to the denizens of the spirit world to ask for a successful performance.

Storytelling in Sabah and Sarawak

Storytelling is an important part of the oral traditions of the indigenous communities of Sabah and Sarawak. The relating of genealogies, folk tales and local history, word play, reciting myths and chanting sacred narratives all form a valued part of these peoples' lives. They also express and serve to transmit social and cultural values. However, urbanization, the spread of literacy and the mass media into the countryside have been at the expense of some traditional narrative forms.

Most storytelling takes place in the late evening after the day's work is done. In Sarawak's Bidayuh society, stories told in the longhouse gallery attract a large audience of both sexes, young and old.

A solo singer (right) and chorus performing a folk tale in a Punan Bah longhouse in the Upper Rajang River region of Sarawak.

Folk tales

In most traditional communities, folk tales are told for entertainment and sometimes to give moral instruction to the young. They are known by various names in different languages, such as *tangon* (in the Kadazandusun language), *tutunungon-tutunungon ru tuu-lair tali* ('tales of long ago' in Timugon Murut), *liton* (Ida'an) and *iringa* (Iranun) in Sabah. Among the Bidayuh of Sarawak folk tales and fables are known as *dondan*, while the Kenyah, Kayan and Penan generally refer to them as *suket*. There are three types of Penan suket: *suket jian* (good stories), *suket saat* (bad stories) and *suket kelete* (playful stories). The suket jian relate the adventures of folk heroes or are about 'good people' (*kelunan jian*), ordinary people who are always successful in whatever they do. Suket saat are stories about 'bad people', those who are lazy, stingy, and envious, and frequently go hungry and lead difficult lives. The suket kelete are about witless people or fools, and are typically told as comic tales. Suket may also feature animal characters, or, at times, both animal and human characters together.

Also popular in Sarawak are the *ensera Apai Alui*, comic tales which, like the Penan 'playful stories', tell of the misadventures of a fool and sometimes trickster, who is known to the Iban as Apai Alui, Palui, or Sali-ali. These tales are both satirical and instructive and, for comic effect, often turn moral values on their head. Thus, Apai Alui is constantly cheated by his neighbour and is hen-pecked by his wife and in return, he endlessly plots revenge, only to have his schemes rebound in disaster. The Apai Alui stories are thus cautionary tales that warn of the consequences of selfishness and stupidity.

Folk tales are purely fictional and while the range of subject matter is vast, some recurring themes with variations are found. These stories are populated with talking animals, spirits, giants, lost children, old married couples, warriors and other characters. Animal tales are common in most communities. Many tell a moral for young people, similar to Aesop's Fables in Europe, such as *Tuntul om Payou* ('Snail and Deer') of the Kadazandusun in Sabah and *Kulubau am Pipiu* ('Buffaloe and Deer') of the Timugon Murut. Among the Iban of Sarawak, these animal stories (*ensera jelu*) concern, above all, the adventures of the mouse deer and tortoise. In the past, youngsters were often entrusted to the care of grandparents, who would relate these tales just before the children fell asleep at night.

There are also magical tales of romance and marriage. A common theme found in many such stories is that of a sky maiden or fairy marrying a man from earth. Another story theme, used frequently amongst the coastal communities of Sabah, is of a poor couple who give birth to a frog or a fish; when it grows up, he or she turns into a human prince or princess, builds a magical bridge to the palace of a king and marries the royal daughter or son.

Animal tales are often told to teach morals to children. For instance, the story of The Deer, the Goat and the Mouse Deer, tells how a giant who had been stealing their fish was caught.

Epics

Unlike folk tales which are often extemporaneous and of variable form, epic tales usually involve a stylized type of recitation by a skilled performer and can take several nights to complete. Although they may contain legendary or historical material, epics are basically fantasy. An example is the *Darangen* of Sabah's Iranun community, which recounts the exploits of a mythical hero named Bantogen from the land of Iliana Bembaran. Various places mentioned in the epic indicate that this may refer to the island of Borneo. Bantogen is credited with fantastic feats, such as stepping from one island to another or flying on his shield. The recitation of the *Darangen* is often done in a stylized form called *tinubau* which involves slowly walking and gesturing with a woven cloth called *tubau* while narrating the poetry.

In Sarawak, these fictive epics, called *ensera* by the Iban, are composed in poetic language, while *jerita* narratives, told generally in prose, relate events considered to be real or true. Jerita include historical narratives, anecdotes, and eyewitness accounts. Ensera include epics or sagas, sung or related in poetic language with dialogues in prose. The most elaborate concern the Orang Panggau (People of Panggau), the Iban spirit heroes and heroines, who are thought to live along the mythic Panggau-Gelong Rivers in an invisible world intermediate between this world and the upper world of the gods. The ensera Orang Panggau are stories of bravery, travel, war, romance and adventure, and a full ensera may continue over several nights. Ensera are either told in the longhouse or for entertainment during boat journeys or in forest camps while parties are on fishing or hunting trips. Much of the enjoyment comes from the dramatic skills of the teller and beauty of the language used.

Audiences sit on the ground around the storyteller, drinking *tuak* (rice wine) and taking puffs from a bamboo water pipe.

Genealogies

In most of the indigenous communities, there are elderly men and women who are knowledgeable in genealogical information. The *tarsila* or *sarsila* of the Iranun, and the *rang dungo* of the Lundayeh of Sabah, are genealogies which record the histories of various families and ancestors. They are recited in a melodic vocal timbre with melismatic flourishes and ornaments. This melodic recitation not only helps the skilled performer to remember the genealogy, it also provides entertainment and instruction for listeners.

Ritual chants

The verses chanted by ritual specialists and mediums during traditional ceremonies often tell stories. The *rinait*, long verses chanted by Sabah's indigenous priestesses, are an example. In addition to summoning spirits from the cosmos to attend the rituals, the rinait recount happenings such as the creation of the world and the exploits of spirits and mythological beings. Bardic chants of the Sarawak Iban performed during rituals depict the journeying of the gods as they travel to this world, while the chants of shamans sung during curing rituals tell of the travels of the shaman's soul as it seeks to remedy a patient's afflictions. There are also occasions when epics, otherwise told for entertainment, are incorporated into rituals, such as the *sugi* sagas sung by Saribas Iban bards during rites to treat gravely ill patients.

Legends

Legends usually refer to the oral history of a people, and are sometimes associated with topographical features of the local landscape. They are normally told in the house at night by an elder who is renowned for his or her knowledge of oral history. An example of a legend is the Nunuk Ragang (*nunuk* meaning banyan tree, *ragang* meaning red) account of the Kadazandusun from Tambunan, which explains the origins of some of the dialect groups and their villages in the Tambunan district of Sabah. The Nunuk Taragang legend of the Kiujau Dusun of the Keningau plain further south resembles a sequel to the Tambunan account. Apart from the Kadazandusun and the Kuijau Dusun, most other Dusunic groups also have a Nunuk Ragang legend.

Nunuk Ragang

This legend tells of the migrations of many of the Kadazandusun tribes from a site believed to have been located on the Liwagu River towards the southern part of the Ranau District.

1. A group of people living on the Liwagu River used to sun themselves in the morning by sitting up the branches of the huge old nunuk tree.
2. One day, a giant red rooster with golden beak and claws landed in the tree.
3. At its spoken command, the people climbed up into its feathers and onto its wings.
4. As the rooster flew over the mountains and southwest down the Tambunan valley, he dropped various people in different places where they settled.

Nunuk Taragang

The Nunuk Taragang legend explains the dispersal of peoples and jars out from Ranau, down through the Tambunan valley and further southwards onto the Keningau plain.

1. One of the children from the village on the Liwagu River was born clutching a golden egg.
2. A small red rooster with golden beak and claws, and the power of speech, hatched from the egg.
3. The people followed the rooster wherever it travelled.
4. Whenever it stopped to rest, they built a village and stored their large heirloom jars.

Pantun and verse debates

Pantun and verse debates are call-and-response genres in which rhyming verses are composed extemporaneously between two individuals or two groups—one begins with a verse, usually made up of four lines, and the other responds with a corresponding verse. These forms of literary expressions are found in the various indigenous communities in the country. Among the Malays, pantun *is by far the most popular literary expression, finding a place in many everyday situations, both formal and informal. It plays diverse functions, from entertainment and storytelling to the formalization of a marriage proposal and other social situations.*

A *runsay* (call-and-response) performance of the Kota Belud west coast Bajau in which the singers are wearing traditional costumes.

Pantun competitions are common in the Peninsula as well as in Sabah and Sarawak. It is not unusual to see all ethnic communities in Malaysia participating in such events.

Pantun

Usually described as the Malay 'quatrain', a *pantun* is made up of four lines with the a-b-a-b rhyme scheme—the first line rhyming with the third and the second with the fourth. Less common forms of pantun appear in two-, six- or eight-line versions. Pantun is found throughout the country. Despite its importance, however, the origin of the Malay pantun remains obscure due partly to its antiquity.

The pantun is divisible into two parts, the first half being called the *pembayang* (preamble), and the second half termed the *maksud* (meaning or intention). The pembayang may have little to do directly with the maksud. In terms of the structure of a pantun, however, the pembayang is vital, as it establishes the rhyme scheme. The essence of a pantun, however, is contained in the maksud. This is the part that conveys the intention of the pantun reciter. This is not a firm rule, however, and pantun do exist in which all four lines are connected in terms of the development of an idea.

Marriage proposal pantun

Burung kenari cantik memikat
Pandai memukau para hartawan
Datang kemari membawa hajat
Ingin memikat bunga di taman

Captivating indeed is the peacock's beauty
Charming the hearts of the wealthy
With a burning desire in our hearts we come
To pluck the blushing rose in your garden

In Sarawak the pantun may be performed at large or small gatherings to welcome guests or for other purposes. The singer may be a man or woman who sits among those present at the gathering in a longhouse or in a public community venue.

The texts of pantun are thematic and among the Iban are usually sung for specific purposes. Some typical themes are pantun for encouragement (*pantun perangsang*), to praise a certain person (*puji*), for sympathy or regret (*sayau*), for a troubled heart (*tusut ati*), or for a plaintive expression of some kind (*sebana*). Among the Kenyah and other upriver peoples the pantun tells a story, while in the Batang Ai region of Sarawak pantun often refers to popular songs about war, love and friendship.

Among the Iban the pantun is a solo vocal music genre, sung without musical accompaniment. In other styles, the pantun is sung by a solo singer with choral accompaniment. Among the Kenyah in the Upper Rajang River region, for instance, a solo male voice sings the main text of the pantun, while a male chorus sings a sustained, and sometimes a moveable, drone pitch to support the basic intoning pitch of the soloist. The chorus usually sings a nonsense syllable, 'eh' or 'oh.'

In all styles of pantun in Sarawak, the singing is syllabic with simple melodies and little or no vocal ornamentation of the melodic line. In the Iban pantun sometimes the words themselves are slightly modified or drawn out (for example, the word '*ru-ding*' might be sung as '*ru-di-eng*'). This stylistic convention holds the interest of the audience and exhibits the skill of the performer in spontaneously creating and musically conveying the lines of text. In the singing of pantun the audience is entertained not only by the content of the poetry itself, but also by the creative ability of the performer.

A *pantun* melody

The music transcription for some *pantun* is a simple, repetitive tune, abruptly ascending by one octave, then chromatically descending down to the original tone again. Other pantun have different melodies.

Source: François-René Daillie, 1988

Other call-and-response genres

Although the word pantun may not be widely used in the languages of Sabah, many pantun-like genres are performed in various contexts.

Sudawil is a pantun-like genre performed by the Kadazandusun of the interior, particularly from the Tambunan and Ranau areas. It is said to have originated from groups of people calling messages, questions and answers back and forth across the hills. Nowadays it is a musical genre performed by a group of four or five women and a corresponding group of men. The verses sung usually have a poetic meaning.

The Bajau/Sama people of Sabah, particularly those from the north and west coast areas, perform circular stamping dances called *runsay* (or *runsai*, *lunsay* or *berunsai*) as they chant verses called *kalang* (or *kallang*). These verses fall into four-line pantun-like patterns.

The dance formation consists of a line of men with interlocked arms joined to a similar line of women by a hand-held cloth. The dancers move in a circle on a wooden floor while singing verses about people and current events. Statements and ideas are tossed back and forth between the men and women, so that the kalang resemble verse debates. As a resolution is reached about a particular topic, the volume and pace of the chanting increases and the men, and sometimes the women, rapidly stamp their feet in time to the rhythm of the kalang.

Runsay performances usually take place at night during social gatherings as entertainment, and can continue until dawn. These performances often provide socially acceptable opportunities for young men and women to meet, and the kalang can function as a means of matchmaking.

Sometimes, communities from other ethnic groups may sponsor runsay performances for special events. The Iranun often commission lunsay by the Jama Mapun, a Sama group originating from the southern Philippines, for entertainment at their wedding celebrations.

A Kenyah-Badang soloist singing a *pantun* in Sarawak's Upper Rajang River area.

Pamiula is a call-and-response genre performed by the Iranun of Kota Belud. This consists of verses in pantun form sung back and forth between a man and a woman seated on the floor. One of the performers, usually the woman, plays the three-stringed violin (*biula*) which is held in front like a cello. The instrumental introduction before the start of the singing is called *ebpamiula*. If only one performer is present, the verses form a soliloquy. A similar genre called *isun-isun* is performed by the neighbouring Bajau community.

Literary expressions

Type	Purpose	Community/ Location
Pantun	Storytelling, entertainment, formalization of marriage proposal	Throughout the country
Pantun perangsang	Encouragement	Sarawak
Pantun puji	Praise	Sarawak
Pantun sayau	Sympathy or regret	Sarawak
Pantun tusut ati	Troubled heart	Sarawak
Pantun sebana	Plaintive expression	Sarawak
Pantun	Storytelling	Kenyah and upriver peoples, Sarawak
Pantun	Songs of war, love & friendship	Batang Ai, Sarawak
Sudawil	Musical verse debate	Kadazandusun, Sabah
Runsay (or runsai, lunsay or berunsai)	Stamping dance/verse debate	Bajau/Sama, Sabah
Pamiula	Call and response	Iranun, Kota Belud, Sabah
Isun-isun	Call and response	Bajau, Kota Belud, Sabah
Daling-daling	Verse debate	Suluk and east coast Bajau, Sabah
Dikir Barat	Verse debate	Kelantan

The Daling-daling dance is usually performed at weddings. Female dancers wear long spiked brass fingercaps (*janggai*) and the *malkota* headdress.

Another pantun-like genre accompanies the Daling-daling dance performed by the Suluk and sometimes the Bajau communities on the east coast of Sabah. The music accompanying this dance consists of a man and a woman singing pantun-like alternating verses separated by the refrain 'daling-daling'. One performer strikes the side of the frame of a wooden xylophone (*gabang*) with two sticks, while the other hits a single-headed wooden drum with a pair of beaters. The instruments form a rapid rhythmic accompaniment to the singing. The extemporaneous verses are humorous and refer to people and events surrounding the celebration. When only one singer is present, his verses provide a humorous commentary on the proceedings.

Dikir Barat

Dikir Barat is a form of verse debate involving two teams of participants which possibly evolved from Islamic religious chanting (*zikir*). Found principally in the east coast state of Kelantan, Dikir Barat has become a social phenomenon with political and other messages.

A Dikir Barat team may consist of as many as 15 performers, the leader (*juara*) and the composer of the improvised lyrics (*tukang karut*). Musical themes are generally lively and simple. As such Dikir Barat allows for popular participation. Pantun in Dikir Barat are created extemporaneously by the tukang karut. Other members of the team serve as background voices, clapping rhythmically, repeating a quatrain after the leader or singing a choric passage throughout a performance.

In Kelantan, Dikir Barat competitions are regularly held, and it has also found its way into radio and television programmes.

TOP: The lead singer in a Dikir Barat performance improvises and sings lyrics, while the chorus repeats each line of the sung lyrics in call-and-response style.

BOTTOM: Dikir Barat performances are accompanied by an ensemble of hand-held frame drums (*rebana kecil*), a single knobbed gong (*tetawak*) and sometimes an oboe (*serunai*).

Sudawil

In this *sudawil*, which was composed by Stephen Mail from Kampung Nambayan, Tambunan, the first and fourth lines of each verse rhyme while the second line rhymes with the third. The sudawil discusses the cultural uniqueness of the Kadazandusun and other native peoples of Sabah.

Posowito ku oh kalawang Tinadtalan do kuron Kada olingai nantadon Hilo id Nunuk Ragang	I hung up my basket Filled with old things Do not forget your roots At Nunuk Ragang
Tataso ku loh tiwak Kotungai loh gaggangou Ilo no soroon tokou Susuion nod tanganak	I slashed the palm shoot Fell on the hive This is what we should remember Tell it to your children
Garabo ku oh bambangan Katatak oh sompuru Kanou no sumompuru Maya do kuobasanan	I threw at the bambangan fruit A bunch fell down Let us unite (as in a bunch) Through our culture

Translated by Laurentius Kitingan

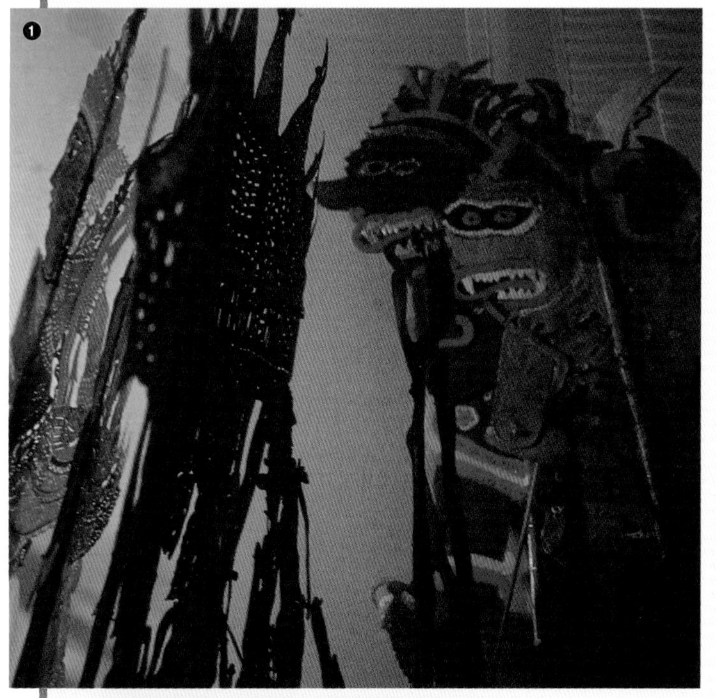

1. Wayang Kulit Siam traditionally uses a Malaysian version of the *Ramayana* story but sometimes also features sketches.

2. Chinese puppet theatre is usually performed to celebrate the birthdays of Chinese temple deities.

3. A Chinese shadow play puppet of the Monkey God made by students at Universiti Sains Malaysia.

4. Shadow play puppets are manipulated by a puppeteer who presents the story through narration, singing and dialogue.

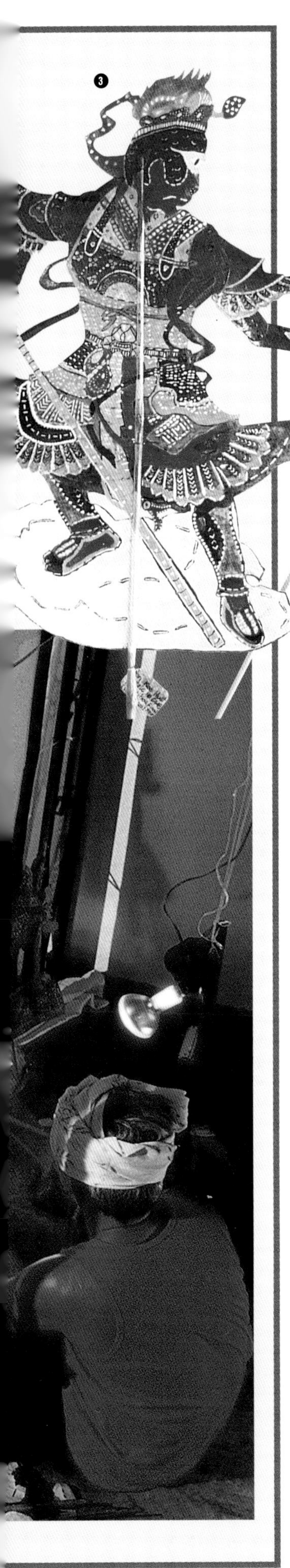

PUPPET THEATRE

Southeast Asia has a rich tradition of puppetry, a theatre form varying in style within the region but, at the same time, demonstrating many similarities. Puppets are made of various materials—cloth, wood, clay, skin and leaves—and may take the form of glove puppets, rod puppets, or hand or finger puppets. Manipulation techniques depend on the figures used and the intended effect.

The most visually exciting puppet theatres in Southeast Asia include the marionette theatre of Myanmar, the water puppets of Vietnam, and Chinese puppetry. Shadow play (Wayang Kulit), however, remains the most popular form, appearing in two forms—one using single-character figures and the other using large, composite figures as in the Cambodian Nang Sbek Thom and the Thai Nang Yai. The former is by far the most widely distributed, being active in Malaysia, Indonesia, Thailand and Cambodia.

The best-known example of shadow play is the classical Javanese Wayang Kulit Purwa, which is also active in other parts of Indonesia as well as the southern sections of the Malay Peninsula, particularly in Johor. In addition, three other styles of shadow play are active in Malaysia: Wayang Kulit Gedek, which represents a southward expansion of the Thai Nang Talung and continues to use the Thai version of the *Ramayana* story; Wayang Kulit Melayu which developed as a result of the borrowing of the Javanese Wayang Kulit Gedog based upon the story of the Javanese hero Panji; and Wayang Kulit Siam, which uses a Malaysian version of the *Ramayana*.

Historically Malay shadow play has been the repository of the indigenous belief system and literary traditions. While essentially serving the purpose of providing entertainment, it also plays an important part in traditional ritual situations, particularly on occasions marking the paying of homage to teachers. The length of time—up to five years—devoted to training a puppeteer indicates the complexity of the training process itself. The apprentice learns the art of puppet manipulation, develops a suitable repertoire, and masters the music. These skills are required in presenting Wayang Kulit. In addition, he may also make puppets and musical instruments, as well as conduct rituals for healing and exorcism, thus continuing in many ways to be an important member of his community.

Although an ancient tradition, Malaysian puppetry has suffered a decline due to several factors—economic, political and cultural. Wayang Kulit Siam has, on occasion, been banned in Kelantan. There are few troupes left and those remaining are finding new ways of maintaining Wayang Kulit through adapting to changing circumstances. As a result, new emerging forms have replaced the classical style, presenting comedy skits rather than serious stories, and using figures that bear little resemblance to the traditional ones. While artistically less impressive, such forms may eventually be the only ones keeping the Malay shadow play alive.

Wayang Kulit puppet created by Universiti Sains Malaysia students in an experimental project.

Malay shadow theatre in Southeast Asia

The ancient art of shadow puppet play has been in existence for over two millennia, finding its greatest concentration in Southeast Asia. Centuries of cross-cultural exchanges in the region have led to its localized reworking, resulting in a flowering of styles. The Malaysian shadow puppet play, Wayang Kulit, *is essentially an adaptation of regional styles into those that are unique to this country.*

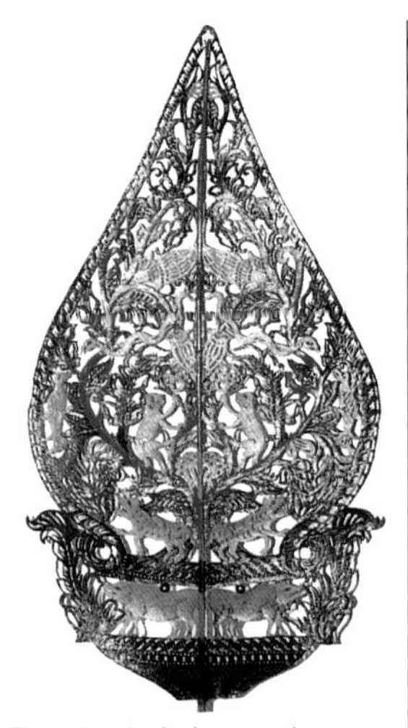

The *pohon beringin* puppet is very important in Wayang Kulit. It is the symbol of the cosmos and the tree of life, and marks the beginning and the end of a performance. This symbolism is present in Indonesian shadow play as well.

Wayang Kulit in Malaysia

Four forms of shadow theatre exist in Malaysia. They are Wayang Kulit Siam (sometimes referred to as Wayang Kulit Kelantan), principally found in Kelantan; Wayang Kulit Gedek, active in Kedah and Perlis; Wayang Kulit Melayu, associated with Kelantan; and Wayang Kulit Purwa which developed in Java and is performed only in Johor.

Whilst these Malaysian forms of Wayang Kulit feature unique local characteristics, their relationship with other Southeast Asian shadow theatre styles remains strong. Variations occur in the puppet designs, literary aspects and aesthetic considerations, while similarities are most evident in the belief systems and rituals contained within some regional styles. Influences from Hinduism, Buddhism and Islam are also clearly evident.

Origins and development

Theories for the origins and early development of the shadow play in Southeast Asia are equivocal, linking the genre with either animistic rituals, ancestor cults or supernatural sources. While some opinions prescribe Javanese origins, it appears more likely that shadow play spread from the Indian sub-continent to Southeast Asia in two directions. The northward flow took it to Cambodia and Thailand, and the southward flow introduced it to Java. From these regions, the shadow play entered the Malay Peninsula.

The origins of the Malaysian Wayang Kulit Purwa and Wayang Kulit Gedek can be explained in terms of this northern and southern flow. Wayang Kulit Purwa is a product of direct transplantation into Johor by Javanese immigrants in the 19th century, and Wayang Kulit Gedek is a local variation of the Thai Nang Talung shadow play. The third style, Wayang Kulit Melayu, is an obvious borrowing from the Javanese Wayang Kulit Gedog. It was introduced into Kelantan as a direct result of court efforts in the 19th century. However, the origins of Wayang Kulit Siam, the most important of the four Malaysian styles, remain unclear.

Wayang Kulit Siam

Despite its name, Wayang Kulit Siam is more strongly influenced by Java than Thailand. It is very

Puppet design

In terms of iconography and design in Malaysian Wayang Kulit, connections with cultures beyond Malaysian shores are apparent. Indian influence is evident in the colour symbolism. Aesthetic influences from Thailand and Java are obvious, besides religious influences from Hinduism and Buddhism.

Javanese influence

Whilst Malay aesthetic considerations have given the principal characters their general shapes, ideas are also derived from Islam and Javanese antecedents. For instance, the shape of Pak Dogol, the senior clown in Wayang Kulit Siam, and other comic figures has been traced to Semar, the Javanese god-clown. Also, the Maharisi puppet is believed to be a direct derivation from its Javanese equivalent.

Figures such as the Jayadrata puppet from the Indonesian Wayang Kulit Purwa are found in Wayang Kulit Siam.

Thai influence

Thai iconography is seen in the figures of Wayang Kulit Siam, the most prominent feature being the headgear worn by the Seri Rama, Laksamana and Sirat Maharaja puppets. In addition, Seri Rama's bird-like costume is derived from that of the lead male dancer in the Thai Menora dance theatre.

Wayang Kulit Gedek figures, especially divine, royal and demon figures, come from the Thai Nang Talung which derived its own designs from the refined Nang Yai, based upon temple iconography and mythical beings in traditional Thai art. The fact that many of the more prominent of the Wayang Kulit Siam figures are made to stand upon serpents or dragon-shaped boats indicates a return to a detail within the Malay version of the *Ramayana* itself (*Hikayat Maharaja Wana*), or possibly the borrowing of an image from Indochina.

LEFT: A mural at Wat Suwannaram in Thonburi, Thailand, depicts iconography which is also represented in Malaysian shadow play figures.

RIGHT: Seri Rama's headgear and long fingernails are indicative of Thai influence.

likely that this style was derived from the Javanese Wayang Kulit Purwa, imported into Kelantan towards the end of the Hindu Majapahit period in the 14th century—and before Wayang Kulit Purwa itself underwent drastic transformations in iconography and performance techniques as a result of Muslim efforts to render the genre compatible with Islamic mores.

These changes did not occur in the Balinese version called Wayang Kulit Parwa, with which Wayang Kulit Siam also shares pronounced similarities. Links between the three forms are seen in the rituals, and in the comic characters. Most significantly, an important ritualistic style of play using the story of the demon Betara Kala (a negative form of the Hindu god, Shiva) appears in all three forms, making it highly likely that the earliest styles of Wayang Kulit in Java, Bali and Kelantan have a common origin. Other equally strong links are seen in the region's diverse shadow puppet play styles.

Repertoire

Classical styles of shadow play derive their repertoire from the Indian epics, *Ramayana* and *Mahabharata*. In Java, greater importance is given to the *Mahabharata*, while Thailand features only the *Ramayana*. Malaysia's Wayang Kulit Siam and Wayang Kulit Gedek have the *Ramayana* as their principal story. The *Ramayana* and *Mahabharata* both underwent considerable transformation and development in Southeast Asia. Many different localized versions of the epics exist. These versions, some of which have remained in the oral tradition to this day, eventually became the source for the shadow play's extensive dramatic repertoire.

In many instances, apart from the principal plots of the epics, extension or branch stores were developed locally. Principal characters continue to play a role, but a whole range of new characters was also created for these branch stories, which over the years have become the mainstay of Wayang Kulit performances. This is the case in Kelantan Wayang Kulit Siam, where performances featuring branch stories have for several decades been overshadowing those utilizing the classical repertoire.

Islamic elements later coloured the Malay *Ramayana*, and in the case of the shadow play, played the role of expanding the repertoire and removing elements such as theatre rituals that were unacceptable from the Islamic point of view. Unlike the Javanese Wayang Kulit Purwa, however, the Malay shadow play styles did not attempt to introduce Islamic teachings through performances. The focus thus remains on entertainment.

Borrowings from within regional styles have been inevitable. Wayang Kulit Gedek uses the Thai version of this epic, the *Ramakien*, but without its Buddhist themes. The *Ramayana* used in the Kelantanese Wayang Kulit Siam, on the other hand, is closer to the Malay and Javanese literary versions of that epic. Wayang Kulit Melayu continues to use the original source of its parent form Wayang Kulit Gedog—the Javanese Panji romance—while Wayang Kulit Purwa uses the *Mahabharata*. In addition, the shadow play styles in Java, Bali and Kelantan have demonstrated a strong tendency to innovate, especially in the creation of new stories which use the characters from the original ancient epics.

Due to certain restrictions imposed upon puppeteers in recent years, new shadow play styles have begun to emerge, for which new characters have been created. These new Wayang Kulit forms avoid Hindu or Indian elements, including the *Ramayana*, which have been the source of controversy. The newly created stories present comedy skits rather than established literary material.

Semar

Semar is a pre-Hindu Javanese god who features as a clown in several important Wayang Kulit stories. Semar was brought to the Malay Peninsula with the Javanese shadow play. In Wayang Kulit Siam, he is known as Pak Dogol. All the ugliest features that may be found in the human anatomy are represented in Semar. Renouncing his heavenly abode, he came down to earth in this ugly, misshapen, androgynous form to act as the protector of heroes.

Wayang Kulit Siam: The Kelantan shadow play

Wayang Kulit Siam is the principal Malaysian shadow play style and one of the oldest traditional theatre forms in the country. Its origins are unclear, but it is believed to be a derivation of ancient Thai and Javanese styles. Having absorbed religious, cultural and artistic influences from diverse sources, it has evolved locally into a typically Malay art form, and reflects Malay aesthetics. In Kelantan, its base, about a dozen puppeteers remain active but this number is rapidly diminishing.

This archive image of a Wayang Kulit Siam theatre from the late 19th or early 20th century indicates that staging methods have barely changed.

Wayang Kulit Siam is found in Kelantan, Terengganu, Pahang and the Patani region of southern Thailand.

Origins and history

Wayang Kulit Siam's origins and history have been a subject of much debate (see 'Malay shadow theatre in Southeast Asia'). Historically, there is no epigraphic evidence to indicate the period within which it developed. Culturally, it is Thai-Malay in character—evidenced by the dialect used in performance. Javanese influence is also present, seen most clearly in the design and construction of the puppets, suggesting a link between Wayang Kulit Siam and the ancient pre-Islamic version of the Javanese Wayang Kulit Purwa.

While taking inspiration from diverse sources, Wayang Kulit Siam developed within the context of local Malay cultural dynamics. Wayang Kulit Siam is, in effect, a unique product of cultural and religious fusion. This is evident in its repertoire and in some of the rituals associated with its performance (see 'Wayang Kulit Siam: The *dalang*, his puppets and stories' and 'Wayang Kulit Siam as ritual').

Areas of performance

Wayang Kulit Siam is found in Kelantan, Pahang, Terengganu and the Patani region of southern Thailand. It is still performed in its base in the east coast state of Kelantan, albeit on a diminished scale and despite disapproval from the state's religious authorities based on the use of rituals contrary to Islam.

Offerings for the spirits

Offerings prepared for the spirits are typical of all traditional theatre genres in Kelantan, and include yellow glutinous rice (*pulut kuning*), parched rice (*bertih*), turmeric rice (*beras kunyit*), a fried egg, cakes and fritters, betel leaves and betel nuts, rolled cigarettes and tobacco, cotton thread, money for services rendered (*wang pengkeras*), and incense or benzoin (*kemenyan*).

Innovations have been made to render Wayang Kulit Siam more attractive to modern audiences. Puppets are painted with translucent ink so that coloured shadows are cast, rather than the usual black silhouettes.

Parts of the theatre

1. The theatre (*panggung*) comprises the entire stage structure. It is a metaphor for the universe.
2. The screen (*kelir*) symbolizes the world with images of peoples passing through.
3. The lamp (*lampu*) symbolizes the sun. It gives life to the puppets. Traditionally only the puppeteer (*dalang*) could turn the light off and on.
4. The pohon beringin is the tree of life. It represents the elements (water, earth, air, fire). It is always the first puppet to move, symbolizing the beginning of life in the universe. It is also the figure that closes a theatre.
5. The puppeteer (*dalang*) narrates the story whilst manipulating the puppets on screen. He also conducts the orchestra.
6. The puppets' wooden handles are stuck into the banana stem (*batang pisang*), which symbolizes the earth.
7. The music is provided by an orchestra of between seven and 10 musicians on pairs of deep-rimmed hanging gongs (*tetawak*), small bossed gongs (*canang*), hand cymbals (*kesi*), double-headed barrel drums (*gendang*), single-headed goblet shaped drums (*gedumbak*), standing drums beaten with sticks (*gedung*), and a double-reed oboe (*serunai*).

The theatre

The Wayang Kulit Siam theatre (*panggung*) is a simple operating box raised about a metre above the ground, measuring about three metres in breadth and about four metres in length. The front opening is approximately three metres between floor and roof, while at the rear the opening becomes smaller, usually just enough to allow a person to enter through a door placed at the back wall to which access is gained by means of a simple ladder. The side walls seldom, if ever, have windows and the front of the theatre, completely open, is concealed by means of a screen (*kelir*) stretched tight across the opening. This is the screen on which the shadows of the figures are projected. It tilts slightly inward, facing downwards. Spectators sit on the grass or on benches.

A traditional-style panggung is made of wood and thatched palm leaves. In the choice of a site for the panggung, certain precautions are taken to conform to ancient beliefs regarding the presence of spirits and malicious influences in the environment. The theatre is constructed with the same taboos applicable to a Malay *kampung* (village) house, requiring invocations by a shaman (*bomoh*) and special offerings to spiritual beings.

The Performance

A Wayang Kulit Siam performance comprises the theatre; the puppeteer, his puppets and the stories; and the orchestra and the music (see 'Music of the Malay shadow play').

Theatre opening ceremony (*buka panggung*)

Following the construction of the theatre, a lamp is hung behind the screen, and a pair of banana plant stems (*batang pisang*) is placed in front of the puppeteer (*dalang*) with the puppets' wooden handles embedded in the stem. The theatre opening ceremony is then performed by the dalang or a qualified shaman.

This is conducted on the first night of performance only, as a form of salute to the teachers and spirits, and to prevent attacks by malevolent or disgruntled spirits. It is also believed to enhance the puppeteer's standing in his community and to ensure a successful performance.

Ritual formulae (*mantera*) are read, the teacher's rice (*nasi guru*) is prepared and offered to the spirits, and the musical instruments are consecrated. The orchestra plays a selection of musical pieces to signal the opening of the performance.

Prologue

The apprentice puppeteer or a regular dalang performs the prologue (*bahagian dalang muda*), which serves to attract a crowd and to set the atmosphere for the actual performance. The prologue also has ritual significance. It is played to glorify Seri Rama—the principal character—and introduces the warriors in his kingdom.

The prologue begins with the leaf-shaped puppet (*pohon beringin*) moving off-screen and the sage puppet (Maharisi) enters, reciting a Thai charm. The battle of two godlings (*dewa panah*) follows. Seri Rama then enters, followed by his warriors who pay their respects to him, and inform him that everything is well in his land of Siusia Mendarapura. A song praising Seri Rama is sung and all the puppets exit.

Main performance

An instrumental piece (*lagu tukar dalang*) is played indicating the change of dalang from apprentice to the master. The senior dalang performs the story selected for the evening and, if necessary, continues on subsequent evenings until completion of the engagement. Performances come to a close on the final night with the theatre closing (*tutup panggung*) rituals. Uncooked rice mixed with turmeric powder is scattered all over the *panggung* area after reading of incantations.

The Wayang Kulit orchestra in a teaching situation at the Akademi Seni Kebangsaan.

Wayang Kulit Siam: The *dalang*, his puppets and stories

Wayang Kulit Siam is a collection of traditions manifested in the local interpretation of the Indian Ramayana *epic. As a play of shadows, puppet movement, music, dialogue, chanting and narration must synchronize in order to infuse shadows with life and vigour. The central figure in a performance is the master puppeteer, and the puppets are his means of conveying the story to the audience.*

Puppeteering skills and training

A shadow play performance hinges on the master puppeteer (*tok dalang*). He manipulates the figures, provides voices to the characters and develops the story through dialogue, narration, commentary, and the use of songs. In addition he conducts the orchestra and functions as a shaman (*bomoh*), sometimes extending this role beyond the theatre to serve the village community as a healer. He is a skilled puppet-maker, craftsman and musician.

Puppet-making is a required skill for a Wayang Kulit Siam puppeteer. It is a skill that is most difficult to learn. Only a small number of puppeteers in Kelantan still make puppets. With declining performances, puppets are often made for private collectors rather than performance, which gives a few skilled puppeteers a lucrative source of income. Puppet-making is also taught as part of a course at the Akademi Seni Kebangsaan (National Academy of Arts) in Kuala Lumpur.

A trainee puppeteer (*dalang muda*) enrols with an established puppeteer. The art of the dalang is rarely handed down in a direct line of descent. Generally, an individual becomes a dalang because he receives intense pleasure from watching Wayang Kulit, and is thus said to be suffering from an illness of the soul referred to as *angin* Wayang Kulit (see 'Belief systems of traditional theatre'). The cure for this is the opportunity to perform. The trainee dalang has to master each musical instrument in the *wayang* troupe, and the entire music repertoire. He then rises to rank of apprentice (dalang muda), performing the opening prologue (*bahagian dalang muda*).

The prologue is the practical vehicle for learning the art of bringing a collection of shadowy figures to life on screen. As the apprentice performs, he learns narration and singing techniques, and the wayang's dramatic repertoire. He must also be skilled in the intricacies of puppet manipulation, which must be coordinated with the music played by the orchestra that is controlled by him. Upon performing a ritual Wayang Kulit Siam where he pays respect to the teacher (*sembah guru*), the apprentice is acknowledged as a full-fledged dalang. The dalang's skills are taught to a small number of persons, and are often lost forever when a dalang passes on.

Famous *dalang*

Awang Lah bin Pandak was the leading *dalang* during the years after World War II. He hailed from a long line of puppeteers beginning with Kelantan's first puppeteer, Erik. In the early 1960s, Awang Lah accepted Hamzah Awang Amat as his pupil. Awang Lah passed away in 1973.

The late Dalang Hamzah Awang Amat was Malaysia's most renowned puppeteer, and a National Arts Laureate. He taught Wayang Kulit Siam at the Akademi Seni Kebangsaan and had performed internationally. He was also an accomplished musician, craftsman and shaman. He passed away in 2001 at the age of 60.

Dalang Dollah of the Baju Merah troupe performs from his base in Tumpat, Kelantan. A child prodigy at the age of nine, he formed his own troupe when he was 19, and has been performing for half a century. Popular among village audiences, he is renowned for infusing traditional stories with fresh modern elements.

Art of making puppets

Cowhide (or sometimes goatskin) is dried and treated before it is scraped and shaved to the required thickness. The design of the puppet is drawn onto the hide. The shape of the puppet and its intricate filigree is then carved out with a small chisel. Noble characters are finely filigreed and augmented with gold paint. Enamel or water-based paint or vegetable dye is applied onto both sides of the puppet. The colours follow stylistic requirements that have become a matter of convention—green for Seri Rama, gold for Sita Dewi, red for Ravana and white for Hanuman.

A narrow piece of split wood is attached to the length of the body and a smaller bamboo stick is attached to one arm as a handle for articulating movement. Some puppets have both arms articulated, and others may have moveable jaws. The figures are perforated so that designs of jewellery and other details become manifest when light is placed behind them.

Noble characters

Hanuman

Maharisi

Laksmana

Sita Dewi

Seri Rama

Stories of the Wayang Kulit Siam

The principal Wayang Kulit Siam tale is a cycle of stories based on the *Hikayat Maharaja Wana*. This is one of the two major literary Malay versions of the Hindu epic, the *Ramayana,* the other being *Hikayat Seri Rama*. The original cycle is collectively known as *cerita pokok* (trunk story), which is performed in the Kelantanese-Patani dialect of Malay. Stories most popular amongst Kelantanese puppeteers are the many extension or branch stories (*cerita ranting*) of the *Ramayana*. These are wholly or partly invented accessions to the basic story of the epic.

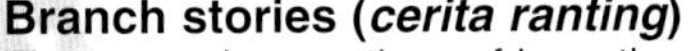

Trunk story (*cerita pokok*)

In the past, in-depth knowledge of the cerita pokok was an important element of a *dalang*'s training—the entire saga taking about 45 nights to complete. Currently, dalang utilize only selected episodes such as the competition for Sita Dewi's hand and her rescue from the dastardly king Ravana. The cerita pokok is, however, not as popular as the extensive collection of cerita ranting.

Synopsis of the *cerita pokok*

The main story is the *Ramayana*. Seri Rama (a prince) and his wife Sita Dewi are banished into the forest by his father upon the instigation of his stepmother. In the forest, Sita Dewi is kidnapped by an evil king, Ravana, and is spirited off to his kingdom.

Seri Rama is stricken by grief. He befriends the monkey kings, Hanuman and his brother Sugriva. They help him find Sita Dewi. Hanuman locates Sita Dewi and reassures her of Seri Rama's love. A battle ensues between Ravana's army and Seri Rama with his monkey army. Ravana is defeated, and the couple is reunited.

They return to Seri Rama's kingdom, but Sita Dewi is made to prove that her purity is intact. She walks on fire without being hurt. Later, aspersions are again cast on Sita Dewi's character. She is banished to a hermitage. There, she gives birth to twin sons, and tells her story to Maharisi who writes it down. Her sons grow up. They meet Seri Rama and they challenge him. It ends in a truce, and Seri Rama discovers their identity. The family is reunited.

Branch stories (*cerita ranting*)

These are the creations of inventive dalang, derived from the *Ramayana* cycle, 'the Panji tales' and other indigenous legends. Whilst using characters from the *Ramayana,* each branch story is a single, complete, and independent unit. In chronological terms, these stories take place after the death of Ravana. A large number of branch stories has existed for generations, handed down from dalang to dalang through the oral tradition. Practising dalang continue to creatively expand the ranting repertoire to this day.

Themes of *cerita ranting*

- The minor *Ramayana* characters seek spouses and their mettle is tested before winning princesses as wives.
- A disgraced deity kidnaps Sita Dewi in order to get Seri Rama to help him re-ascend heaven. He is 'killed' by Seri Rama and reinstated to his divine form.
- Sita Dewi is kidnapped by Ravana and subsequently rescued. Parallels the main *Ramayana* story.
- Seri Rama's kingdom is invaded by territory-hungry monarchs. The invading forces are usually defeated.
- Seri Rama has a weakness for pretty women. He marries a number of them. Wives are also acquired by him as booty in successful battles. He leaves a string of families in various places. They are all ultimately reunited.
- Seri Rama abandons Sita Dewi in search of extra-marital love and adventure. She, in disguise, faces him in battle, impresses him and they are reunited.
- Seri Rama's territories are invaded by disgruntled kings in search of their daughters/spouses who have been kidnapped by members of Seri Rama's family. The invading forces are either defeated, or the princesses are returned after a peace agreement is concluded.
- Seri Rama banishes his faithful warriors for various misdeeds. Reconciliation is finally effected through elaborate intervention of the gods.

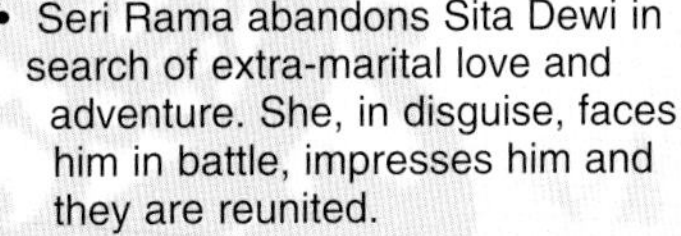

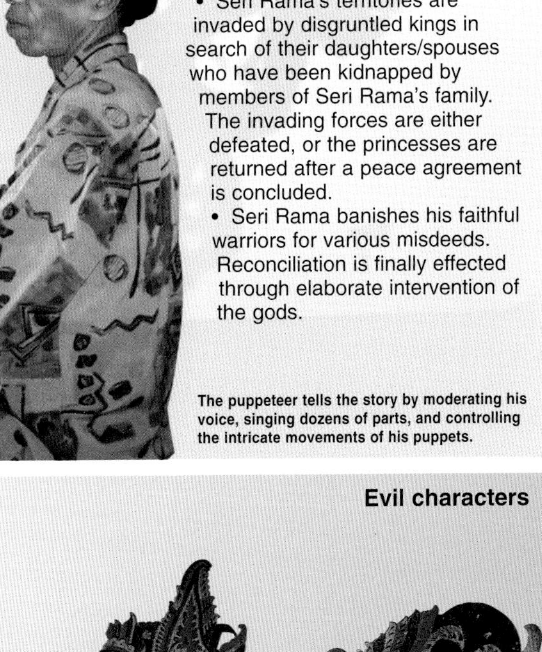

The puppeteer tells the story by moderating his voice, singing dozens of parts, and controlling the intricate movements of his puppets.

The puppets

The *orang kampung* (villager) puppet is a comic figure in *Wayang Kulit.*

A Wayang Kulit Siam set consists of about 60 figures, their size varying from about 15 centimetres to more than 60 centimetres in height depending upon the character. The figures of noble characters, such as Seri Rama (the hero of the *Ramayana*), his brother Laksmana, and his wife, Sita Dewi, are slim and tall while those of the ogres are large and bulky. Most figures are carved with faces in profile, with the body positioned directly frontal and both feet pointing in the same direction. In the case of the ogres, their faces are carved in three-quarter profile and eyes may be visible. Heroic and evil figures have a single articulated arm, jointed at the shoulders, elbows and wrists. Refined or coarse figures are identifiable, apart from their bulk, from details such as nose and mouth shapes and sizes, the eyes, length of their fingernails, and their stances. The heroic ideal is elegant and refined, and a calm exterior indicates strong spiritual qualities. Comic figures have both arms articulated, this being an apparent Javanese influence in puppet design.

Evil characters

Wayang Kulit Gedek, Melayu and Purwa

Three other forms of shadow theatre performed in Malaysia are Wayang Kulit Gedek, Wayang Kulit Melayu and Wayang Kulit Purwa. Derived from either Thai or Java styles of shadow play, they have absorbed local cultural nuances and developed distinct styles. Wayang Kulit Gedek, in particular, is an eclectic blend of modernity and tradition. It has been remarkably reactive to changes in Malay society, and is a medium for social comment in villages. Performances of all three styles are on the decline.

The colourful, intricately carved and delicately drafted Wayang Kulit Gedek puppets are an interesting mix of traditional and modern characters, representing refined, coarse and clown types.

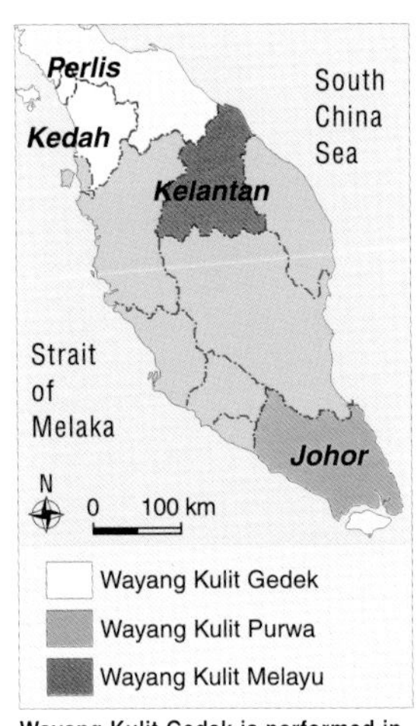

Wayang Kulit Gedek is performed in Kedah and Perlis; Wayang Kulit Purwa in Johor; and Wayang Kulit Melayu in Kelantan.

Wayang Kulit Gedek

Wayang Kulit Gedek is derived from the Thai shadow play Nang Talung. It was initially performed within Thai communities of the northern Malay states of Kedah and Perlis. A stylistically distinct version of the Nang Talung became consolidated locally in the 1930s. This new form, Wayang Kulit Gedek, used similar puppets, musical instruments and, to some extent, a common repertoire. Some of the Buddhist ritual elements of Nang Talung, however, were discarded.

The puppeteers (*dalang*) use local dialects but prefer the southern Thai dialect in invocations, incantations, and songs. Episodes are often selected based on their potential for humour, allowing the dalang to make use of the comic sections to highlight contemporary issues, and to use this form of shadow play as a vehicle for social comment and social critique through scripts.

Principal puppet characters are obtained from southern Thailand. Local puppet-makers only make some of the less intricate comic characters, stage properties such as trees, palaces, and modern conveniences such as aeroplanes or motorcycles.

Wayang Kulit Purwa puppets are highly stylized and crafted to express character.

A whole set of these puppets is a curious mixture of figures designed in the conventional style, and those outrageously modern. The dalang keeps his puppets in one or more folios made of thatched or plaited split bamboo. A set may consist of between 100 and 200 figures, including accessories such as weapons, vehicles and trees. In an average performance, however, about 30–40 are used.

A Wayang Kulit Gedek performance commences with theatre opening rituals. The offerings are made, the theatre building is blessed (*buka panggung* or *buka balai*), the musical instruments are consecrated (*buka alat-alat muzik*), and the dalang undergoes ritual preparation for the performance (*pemujaan diri dalang sendiri*). Rituals also include the consecration of the banana stem (*pemujaan batang pisang*) on which the puppets are to be placed during performance; and the drawing of a ritual symbol (*lukisan gambar-rajah*) on the stem.

The dalang then introduces the sage (Maharisi), the godling with an arrow (Dewa Panah), and a refined godling (Pi Phrai) who is the dalang's representative (*wakil dalang*). The Maharisi figure moves across the screen several times from the dalang's right to his left, and is placed in the banana stem. Maharisi does a salutation gesture (*sembah*) and recites a charm in the Thai language before exiting. The figure of Phra Isuan (the god Indra) seated on an ox is next to be played.

Finally, Pi Phrai is introduced to the audience. He salutes three times, moves across the screen and then salutes a fourth time before lying down flat across the screen. Face downwards, he performs a salutation to the earth thrice. Next, facing up, he salutes the sky twice. The figure goes off-screen for a moment and then re-enters, and addresses the audience on behalf of the dalang, seeking the audience's indulgence and forgiveness for any mistakes the dalang may make in the performance. While the theatre opening rituals take place only on the opening night, this opening segment of the play is re-enacted each night of the performance.

The actual story opens with the pair of clowns, Kieau and Ai Tong. They introduce the dalang and provide a synopsis of the events that are to unfold in the play. The performance may last one or more nights, depending on the story selected and the invitation extended to the troupe. As the events and the dalang's dialogue are improvised, there is much flexibility within a performance. No two performances, even by the same dalang, are ever exactly the same. Performances end with a simple theatre closing (*tutup panggung*) ceremony.

Wayang Kulit Purwa

Wayang Kulit Purwa is believed to be the oldest form of Southeast Asian shadow play. This elegant and refined shadow theatre flourished in Java during

The *pohon beringin* puppet is employed to represent a variety of objects such as mountains, trees or caves. It also possesses ritual significance.

the Hindu Majapahit empire. Through Majapahit influence in the 14th century, Wayang Kulit Purwa is believed to have had some impact on the Malay Peninsula, influencing the Kelantanese form of shadow play called Wayang Kulit Siam.

In the 1520s, with the advent of Islam, Wayang Kulit Purwa in Java underwent significant modifications to counter the Islamic prohibition against naturalistic representation of human anatomy. The figures were extensively stylized and crafted to express character and emotion in a visually abstract manner.

This modified Javanese form re-entered the Malay Peninsula in the 19th century, imported by Javanese immigrants into the southern state of Johor. Changes have taken place in the Malaysian style of Wayang Kulit Purwa, resulting in a genre with its own unique characteristics. However, Wayang Kulit Purwa in Johor still retains the essential Javanese style, seen particularly in the use of *Mahabharata* episodes. The dramatic repertoire is extensive and is derived from Kawi (old Javanese) versions of the *Mahabharata*.

A few Wayang Kulit Purwa puppeteers, mainly Javanese immigrants or their descendants, continue to be active in Johor. Performances are conducted in the Javanese dialect, but Malay has recently begun to be used. The incantations continue to be recited in Javanese. Music is provided by a gamelan orchestra and the range of tunes is embellished by songs sung by the dalang. The manipulation of the puppets is considered to be the most important element in the play. A selected episode is completed in one night.

The late Nik Abdul Rahman was a royal *bomoh* (shaman) in Kelantan and a famous Wayang Kulit Melayu *dalang* (puppeteer).

Wayang Kulit Melayu

Derived from the highly refined Javanese Wayang Gedog which uses the Javanese Panji romances as its principal story, Wayang Kulit Melayu is performed only in Kelantan. It is an example of a rare instance in traditional Malaysian performing arts culture where an art form flourished under court support in the 1920s. Puppeteers were sent to Java to learn this form of shadow play where it is active. Royal support reportedly dissipated at the outbreak of World War II and with the onset of the Japanese Occupation.

Rejuvenated during the time of national independence in the late 1950s, Wayang Kulit Melayu was restaged for a folk audience, rather than as royal entertainment. However, its classicism translated poorly to its new audience base, and it gradually lost popular support.

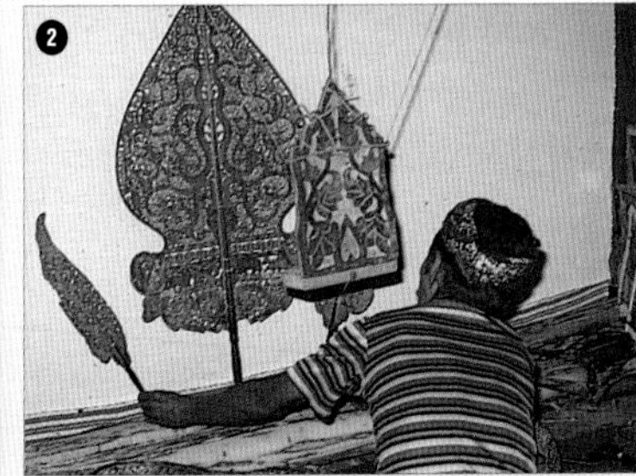

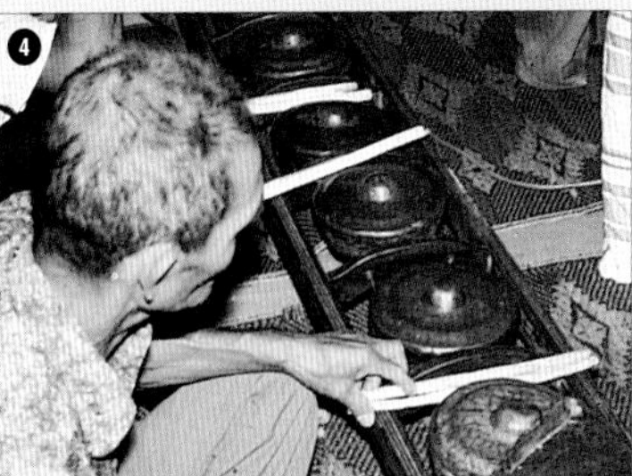

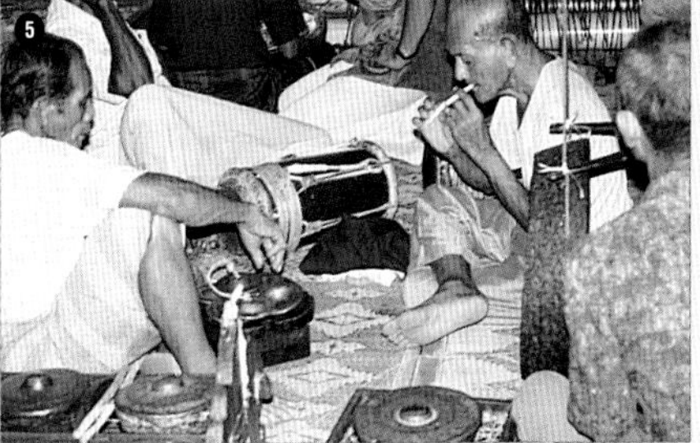

1. Close-up of the puppets.
2. The *pohon beringin* puppet is the first to be played.
3. The performance is long and solemn, involving many characters.
4. The orchestra includes a gamelan—clear evidence of Javanese influence.
5. Musicians watch the performance closely for their cue to play.

Wayang Kulit Gedek

Wayang Kulit Gedek puppets are made of goatskin. They are delicate, colourful and translucent, with intricate carving and perforated designs. Conventional figures are characters from classical mythology—gods, demons, semi-divine heroes and legendary princesses. The modern figures include pirates, soldiers, buxom ladies dressed in the latest Western fashion or tight-fitting sarongs and blouses with plunging necklines, and cigar-smoking gentlemen in suits, ties and top hats.

Generally, only one arm of each puppet is articulated. The fixed arm wields a weapon, such as a sword or bow in the case of male characters, and a bouquet in the case of female ones. Clowns, servant-attendants and peasants have both arms articulated. In addition, their lower jaws are often moveable.

Types of puppets

Type	Role	Characteristics
Refined (*halus*)	Divine or semi-divine heroes, princesses and certain demons (*yaksha*).	Decorated with elaborate clothing and jewellery; tendency to be physically small, with the exception of demons.
Coarse (*kasar*)	Demons and rough or uncouth human characters.	Bulky with protruding eyes and teeth, visible gums and long claws.
Clowns	Comic servant-attendants.	Painted in dark colours so that they emerge as bold shadows.

Performance elements

Dramatic repertoire	Musical repertoire	Instruments
Ramakien (Thai version of the *Ramayana*).	Pieces for walking.	Pair of inverted gongs (*canang*)
About 20 stories adapted from Thai and Malay folk tales and romances, borrowed from Nang Talung or derived from Middle Eastern/Indian sources.	Pieces for war.	Single-headed stick drum (*geduk*)
Newly invented stories used as a vehicle for social comment.	Pieces for bathing, relaxing or courtship.	Single-headed hourglass-shaped drum (*gedumbak*)
	A wide range of non-*wayang* tunes derived from local folk music, and Malay and North Indian films.	Pair of hand cymbals (*kesi* or *cing*)
		Double-reed oboe (*serunai*)
		Pair of suspended gongs (*tetawak*)
		Wooden clappers
		Modern instruments are sometimes used

Chinese puppet theatre

Three-dimensional Chinese puppet theatre was brought to Malaysia by Chinese migrants in the 19th century. These are glove puppets (po-te-hi)*, performed in Hokkien, rod puppets* (cha-ka-lei)*, performed in Teochew, and string puppets or marionettes* (cha-ke-re) *performed in Hokkien. The puppet theatre is similar to Chinese opera in style and content, but with more realism. Performances are conducted on makeshift stages in temples or open areas, usually during religious festivals and to celebrate the birthdays of deities.*

Rod puppets are about 25 centimetres high with expressively sculptured and painted faces.

Types of Chinese puppets

Chinese puppets for theatre may be divisible into three-dimensional varieties (rod, glove and string puppets) and two-dimensional (shadow puppets). Of these, three-dimensional puppet theatre is performed in Malaysia, using glove, rod and, on rare occasions, string puppets. Chinese puppet theatre is urban-based and performances are usually held in towns and cities with a significant Chinese population.

Rod puppets

Rod puppets are dolls that are operated by three wooden rods. The puppeteer holds a central rod to which the puppet's head is attached with one hand and manipulates the other two rods that are joined to the wrists of the puppet's arms with the other hand. Objects such as swords, fans and canes may be affixed to the hands of the puppets which are in the form of a clenched fist with a hole through it. Other puppets have fingers pointing in the requisite finger position in live opera. The female character has her thumb touching the middle finger and other fingers extended. The male character has his thumb touching the ring finger and the index and middle fingers extended. These characters can also hold brooms, spears and other objects with their two arms.

Glove puppet theatre originates from Quanzhou, a city in Fujian province in China. This form of theatre derives from the tradition of the puppeteer travelling from village to village with a sack full of puppets.

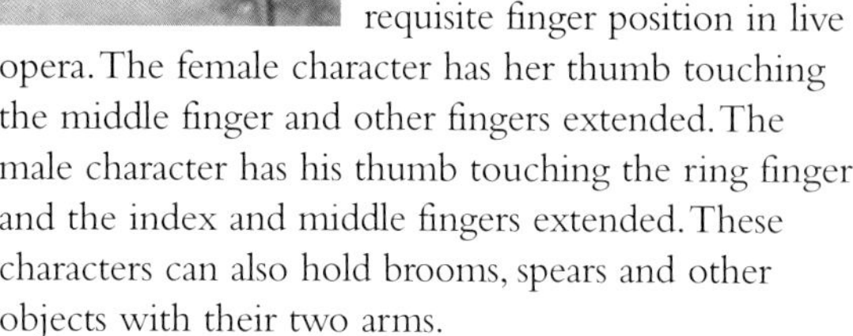

Glove puppets

The glove puppet is a cloth bag fitted over the hand. It consists of a head, hands, feet and a costume shaped like a three-fingered glove. The puppeteer manipulates the doll by inserting his hand through the cloth costume which has some framework around the shoulders. The index finger controls the head, while the thumb and middle finger control the puppet's arms. Puppets vary in size according to the personality portrayed.

Costumes and characters

Each puppet troupe has between 40 and 100 puppets, ranging from the highest social status (the king) to the lowest (the servant). Puppet heads, originally brought from Fukien province in China, are carved of wood and coated with wax. Sometimes special facial features are designed with fine clay. As in live opera, one can discern the character of a puppet by its facial features and its costume. The facial features define the role type: male (*sheng*), female (*dan*), clown (*chou*) and the painted face (*jing*). The colour and decorations of the costumes define the type, rank and status of the character (see 'Chinese opera').

Costume decorations are based on symbolism found in Chinese art and literature. The phoenix and the dragon, symbols of prosperity and fertility, are used as imperial emblems on stage costumes. The plum blossom, regarded as the symbol of long life and femininity, decorates the costumes of female characters. The various puppet character types have shoes sewn to their cloth legs. High black satin boots with thick white soles are usually worn by male roles for military and official occasions. Women wear flat-soled slippers of various colours.

In some ways, a greater degree of realism exists in puppet theatre than on the live stage. Cardboard horses can be used in the puppet theatre whereas in the live theatre only the horse-whip is used to represent the horse. Puppets can juggle with weapons, and throw them at the enemies during fighting scenes. Cloth animals also appear on stage.

The performance

The percussion ensemble plays for about half an hour to announce a performance. This is followed by a prologue which begins with a thanksgiving ceremony known as Tiaojiaguan performed by a

Facial features

The eyebrows of male, female and clown roles are finely pencilled in a slight curve. In the case of the painted face, straight brows which are broad at the top and narrow down towards the nose indicate good characters with dignity while slightly curved, upturned or drooping ones represent cowards or bad characters that are restless. Eyebrows which are dotted with broken patterns indicate ferocity and hostility. Gentle characters are given small eye-sockets while more rough and crude characters are given larger eye-sockets.

mute white-faced character who moves across the stage holding a scroll to welcome the audience and to wish them prosperity. The stagehand then brings the Prince puppet (Taizi) and presents it to the temple deity. The stagehand returns with a red packet and biscuits to wish the troupe good fortune. The actual story is then played.

The puppet theatre shares an almost identical repertory of stories with live opera. Stories from the 'Romance of the Three Kingdoms' and 'Journey to the West' are popular.

Music of the puppet theatre

The music of the puppet theatre consists of different melody and speech types as well as percussion music, each associated with a different dramatic function. No scores are used, and music is learnt by rote.

The most commonly used melody type is the seven-worded tune (*qizidiao*). The slow and melancholy version is sung during scenes of sadness while the fast version is used to express anger or happiness, or to describe a scene, action or thought. Glove puppet theatres also perform the so-called 'small tune' or *xiaodiao*, and a large repertoire of happy and sad tunes, each identified by a name taken from sources such as popular tunes.

Common speech types comprise chants on one or two notes delivered with regular beats played on the woodblocks and with syllables that rhyme at the end of each phrase. These chants are usually sung by puppets who are praying to Buddha, or by comic characters who act as narrators.

The percussion ensemble announces the beginning and end of the show, change of scenes, exits and entrances of puppet characters, fighting scenes and other dramatic passages. There are very few syncretized aspects to the music; sometimes an electric guitar and keyboard are added.

Physical characteristics

Wigs made from real hair are fixed permanently to the heads of the puppets. The coiffures indicate the social status of the wearers. Puppet heads also have beards and whiskers fixed. The shape, size and colour of the beard help in identification. Comedians usually have a moustache. Powerful characters of high status can be recognized by a long, full, black, grey or white beard which covers the mouth and reaches the puppet's chest.

There are only a few puppet troupes left in Malaysia. Troupes are small, comprising seven to 10 members. Audiences for the puppet theatre are mainly drawn from the ranks of children and the older generation who bring the very young. Most of the younger generation cannot understand the intricacies of the art and are not familiar with the themes and tunes.

Chinese puppet musical ensemble

The musical ensembles of the glove and rod puppet theatre are divided into the civil (*wen*) and military (*wu*) sections, although exact instruments used may vary. In the glove puppet ensemble the wen section consists of a coconut shell fiddle (*yehu*), moon guitar (*yueqin*) and two-stringed fiddle (*erxian*). Sometimes a bass guitar and ukulele are added. The wu section comprises drums (*gu*), clappers (*ban*), cymbals (*bo*), gongs (*luo*) and woodblocks.

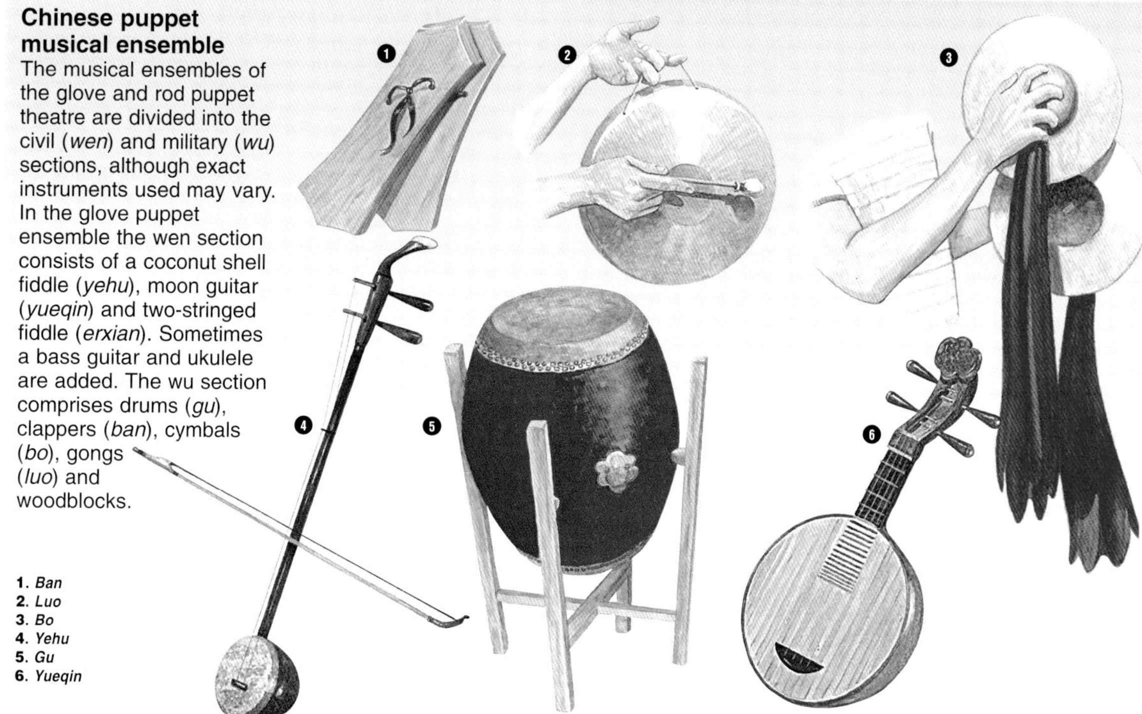

1. *Ban*
2. *Luo*
3. *Bo*
4. *Yehu*
5. *Gu*
6. *Yueqin*

String puppets are painstakingly carved out of wood, with the faces painted. Their clothes are usually made of silk and attached to their bodies are eight to 30 strings which help bring them to animated life.

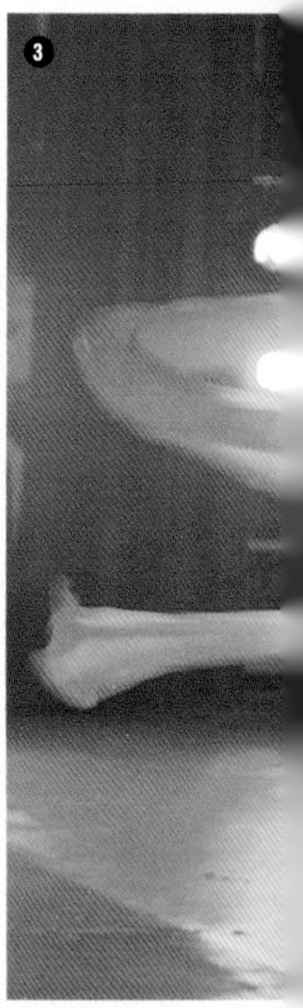

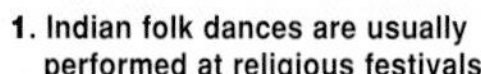

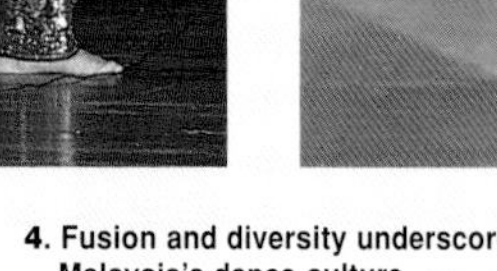

1. Indian folk dances are usually performed at religious festivals.

2. Mak Yong is a fusion of ritual, dance, song, music and stories.

3. Foreign dance cultures, such as that from China, have produced hybrids of dance genres in Malaysia.

4. Fusion and diversity underscore Malaysia's dance culture.

5. The Orang Asli's dance idioms are taken from their natural environment.

6. The traditional dances of the indigenous people of Sabah and Sarawak are rooted in animism.

DANCE AND DANCE THEATRE

Malaysia's dance heritage has evolved from centuries of cross-cultural exchanges between peoples and traditions. The Orang Asli and the numerous indigenous peoples of Sabah and Sarawak, who own the oldest dance traditions in the country, have dance movements that are closely associated with symbols and metaphors of the forest, rivers and highlands which form their habitat. These dances, whilst enriched by inter-borrowing from newer Malay dance culture, retain the ritualism of their ancient animistic belief systems.

Malay dance traditions range from court dance traditions, folk and social dances to ancient and popular dance theatres, and new creative dances. Over the centuries, the Malays have synthesized and acculturated elements of foreign dances and ingeniously incorporated them into their own performances. Malay dance traditions have been influenced by the dance cultures of India, the Middle East, China and Portugal. This fusion and diversity have become part of Malaysia's dance legacy.

Ancient rituals, stylized dance movements, acting, singing and the playing of musical instruments are fused and presented as dance theatres in the form of Mak Yong and Menora. Similarly, the ancient martial art of *silat* has been incorporated with storytelling, acting, singing and music in the Randai dance theatre. Mak Yong, Menora and Randai are three instances of dance theatre that are rooted in ancient Malay beliefs and customs, at the same time exhibiting influences from abroad. The Thai-inspired Menora has its roots in the ritual performance of old Buddhist texts while Randai was brought over by Minangkabau Malays from Indonesia.

Malay folk dances are closely affiliated to the dances of areas around the Strait of Melaka, the Riau Archipelago, the Sulu Sea and the South China Sea. Joget, Inang, Asli and Zapin are four such pan-Malay folk dances that are performed nationwide either as social dances or as choreographed pieces. These forms show, in turn, regional variations. The different dance styles reflect the subtle cultural nuances of each region despite the borrowings and exchanges of dance styles between the states in Malaysia. These have enriched the Malay folk dance repertoire over the centuries.

Dances from beyond Southeast Asia have also had a lasting impact on Malaysia, such as Indian classical and folk dances. The influence of many dance cultures from Asia, the Middle East and Europe on Malaysia's dance tradition has produced hybrids of dance genres. Indigenous dance traditions have either remained in their original forms or have been assimilated into newer traditions without forgoing the distinctiveness of their Malaysian identity.

Indian dances have influenced other dance styles in Malaysia.

Earliest dance forms

The oldest dance traditions in Peninsula Malaysia belong to the Orang Asli. This lively indigenous performance tradition was thriving before the coming of other Malay peoples into the land. The early Malay dances are manifestations of the ancient harmonious relationship between the Orang Asli and nature. They feature dance idioms that reflect the flora, fauna and their habitat. Dance fulfils ceremonial, social, and in some instances, healing functions within these indigenous Malay communities.

Orang Asli dances in modern times sometimes use contemporary costumes and stage settings alongside traditional musical instruments.

Location of Orang Asli

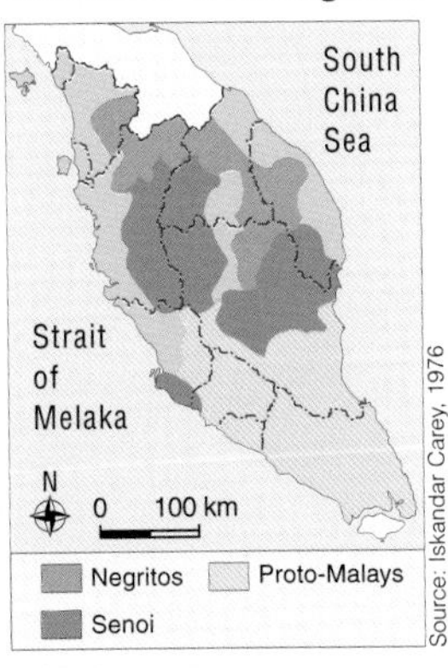

The Orang Asli of Peninsular Malaysia are generally divided into three main groups: the Senoi of the north and central interior rainforests, the Negritos (or Semang) in the northern region of the Peninsula, and the aboriginal or proto-Malays in the southern region. These groups and their sub-groups are:

Senoi:
Temiar, Semai, Jah Hut, Che' Wong, Semoq Beri and Mah Meri.

Negritos:
Jahai, Batek, Mendriq, Lanoh, and Kintak.

Proto-Malays:
Jakun, Temuan, Semelai, Orang Laut and Orang Seletar sub-groups.

Dance and the natural environment

The Orang Asli's dance tradition is subdivided into three groups: dances of the Semang or Negritos, dances of the Senoi, and dances of the proto-Malays. Of the three groups, the Negritos and Senoi are closely connected with the rainforest, while the proto-Malays are coastal-based. The Senoi, the largest Orang Asli group, inhabit the highland areas. The Negritos dwell in the lowland tropical forests, and the proto-Malays live on the fringes of the forest, river banks and mangrove swamps.

The dances of the Negritos and Senoi are intimately related to the forest while those of the proto-Malays represent movement idioms from the flora and fauna of mangrove swamps, rivers and seas.

Dance in the rainforest

To the Senoi and Negritos, the rainforest is not just familiar landscape. It also houses the spirits and souls of their ancestors. Discreet behaviour and care are needed to maintain the balance between man and nature. The Senoi and Negritos believe that everything in the forest is potentially animated and has a soul. Contact between them and the souls of the forest is made through dance and music.

This is best exemplified by the Temiar people's Sewang dance ritual. The Temiar believe in the power of dreams. One may dream of a plant's 'head soul' (*halaq* or spirit-guides who appear in dreams in the shape of fruits, trees and flowers). This soul is able to bestow songs upon the dreamer. The songs received —dreamsongs—become sacred and communal, shared during the Sewang ritual dance ceremony. They are viewed as the secret path to a harmonious co-existence between man and the forest. The receivers of dreamsongs become the medium between the spirit guide and the ordinary man.

Dance of the proto-Malays

In contrast, the dances of the proto-Malays are closely associated with social events. The Orang Laut and Orang Seletar, for example, perform dances to celebrate weddings, community feasts and other social gatherings.

The Orang Seletar (who live in mangrove areas and along the rivers of southern Johor), and the Orang Laut (who inhabit Johor's southwest coastal shores) live near Malay villages. Their dances display stylistic similarities with Malay folk dances. Musical instruments consisting of a small gong, a violin, and a drum are often borrowed or purchased from the Malay villagers. The songs accompanying their dances are sung in quatrains (*pantun*) by the dancers and musicians. While there are shared performance elements with the Malays, the dance metaphors are more reflective of the natural environment.

The Orang Seletar's dances of the Ketam Bangkang (a species of mud crab), Kepah Ngo'ngai (edible bivalve molluscs), Beting Kepah (shallow shoals of molluscs), Ketam Bongai (riverine crabs) and Gongong (gongong shellfish) are about aquatic

fauna. The subjects of their dance are the crabs, shellfish, shallow shoals and edible molluscs that provide them with food and subsistence. Like their dances, the lyrics of the songs are composed to depict real but amusing behaviour patterns of the crabs and shellfish.

Dance movements are stylized imitations of crabs or molluscs climbing up and down floating tree branches, entering and exiting holes in the ground, or gestures of people picking up crabs and shellfish from shallow shoals or river banks. The dances are casual and joyous, allowing much interaction between performers and spectators. They are performed in the evenings and may last till dawn.

Another group of proto-Malays, the Temuan of Gunung Ledang in Johor, are a land-based community and their dances imitate movements of forest primates such as the slow loris, monkeys and gibbons. The animals' antics in the forest inspire Temuan women to craft dance movements about them. Tarian Konkong and Siamang Tunggal, for instance, are performed while dancing in circles to the accompaniment of *keranting* (bamboo zither), *kong-kong* (bamboo tubes), *tong-tong* (wooden xylophones), and *serunai* (bamboo oboe). Temuan men play the music ensemble, with senior Temuan women occasionally assisting. The dances are joyous and playful, and celebratory of nature and its wonders.

Sewang ritual

The Temiar's dreamsongs are imparted through dance during the Sewang ceremony. Dance movements are ambulatory with gentle swaying. The dancers make forward, sideward and backward stepping movements in a circular formation on a sprung floor of bamboo slats. They bend and sway their torsos, swinging their arms in front of their bodies. There is a sense of looseness of the arms and body as the dance picks up momentum to the rising crescendo of the chorus.

Bamboo stamping tubes are used to accentuate the dreamsong and the dance movements. As the rhythms of the bamboo stamping tubes become more divided, the dancers bend their torsos lower, singing a higher pitch. The dancing and music eventually reach frenzied heights, with both dancers and musicians reeling between conscious and subconscious levels. The dancers perform rapid low-level jumps while rolling their heads sideways as the song becomes louder. Some of the dancers would faint and are placed near the centre of the dance circle to be revived by the spirit-medium. When the frenzy subsides, the dance is performed anew from beginning to end. This cycle of dance continues into the early morning until exhaustion takes its toll over the entire ensemble of performers.

Scenes from a 1970 Temiar ritual seance. These ceremonies are said to be the means by which dreamsongs from spirit guides are imparted.

Dream theories and healing rituals

First introduced to the rest of the world in the 1930s when sociologist Kilton Stewart visited the Temiar, the Orang Asli group's Sewang ritual has long been a source of inspiration and fascination for Westerners. In his *Dream Theory in Malaya*, Stewart writes: 'Senoi psychology falls into two categories. The first deals with dream interpretation, the second with dream expression in the agreement trance or cooperative reverie.... The average Senoi layman practises the psychotherapy of dream interpretation as a regular feature of education and daily social intercourse.'

These 'healing arts' have attracted anthropologists as well as musicologists to study, record and transcribe Temiar rituals. Marina Roseman, who lived with the Temiar for two years, suggests in her book *Healing Sounds from the Malaysian Rainforest: Temiar Music and Medicine* that the gestures and sounds of dance and music acquire a potency that can transform thoughts, emotions, and bodies.

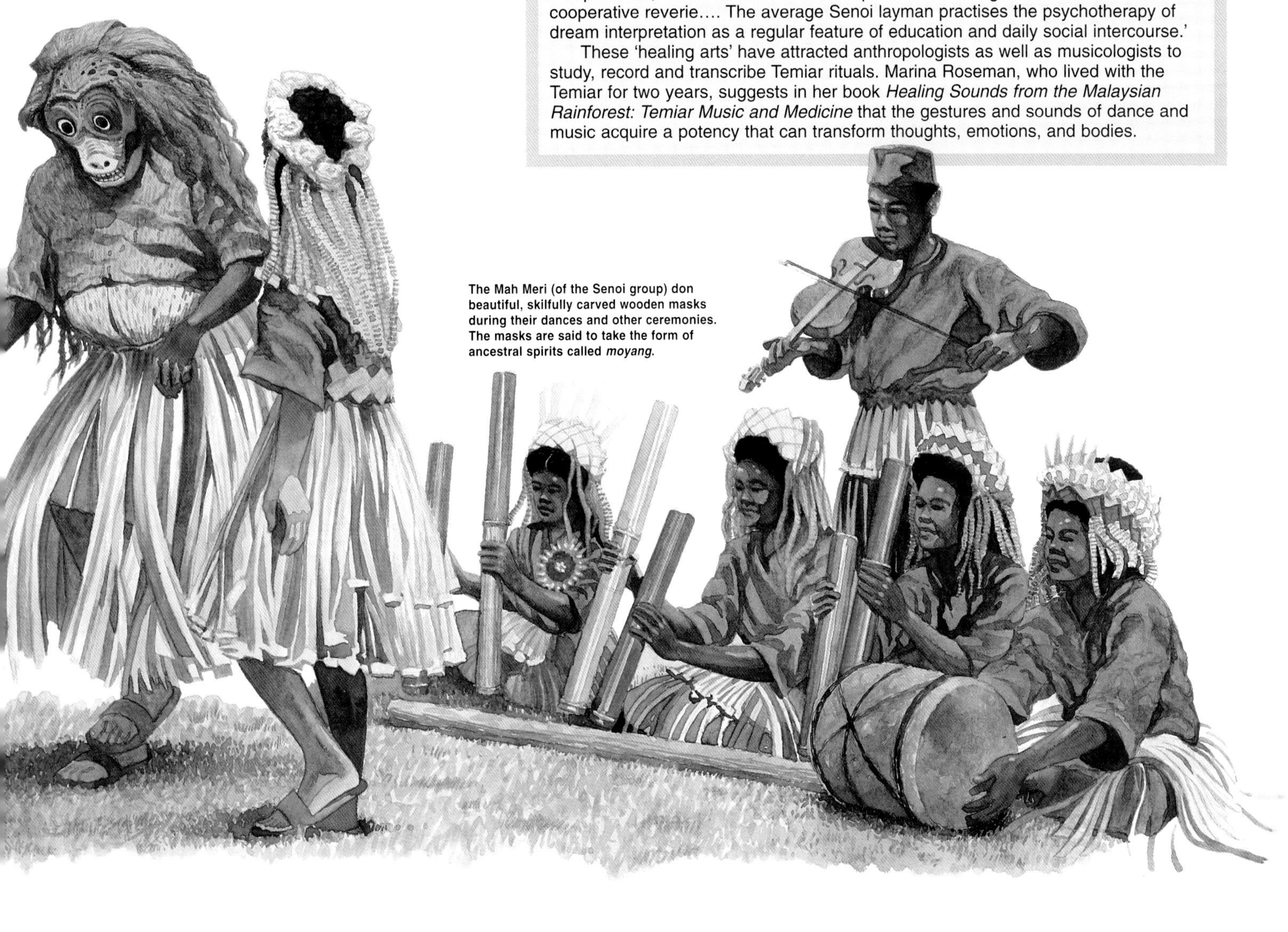

The Mah Meri (of the Senoi group) don beautiful, skilfully carved wooden masks during their dances and other ceremonies. The masks are said to take the form of ancestral spirits called *moyang*.

Mak Yong: Ancient folk theatre

Mak Yong is the oldest living example of Malay dance theatre and is the least subject to external influences. Developed from animistic beliefs and shamanistic activity, Mak Yong's origins are linked to divine sources. It is an arabesque of rituals, song, dance, stories and music, once performed only by women. Mak Yong in its original form is now rarely performed in its Kelantanese homeland for religious and economic reasons.

Mak Yong performances are found in Kelantan, Terengganu and the Patani region of southern Thailand.

Origins and history

The origins of Mak Yong are mired in mystery and folklore. Its roots sink deep into animism and shamanistic beliefs, as illustrated by the symbolism and spiritual meanings of the stories and dances. Performed in the villages of Kelantan, Terengganu and the Patani region of southern Thailand, its form and substance have barely changed over the last 100 years. Performances are either for entertainment or ritual purposes. Ritual performances are usually performed in combination with the most important of Malay shamanistic dances—the Main Puteri—which shares a similar spiritual essence (see 'Belief systems of traditional theatre').

Mak Yong is essentially a folk art. For a brief period early in the 20th century, the genre received support from the Kelantan palace. However, the attempt to create a classical version of Mak Yong failed to materialize (see 'Mak Yong's court sojourn').

There are very few remaining Mak Yong troupes. Performances in urban areas are extensively modified to meet the expectations of modern audiences. Rural performances are more in keeping with tradition, but are rare.

Menghadap rebab is the finest elaboration of Mak Yong dance. Of deep spiritual significance, it involves saluting the *rebab*, which symbolizes the guru. This opening dance is an essential part of the performance.

Conventions

Mak Yong performances are guided by certain basic conventions. The theatre (*panggung* or *bansal*), a temporary structure made of bamboo and thatched palm leaves (*attap*) approximately four by five metres in size, must be constructed in an east-west alignment. Traditionally, the panggung is built at ground level, but now is usually elevated for better audience visibility. Ground-level panggung are still used in ritual Mak Yong performances.

The principal musician, who plays the three-stringed lute (*rebab*), must sit on the panggung's eastern side close to the central post (*tiang seri*). Other stage conventions relate to the positioning of the performers, the start of the orchestra, as well as precautions and prohibitions to be observed in handling the paraphernalia, particularly the musical instruments as they are believed to have ritual and spiritual significance.

Most of the action takes place at the centre stage (*gelanggang*). All members of a troupe remain onstage throughout the performance, even when they are not performing. While technically offstage, the performers sit on the floor around the edges of the stage, from where they continue to contribute to the play as chorus members (*jung dondang*).

Few stage or hand properties are used—a few strands of bamboo tied together in a wand (*rotan berai*), a dagger (*keris*) and wooden swords (*golok*). A theatre opening ritual (*buka panggung*) and a similar theatre closing ceremony (*tutup panggung*) are mandatory. The buka panggung involves a series of invocations addressed to a host of supernatural beings and spirits. Offerings are made by a shaman (*bomoh*). He seeks the spirits' blessings, and ensures that the spirits will aid the performance to a successful completion.

Performances begin, as a rule, after the late evening prayer (*isyak*). Prior to the buka panggung rituals, the musical instruments and the musicians take their places. The east-west alignment of the theatre allows the performers to face both the *rebab* and the direction of the rising sun during their opening dance. This is known as *menghadap rebab*, intended to salute the rebab. This sequence changes for the more elaborate ritual performances.

Heavenly being

Changing faces

Often the faces of performers were painted to show the qualities of each character. Pictured here are Mak Yong costumes from the early 20th century. Modernization of the theatre form has led to costumes being replaced by glitzier accoutrements.

Male lead character

Ogre

Female attendant

Clown

Performance elements

From a single story, 'Dewa Muda', the Mak Yong repertoire has been expanded to 12 stories. Other stories are 'Dewa Pechil', 'Dewa Indera-Indera Dewa', 'Anak Raja Gondang', 'Gading Bertimang' and 'Raja Tangkai Hati'. All deal with the adventures of gods, mythical princes and the supernatural. The sources of these stories remain unknown with the exception of 'Anak Raja Gondang', which comes from the Buddhist *Jataka Tales*. It is likely that the remaining stories are derived from the extensive indigenous mythology of the Kelantan-Patani Malays.

In rural performances, the cast comprises eight to 10 performers. Between 20 and 25 performers may take part in a more sophisticated performance. Additionally, there may be four to six musicians in a large professional troupe. The orchestra consists of three main instruments: the most important being the rebab, a pair of double-headed barrel drums (*gendang*) and a pair of hanging gongs (*tetawak*). (See 'Music of Mak Yong, Mek Mulung and Jikey').

The Performance

Following the theatre opening, the Mak Yong actresses enter for the *menghadap rebab* dance. It leads to several other sung pieces to the accompaniment of dances, performed either in groups or as solos. Then the king (Pak Yong), having bid farewell to his wives, sets out to seek the elder clown (*peran tua*), and sends him to seek the younger clown (*peran muda*). The Pak Yong then introduces himself and establishes which of the Mak Yong stories is to be performed. This sequence fulfils the function of introducing the main characters and the gist of the story to the audience.

The story then unfolds. In most Mak Yong stories, the tale begins with the Pak Yong wishing to have a dream interpreted, as in 'Dewa Muda', or to go on a long journey, as in 'Anak Raja Gondang'. The story is continued on subsequent nights, picking up from where it stopped the previous night. A performance may last a week and on the final night ends with a ritual closing ceremony.

Roles in Mak Yong

Role	Characters	Purpose
Pak Yong	The lead role of king (*raja*) or prince (*raja muda*). Divided into *pak yong tua* (elder king) and *pak yong muda* (younger king).	Traditionally played by a woman, the role has spiritual importance. The notion of god-kingship gives the *pak yong* an aura of divinity.
Mak Yong	The female lead. Sometimes divided into the *mak yong* (queen) and *puteri mak yong* (princess).	The main female character, pivotal to the story. Always played by a woman.
Peran/pengasuh	Two main roles of male attendants—*peran tua* (elder clown-servant) and *peran muda* (the younger clown/servant).	They serve the main characters and act as companions. Deeply spiritual, the roles are traced to the Javanese pre-Hindu god Semar.
Inang	Two roles of female attendants—*inang sulong* (the elder) and *inang bongsu* (the younger).	Female attendant and companion to the female lead characters.
Tok wak	Elderly man who may be the royal astrologer (*tok nujum*), fortune teller, royal executioner, and a range of royal craftsmen.	A highly interesting and multifaceted character who fulfils defined functions within the story.
Dewa	All the benevolent gods, goddesses and spirits.	They introduce the 'other worldly' element into the story, usually performed by men.
Jinn/gergasi	A range of negative characters featuring genies and giants. They vary in spiritual power and malevolence.	Nasty creatures who plague the main characters and enhance a sense of drama.
Orang darat	A range of village folk of both sexes who are, essentially, country bumpkins.	Provide comic relief and contrast to the high drama of the play.

Body language
Movements of the hand, arms, feet and torso combine to form sequences which identify role types and emotional nuances. Hand movements (*ibu tari*) are not precise in usage and meaning, varying from one Mak Yong diva to another. Illustrated here are some basic movements, possibly adapted from the ancient Indian treatise, the '*Natyasastra*'.

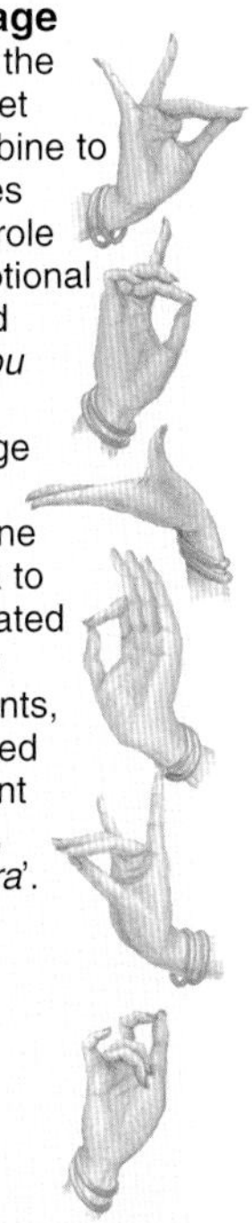

Randai

Randai is a form of dance theatre of the Minangkabau people of Negeri Sembilan. It fuses the silat *art of self-defence, stylized dance, songs and plays based on an extensive traditional storytelling repertoire. The silat dance is the conveyance for the acting, dancing and storytelling. This dance theatre form illustrates the continuing existence of independent cultural spaces for expressing Malaysia's rich ethnic diversity.*

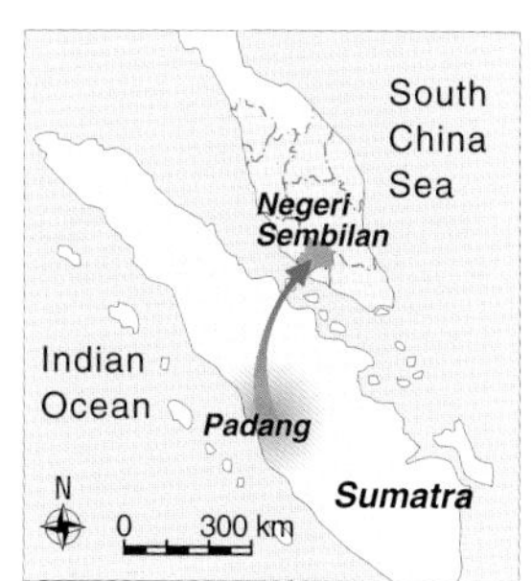

The Minangkabau Diaspora beyond Sumatra has resulted in Minangkabau settlements being established in various parts of Southeast Asia, including Malaysia.

Silat and dance

In the traditional Minangkabau villages of West Sumatra, the art of *silat*, which is a martial arts form, and its lore and legends, are taught to all young men. The training is conducted in the *surau* which is not only a Muslim place of worship but also a community centre. Training in silat is divided into two levels. Amateurs and young men initially receive instruction in basic silat stances, martial prances, hand and body manipulation techniques and the building up and control of stamina. The students then learn combative manoeuvring with the hands or with hand-held weapons. Duels between silat performers become more intricate when the *keris* (dagger) is used. At this point the art becomes *Pencak Silat*, the form of silat intended for self-defence.

Pencak Silat, when performed as dance to the music of the *taklempong* (horizontal knobbed gongs), drums, and small flutes, is known as Tari Sewah. However, the dance is known as Tari Gelombang when a group of men execute silat movements without weapons for the purpose of saluting dignitaries and special guests at a village celebration, wedding or ceremonial installation of a chief. Tari Gelombang—literally meaning the dance of rolling waves—demonstrates the grace of silat as an elegant dance form—a flow of undulating movements involving various parts of the body.

When a large group of dancers in a circle performs silat dance movements, the dance assumes different forms and functions. It becomes a means of acting, storytelling and singing in the dance theatre style known as Randai.

Silat as martial art

The word *silat* refers to a system of body movements for self-defence utilizing *langkah* (steps) and jurus (movements). Traditional silat harnesses the ability to remain alert and defensive, thus requiring the practitioner to be non-offensive and to only fight when attacked. During training, silat practitioners are drilled in specific movement techniques and styles that are called *pencak*. Thus, *Pencak Silat* means both technical and stylistic movements acquired during training and the act of self-defence through a system of body movements. The langkah is the basic movement structure that aids in responding to shifting body weight as the practitioner coordinates the jurus consisting of a variety of elbow and take-down techniques, twisting of the torso and breaking counter attacks.

There are several hundred styles of Pencak Silat in Malaysia that abide by their own formal curriculum based on the teachings of their *mahaguru* (great teacher).

Randai is traditionally performed in open spaces in the evening. A performance may last several hours. Present-day Randai performances are often staged indoors in community halls or auditoriums.

With the Minangkabau Diaspora, many regional variations of Randai may be witnessed. In Negeri Sembilan, for instance, Randai is performed with its own local flavour, differing from the West Sumatran version. Despite this, Randai remains a living legacy of Minangkabau artistic ingenuity. It forms part of the curriculum at the Akademi Seni Kebangsaan (National Arts Academy). In contrast to the traditional convention, women feature along with men in performances staged by the academy.

Minangkabau culture

The *merantau* phenomenon

As defenders of the Minangkabau social code of conduct and customary laws (adat), the men undergo customary voluntary migration (*merantau*) with the objective of seeking better fortunes in distant places before returning home to marry and build a family of their own. The merantau phenomenon and the Minangkabau Diaspora beyond Sumatra have led to the establishment of Minangkabau settlements in various parts of Southeast Asia, particularly in the Indonesian archipelago and Malaysia. The largest of these is in Negeri Sembilan. Arts, music and dance in Negeri Sembilan are distinctively Minangkabau in form and character.

Minangkabau storytelling

Storytelling, or *bakaba*, was the forerunner of Randai and means 'to tell stories'. Narration of love stories is known as *batalarek*, while stories depicting the heroic deeds of the Minangkabau legendary hero, Si Tongga Maget Jabang, are known as *basijobang* or *basitongga*. Stories are narrated in the form of songs and poetry accompanied by either the *rebab* (bowed lute) or a matchbox. The narrator, known as Sijobang, would take a box of matches and rhythmically tap it on the floor to accompany the poetic rendition of the story. Stories derived from the traditional repertoires of storytellers are performed in Randai.

Elaborate traditional Minangkabau costumes are featured in Malaysian performances of Randai.

Minangkabau storytellers are accompanied by the *rebab*.

Components of a Randai performance

A performance starts with a procession of musicians playing hand-held *taklempong pacik* (knobbed gongs), drums, and a *pupuit* or *serunai* (double-reed oboe) leading the Randai performers into the arena. Following the introduction of the group, the musicians leave the area to sit among the audience, or on the periphery of the performance area.

The dancers begin by executing a salutation dance. This is followed by *silat* dances in a circle with songs sung by a lead singer-dancer. The remaining dancers sing refrains from the song as they dance to the melodic phrases. The song acts as a prologue to the story and play-acting that commences at the end of each dance sequence. The dancers punctuate the melodic phrases and accompanying dance motifs with hand clapping and thigh slapping. Rhythmic mnemonics are at times interjected to accentuate the hand clapping and thigh slapping. When the dancing and singing come to an end, the dancers sit on the ground, still maintaining the circle formation.

The actors of the selected play now enter the circle to commence the play. Actors are usually drawn from the same people who dance the Randai. Female impersonators are required to sit outside the circle of dancers to await their turn. When an act is completed, the dancers resume their silat dance around the circle and begin a new song and dance routine as a prologue to the following act. This sequence of song, dance and acting is repeated until the story is completed.

Play

The dramatic repertoire for a Randai play is derived from traditional Minangkabau stories. The stories are crafted to teach values believed to be an integral part of Minangkabau customs (*adat*). The storyline is simple and extols virtues like filial piety, faithfulness within marriage and the importance of preserving the family's sanctity.

In the play pictured (right and below), a young woman is expelled from the family by a jealous and scheming mother-in-law. She is eventually proven to be of sterling character, the mother-in-law is chastised, and the family is reunited. The arrangement of performers on stage is flexible, but a basic guide is shown in the diagram (far right).

The acting is highly expressive and melodramatic. In this act (left), the patriarch chastises his recalcitrant family, emphasizing the need for a peaceful family life.

Dance

Dancers are attired as warriors but the *silat* movements are executed as a series of undulating movements without the aggressive element inherent in martial silat. The dancers accentuate these movements with hand clapping. The use of silat in Randai demonstrates its versatility.

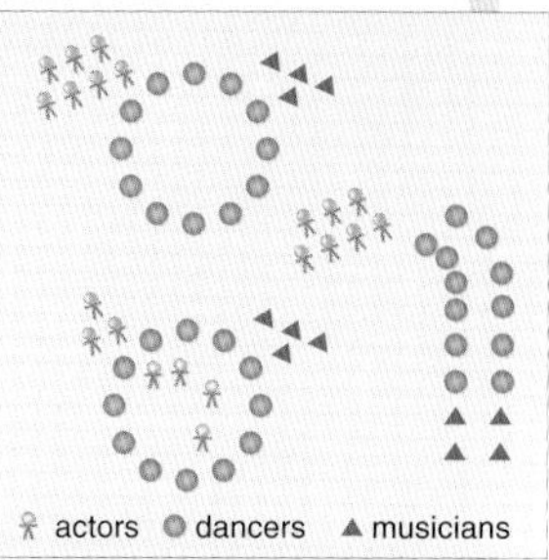

In Randai, silat is featured as dance. Silat movements are executed in between acts and accompany the storytelling. The dance is performed by at least 10 dancers in the form of a large circle. As a dance the movements are graceful and powerful.

Music

The music, played at the beginning of each act, sets the tone for the ensuing story. The basic instruments are gongs, drums and an oboe. The gongs are called *taklempong pacik*—a quintessentially Minangkabau instrument. They are a collection of small to medium sized knobbed gongs (pictured below). Each set is made up of two gongs beaten with padded sticks.

Menora

Menora is a Thai-influenced folk theatre performed with stylized ritual dance, singing and the staging of plays from mythical stories. Rooted in ancient Thai and Malay shamanism, ritual beliefs and Thai Buddhism, it has absorbed elements from other theatre forms such as Mak Yong and Wayang Kulit. Menora is a prime example of cultural, artistic and religious fusion in traditional Malaysian performing arts.

Menora is performed in Penang, Kedah and Kelantan.

Origins

Menora's precise origins are unrecorded. It shares stylistic attributes with the Thai Lakhon Chatri and is believed to have entered the Malay Peninsula with the southward movement of the Thai peoples during the 19th century. Menora is also linked to India due to its strong Buddhist colouring and in the use of the *Jataka Tales*—a collection of 547 stories and tales about the Buddha in his previous lives—in its dramatic repertoire. Menora is currently performed by about five troupes of Thai Malaysians in Penang, Kedah and Kelantan.

Menora's origin myth gives it a strong shamanistic base, ascribing its creation to Mesi Mala, a mythical Thai princess and female shaman. Inspired by a vision of the gods dancing in heaven, she formulated a dance form which was spiritual and curative. Mesi Mala continues to be revered by Menora exponents, especially during the theatre opening rituals and trance sessions which serve to make contact with the gods and spirits. Local animistic beliefs later fused with religious influences, in this case Buddhist. The Buddhist influence is most apparent in the occasions for performance, and its use as a religious offering to Lord Buddha.

BELOW: The theatre opening rituals include making offerings to the Menora dancer's crown, the tailpiece and the musical instruments.

BOTTOM: A Menora performer's aura of magic is enhanced by the make-up.

Types of performance

Ritual performances are staged to effect the wearing of the beaded costume ceremony (*champa noi*) as well as the crowning ceremony (*krob sert*) to mark the graduation of a Menora apprentice, for the release of vows (*kae bun*), and to commemorate deceased Menora teachers (*wai khruu*). Performances may also be held purely for entertainment, during Wesak, in praise of spirit guardians called Datuk Kong (in Hokkien dialect in Penang and Kedah), during the ordination of Buddhist monks, to celebrate Thai weddings and the birthdays of deities, and during fundraising for temples.

Performance elements

In the past, Menora actors numbered only three—the hero, heroine and the clown. The cast was all-male and the three actors would also take on additional roles as required by the story. Female performers are a recent innovation. The number of players has also increased. A troupe comprises the main performer, who may be male or female, two male clowns and a group of female dancers.

The basic instruments used in a Menora performance are the *klong*, a pair of *tab*, the *cing*, the *mong*, and the *pi*. They correspond to the *geduk, gedumbak, kesi, canang* and *serunai* respectively (see 'Music of the Malay shadow play'). The ensemble includes, additionally, the *khrap khuu* (*krek* or *cherek*), a pair of dried bamboo sticks which are knocked together to produce a clapping sound and serve as an instrument to control the tempo of the music. The orchestra plays during dances and trance-induction ceremonies. While the story is played, the orchestra is silent, but plays to punctuate dramatic moments.

The dance repertoire comprises a series of dances performed solo by the main performer or in groups by dancers depicting mythical birdmaidens (*kinnari*). Most of the floor patterns are circular or formed in a figure of eight. Footwork is apparent, and outstretched arms with the fingers bent back are a constant feature. A dance may last several hours before the story (*lakhon*) is eventually performed.

It is believed that the dance vocabulary forms the backbone of Menora's ritualism as the ancient version of Menora may have been performed purely as an extended dance piece without an associated story. The movements are therefore directly linked to its creator, Mesi Mala. Beginning with just one story called 'Manohra' adapted

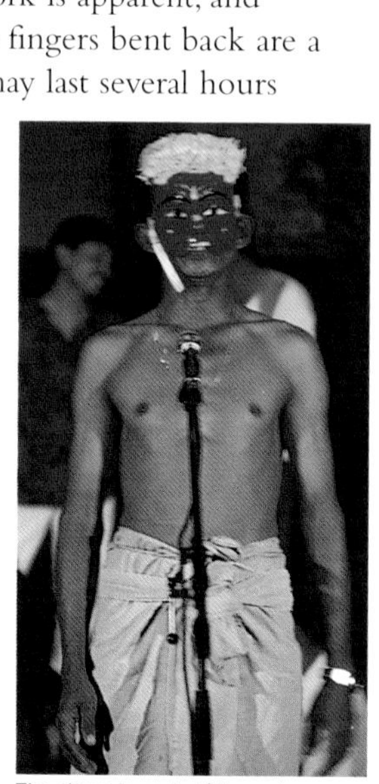

The clown is part of Menora's original all-male cast of only three.

Dance of the Master

The 12 basic original dance movements combine to create a highly dramatic piece called Dance of the Master (*Mae Bod*). Six of these postures are illustrated here. Menora's dance movements are ancient, with attributes that demand skill and acrobatic flexibility. They can no longer be properly executed and are thus seldom attempted. New directions in dance movements are done to please modern audiences, and do not enhance the performance spiritually or aesthetically.

Dressing the dancer

The costume of the main Menora performer is very elaborate. It consists of a tiered crown (*sert*) which is only worn by ritually initiated performers, a beaded overshirt or tassled shawl (*sang wang*), a beaded neck piece (*klong khor*) and pendant (*tab suang*), pleated cloth (*rad saphok*) worn over a pair of long trousers, a structured tail-piece (*hang hoong*, inset), and colourful lengths of cloth (*hoay naa* and *phaa hoay*) tied around the waist with a centrepiece buckle (*phan meng*). There are two pendants (*phik nok naang end*) hung at either side of the performer's waistline. The costume includes bangles (*kamlai*) and long beaded or silver, curved fingernails (*lap*). Dressed in this manner, the dancers are said to imitate the movements of a mythical bird (*nok insi*).

from the *Jataka Tales*, the dramatic repertoire expanded to include 12 stories. The Manohra tale is now used purely for ritual performances.

The west coast style of Menora performed in Kedah and Penang retains its originality but uses Penang Malay together with Thai and the Hokkien dialect. In the east coast, the Kelantan Menora has integrated elements of Mak Yong and evolved into a distinctive style called Menora Mak Yong.

The Performance

The opening of a Menora performance is marked by the carrying of the instruments to the performance area. The theatre is consecrated (*bert roong*), and the musical prelude (*long roong*) is played. The troupe leader or shaman sings a salutation song for departed Menora teachers accompanied by the chorus.

The song and dance segment begins with the apprentice performer doing an introductory piece, followed by a dramatic dance by the principal Menora dancer, which may last several hours. The whole troupe then takes to the stage and acts out the story for the evening. As the performance draws to a close, the drama becomes pantomime in style. This is the cue for the play to cease, and is performed in either song or dance, with improvisation and adaptation to an audience's tastes. A ritual closing of the theatre ends the performance.

Shamanism in Menora

In ritual Menora, the trance sessions performed directly after the theatre opening crystallizes its shamanistic base. These sessions may comprise any number of trancers. Contact with the gods and spirits is effected through these sessions. It is this shamanistic base which sustains Menora as a dance form, and the animistic rituals are preserved within its Buddhist performance context. In the villages of Kedah and Kelantan, Menora is still steeped in its ancient, sacred aura. In performances staged in urban areas, the ritual elements are reduced and dance movements are often modernized.

LEFT: The Menora stage uses elaborately decorated backdrops and side curtains. The stage is constructed from thatch and bamboo and is elevated only for non-ritual performances.

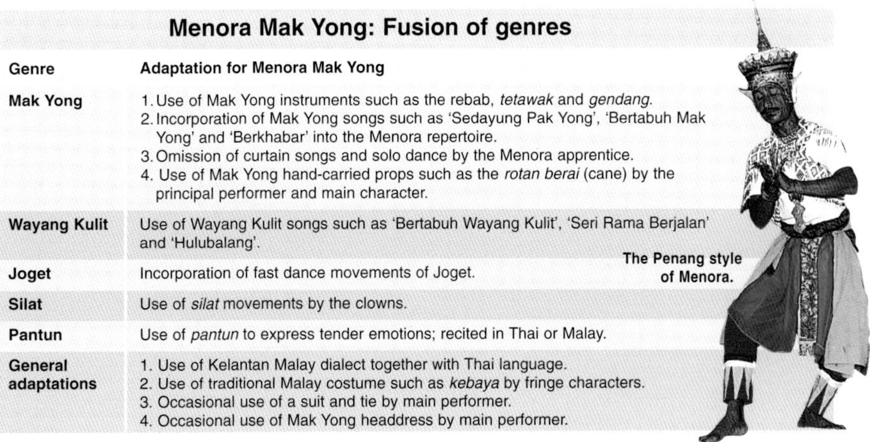

Menora Mak Yong: Fusion of genres

Genre	Adaptation for Menora Mak Yong
Mak Yong	1. Use of Mak Yong instruments such as the rebab, *tetawak* and *gendang*. 2. Incorporation of Mak Yong songs such as 'Sedayung Pak Yong', 'Bertabuh Mak Yong' and 'Berkhabar' into the Menora repertoire. 3. Omission of curtain songs and solo dance by the Menora apprentice. 4. Use of Mak Yong hand-carried props such as the *rotan berai* (cane) by the principal performer and main character.
Wayang Kulit	Use of Wayang Kulit songs such as 'Bertabuh Wayang Kulit', 'Seri Rama Berjalan' and 'Hulubalang'.
Joget	Incorporation of fast dance movements of Joget.
Silat	Use of *silat* movements by the clowns.
Pantun	Use of *pantun* to express tender emotions; recited in Thai or Malay.
General adaptations	1. Use of Kelantan Malay dialect together with Thai language. 2. Use of traditional Malay costume such as *kebaya* by fringe characters. 3. Occasional use of a suit and tie by main performer. 4. Occasional use of Mak Yong headdress by main performer.

The Penang style of Menora.

Dances of Sabah and Sarawak

Like the Orang Asli of Peninsula Malaysia, the indigenous peoples of the East Malaysian states of Sabah and Sarawak own some of the oldest dance traditions. They reflect the diverse ethnic communities of the land and are rooted in the ritualism and spiritualism of their ancient animistic beliefs. These traditions are still observed despite borrowing from other dance cultures.

Ngajat dancers don feathers in their headgear, beads and a loincloth (*cawat/sirat*), and carry *parang ilang* machetes and *terabai* hand shields.

Background

The dances of the more than 100 indigenous communities of Sabah and Sarawak are performed during festivities that are either part of agrarian rituals, warrior rites of passage or to celebrate weddings and other social events. The Dusun, Murut and Paitan groups in Sabah often associate their dances with ritual ceremonies. These dances are accompanied by gong ensemble music, and sometimes by ritual chanting by shamans or mediums.

The seafaring groups of Austronesians who ply the seas around the Sulu Archipelago share common ancestral and cultural affinity with the dance and music of the peoples of the southern Philippines. The dances of the maritime Bajau and Suluk, among others, who live in the eastern coastal areas of Sabah, are performed to the *kulintangan* gong-chime ensemble for weddings and other customary feasts, and feature elaborate costumes.

The Iban, Bidayuh, Kayan and Kenyah communities of Sarawak, found along the inland and upper reaches of river basins, share similar dance styles that are gender specific and performed for ritual related activities. Solo dances of male warriors dominate the dance repertoire in all activities that feature dance. The main highland communities of Kelabit, Lun Bawang and the Penan, collectively known as Orang Ulu or upstream people, perform dances that are relatively more subtle in style.

Mongigol-Sumayau dance performed by the Lotud in traditional costume.

Murut dancers leap between bamboo poles that are hit to the rhythms of gong and percussion instruments.

Dances of Sabah

The most well-known dance in Sabah is the Sumazau, but its interpretation and name varies from group to group. Many variations of the dance exist within the large Kadazandusun communities. Some of the styles are associated with places of origin, such as Penampang, Tambunan, Papar and Ranau.

In the dance sequence of the Sumazau, two rows of men and women facing each other execute slow rhythmic movements, their arms outstretched as they bounce on the ball of one foot and lift the other off the floor. In Penampang, their arm gestures are likened to the flight of birds, with the dancers moving their limbs to the pulsating gong beats.

Bidayuh ritual dances used to be performed on various occasions, such as the end of a harvest, and to drive away disease.

An important feature of Sumazau is its association with the spirit world mediated by female shamans or *bobohizan*. The Sumazau in Penampang, for example, is performed to celebrate thanksgiving (*moginakan*), moving to a new house (*magang*), ushering the blooming of padi shoots (*monogit*) and to pay homage to padi spirits (*magavau*). Amongst the Suang Lotud, the dance is called Sumayau or Madsayau. A variant of the Sumazau dance is the Mongigol, a dance performed by the Kadazandusun of Ranau for celebrations and spirit rituals. The Lotud Dusun of Tuaran, another Dusunic group, perform the solemn Mongigol-Sumayau which is very different from the dances of the Kadazandusun. This is used in spirit worship, soul calling and rain-making ceremonies.

Another of Sabah's dances is performed on the *lansaran* by the Murut of Keningau, Tenom, Nabawan, Sepulut, Pensiangan and Tomani. The lansaran is a sprung floor of timber logs fastened with rattan. The dance, which incorporates rhythmic bouncing on the floor, involves male performers jumping high to retrieve trophies or *singkowoton* hung on the rafters. Legend has it that the prize that used to hang above the lansaran was the head of some unwary opponent; these days it's more likely to be money.

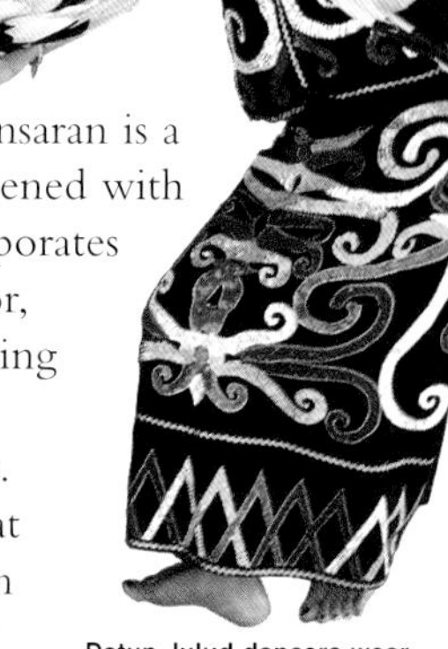

Datun Julud dancers wear elaborate headdresses and hold fans made out of hornbill feathers.

The Bajau of Semporna and the Suluk on the east coast of Sabah don colourful costumes when they perform the traditional Igal and Bolak-bolak, and the more recent Mongiluk and Daling-daling. These communities ply the waters around the Sulu Sea, often borrowing from or extending the dance styles to their kin in the southern Philippines.

The Bolak-bolak is a lively dance accompanied by either the *gabang* (wooden xylophone) or the kulintangan. Inspired and influenced by dances from the Philippines, the movements of the Bolak-bolak are characterized by the clapping of hand-held wooden castanets (bolak-bolak) in the dancers' hands. In the Daling-daling, pairs of performers rapidly step to the front and back of their partners while moving their arms to the rhythms of the gabang, and are accompanied by singing, either by a soloist or two people, and a chorus.

Murut dancers on the *lansaran*.

LEFT TOP: Melanau welcome dance at Kampong Sok.

LEFT BOTTOM: Lotud Sumayau dance.

Dances of Sarawak

In contrast to Sabah's dance traditions, Sarawak's dance culture draws images of courage and tribal affinity. This is best exemplified by the dances of the Iban, Bidayuh and, to a certain extent, those of the Melanau. In the old days, these dances symbolized the virtuosity of male warriors embarking or returning from successful war raids, bringing back decapitated heads of enemies to their longhouses.

The Ngajat dance of the Iban and Bidayuh people and the Kanjet dance of the Orang Ulu are highly revered as dances of courageous men, their forms displaying skills of warfare and dexterity of movements. The dance involves dramatic leaps and jumps, the male dancers augmenting their movements with shrill sounds and flamboyant gestures of bravery.

Female Ngajat dance styles are subtler, slower and softer than the male version. Women usually dance the Ngajat in a linear formation and their gestures are relatively narrower, with pivotal turns on one foot and tilting of the hips. The dance is accompanied by music rendered by gongs and other ethnic percussion instruments. The Ngajat is performed during the Gawai harvest festival, to welcome guests at the longhouse and on other important occasions.

In contrast to the Ngajat, the dances of the Orang Ulu are more supple and pliant. The Kelabit women dance the Datun Julud to emulate the hornbill in flight, with slow, graceful movements of their arms, legs and torso. The dance was once performed to greet returning warriors or to celebrate the end of a rice harvest, as a symbol of happiness and thanksgiving to the gods. The Datun Julud has since become part of entertainment often performed in the longhouse to greet visitors.

The Melanau dances, on the other hand, are closely associated with their traditional activities of fishing and sago harvesting in the coastal areas where they lived. These dances are also closely related to the rites and rituals of life and death. Long bamboo poles are often used by Melanau men as dance properties, which add to the rhythms of the accompanying music.

Dance of the hornbill

The dance idioms of the Ngajat are borrowed from the movements of birds such as the hornbill. Dance gestures include outstretching of the arms and bending of the torso to imitate birds sweeping high in the sky (below). The dancers take side-stepping movements with their feet and rotate their wrists to mimic birds moving delicately on twigs and branches of trees in the rainforest. The dancers always maintain their balance by stretching out their arms as they turn around in clockwise and anti-clockwise directions.

The Mangiluk is a traditional dance of the Suluk community of Sabah.

Mongiluk dance performed on a lepa boat by Bajau of Semporna, Sabah.

Malay folk and social dances

Malay folk and social dances in Malaysia are characterized by the syncretic nature of their repertoires, the result of fusion of foreign influences in dance movements and musical styles with home-grown creative elements. While these dance genres have kept to their original form and structure, improvisations in style and repertoire over the centuries also reflect a conscious process of adapting new ideas to enhance these dances to suit contemporary tastes.

Joget is a popular dance in Malaysia, and is performed at festivals, weddings and on other social and cultural occasions.

Genres of folk dances

Dance means many things in the Malay language. Formally arranged movements as in choreographed pieces fall in the realm of *tari* or *tarian*, which literally means dance performed by trained performers to be viewed. Dances could also be regarded as game (*main*) or gambol (*gencok*), while participatory call and response singing and dancing are referred to as *tandak*. While tarian are exclusive and restrictive, main, gencok and tandak are inclusive and embracing, and are performed as social events to be participated in by all present.

In spite of the exclusive-inclusive dichotomy, there are four main genres of Malay folk dances—Joget, Inang, Asli and Zapin—differentiated by their dance structures, performance elements and accompanying musical styles. Dance styles in different regions in Malaysia vary according to the localization of folk dance traditions. Ronggeng, Tandak, Joget Lambak and Joget Moden, for example, are variations of Joget. Mak Inang Lama, Inang Pulau Kampar and Lenggang Mak Inang are variants of the Inang genre. Similarly, variants of the Asli genre are the Senandung, Gunung Sayang, Melayu Asli and Dondang Sayang dances. The Zapin dance genre, meanwhile, is recognizable in the form of Zapin Melayu, Zapin Johor, Zapin Arab, Zapin Pekan, Zapin Terengganu, Zapin Sindang and numerous others.

Malay folk dance circa 1915–1920.

Zapin

The oldest form of a syncretic folk dance that has survived to this day in Malaysia is the Zapin. It fuses dance and music traditions from the communities of Arabs from Hadhramaut (present-day Yemen), who brought trade and Islam to the Malay World before the 14th century, with Malay dancing styles. Although the foundation of Zapin is in the Arabic *zaffan* and is marked by robust dancing by men, the syncretic Malay Zapin is more subdued and relatively more refined. Until very recently it had remained a male dominated dance genre.

Zapin has evolved into a popular folk dance with regional variations in form and style.

Traditional Zapin performers do not consider Zapin as tarian, but as main or playing a game. Thus to perform Zapin is to play or main Zapin. Zapin is most popular in Johor and is performed in numerous styles associated with the various villages in the state where it is still popular (see 'Zapin').

Joget, Inang and Asli

These three dance genres are believed to have developed through syncretic processes involving Portuguese and Malay influences. Of the three, Joget is the most popular. It became the most commonly performed social dance during the 20th century when taxi dancers at amusement parks, dance halls, mobile dance stages and cabarets incorporated Joget in their repertoires. Until the 1960s, Joget was an integral part of the Ronggeng repertoire that also included elements of the Inang and Asli dance styles.

The word *joget* denotes dance in the broadest sense, but it also refers to a very specific folk dance that has evolved from the syncretic elements of Portuguese folk dances and Malay dancing styles.

It is speculated that Joget was first performed by the Malays of Melaka during the Portuguese period. Joget is assumed to be a Malay version of the Portuguese Branyo, a local derivation of the Brundo or Branle, which was popular in 15th-century Europe. The Brundo or Branle, performed in a circle or in single file, became the basis of the Branyo. The Malays of Melaka performed dances similar to the Branyo to the duple and triple beat of the European Brundo, Branle and local Branyo music. It is also very probable that the Malays of Melaka had choreographed new dances through the syncretization of an older dance called Tandak, thus turning Joget into a new dance form in 16th-century Melaka. The older Tandak, which is still performed in villages in Peninsular Malaysia, Sabah and Sarawak, is the predecessor of Joget. The older Tandak is both a folk and social dance. It is usually performed at wedding celebrations by dancers in pairs, often exchanging *pantun* or quatrains sung to Tandak tunes, and accompanied by a small drum and gong ensemble. In contrast to the Tandak musical ensemble, the Joget ensemble is made up of two *rebana* drums, a gong, a violin or an accordion and one or two singers. Thus, Joget has become a more urbane dance than Tandak with the use of an eclectic musical ensemble. The dance is performed by couples who combine fast hand and leg movements.

Inang and Asli dances have emerged from the syncretic process to become the base dances for many other variants of Malay folk dances. Inang dance is a modernized version of the traditional Mak Inang folk dance. The term *mak inang* literally means wet nurses who were employed by the Malay aristocrats to look after their infants and young children. It was believed that the wet nurses would sing lullabies and folk songs to their young charges while dancing in walking steps. Their dances were often referred to as Tarian Mak Inang, dances of the wet nurses. The dance form, however, eventually became a folk dance moving to a fast tempo set by the rebana and *gendang* drums, and the *biola* (violin) playing the tunes of Mak Inang songs.

Canggung

A popular dance in Perlis, the term *canggung* itself means dancer in the Thai language. The dance (right) shows obvious influences from Thai culture, and is believed to have been created by two sisters, Intan and Lian. It is performed during festivals and at wedding ceremonies, in pairs with the women performers holding handkerchiefs. The dances are accompanied by singing, the lyrics consisting of *pantun* and a chorus: '*Ala canggung, mak si canggung, Canggung, canggung la, la, la, la, le.*' The musical ensemble is made up of a gong, a violin, a pair of frame drums (*rebana*), and a larger drum (*gendang ubi*).

Asli dance

The beginnings of Asli dance can be traced to steps accompanying the singing and exchanging of pantun amongst village folks, referred to as Melayu Asli. An Asli song is identified by an eight-beat phrase in 4/4 time, where the first four-beat phrase has a fixed pattern while the second four beats are usually improvised but are accented by a gong beat on the fourth and eighth beats. Examples of Melayu Asli songs are 'Makan Sirih', 'Gunung Banang', 'Sapu Tangan', 'Asli Selendang', 'Bentan Telani' and 'Asli Abadi'. In the Tepak Sirih Dance for instance, the dancers bring betel leaf sets onto the stage while executing graceful dance movements to the tune of the Asli beat.

Asli dance is characterized by flowing, elegant movements.

As a dance form Asli is popular all over Malaysia and the most refined of all Malay folk dances. Dancers curl and flex their fingers on the fourth and eighth beats while executing slow, flowing and elegant movements resembling the Asyik court dance (see 'Asyik and Joget Gamelan').

Innovations

Both Inang and Asli dances have not only incorporated modern and traditional musical instruments, but also include many eclectic musical arrangements. Inang is commonly used as a base by choreographers to create new dances in the form of Tarian Inang using specific dance paraphernalia, and as a result the dances are often named after them. Tarian Piring (saucer dance), Tarian Lilin (candle dance), Tarian Selendang (shawl dance), Tarian Saputangan (handkerchief dance), Tarian Kipas (fan dance) and Tarian Payung (umbrella dance) are some of the newer versions of Inang dances that have evolved over time. Sometimes, these dances incorporate movements and rhythms from Joget and Asli tunes.

1. Tarian Payung
2. Tarian Lilin
3. Tarian Kipas
4. Tarian Selendang.

Chinese dances

Chinese dances were brought by immigrants in the mid-20th century and initially kept to the original form of folk and classical dance genres found in China. Since then Chinese dances in Malaysia have developed far beyond such replication, and while some of the original forms have been retained, local choreographers have incorporated elements from other ethnic, Asian and Western cultures into their techniques and repertoires, resulting in a vibrant dance movement that is contemporary in treatment and Malaysian in identity.

Hang Li Po features costumes designed by Steven Koh. The princess first appears in Ming Dynasty costume (right), and later in his 'danceable' *kebaya* (top).

Street Opera in Harvest, choreographed by Steven Koh in which he blended Malaysian customs with Chinese dance styles.

Children's dance choreographed by Wong Kit Yaw.

Origins

Chinese folk dances generally fall into five main regional genres—Han, Mongolian, Korean, Tibetan and Xin Jiang—that are performed during festivals and other celebrations. Dances such as *Hong Chou Wu* (Red Silk dance, also known as Ribbon dance) and *Cai Cha Pu Die* (Plucking Tea and Catching Butterfly dance) have dance idioms that reflect the lives of rural Chinese. The latter actually depicts Han (Hokkien) women plucking tea, crossing little streams and trying to catch butterflies on their way home. *An Hui Hua Gu Deng* (An Hui Flower Drum Lantern dance) is a Han procession dance from the An Hui province in which men and women dance together, manipulating fans and handkerchiefs. This communal dance usually takes place in the evening and lanterns are lit to be carried along.

Folk dances are performed to the accompaniment of an ensemble of *gu* (drums), *bo* (cymbals) and *sona* (double reed oboe). Classical dances such as *He Hua Wu* (Lotus dance) are accompanied by a Chinese orchestra. Their elegant movements use the analogy of praising the lotus to emphasize internal beauty.

Development in Malaysia

Chinese dances in Malaysia have their roots in China's dance culture. After World War II and the Japanese Occupation, many Chinese immigrants brought 'Anti-Japanese Occupation' songs and dances to Southeast Asia, including Malaysia. These spread quickly among the Chinese community. In the 1950s, a film on Chinese folkloric arts that was screened in Malaya featured famous folk and classical dances such as Hong Chou Wu, He Hua Wu, Cai Cha Pu Die and An Hui Hua Gu Deng. Local cultural activists and dance enthusiasts replicated these dances. Then in the early 1960s, Lee Shu Fen, a visiting dancer from Taiwan, imparted the basics of Chinese dance *Shen Yun* (body rhythm and melody) to local dance enthusiasts. Her production of *Bai Niang Niang* (Lady White Snake) inspired Malaysia's pioneer in Chinese dance, Steven Koh, to create his own dances.

About a decade later, a performance by the Ying Xing Yi Shu Tuan (Silver Star) performing arts troupe at Kuala Lumpur's National Stadium took local Chinese youths by storm. The performance, organized to raise funds for flood victims in Kuala Lumpur, was filled with famous Hong Kong film stars featuring beautiful songs and folk dances. Following this event, many Chinese associations rapidly formed youth societies to organize music, dance and drama events.

Chinese associations have played a major role in preserving and promoting Chinese dance; for example, the Malacca Malaysian Chinese Association established a dance troupe. Steven Koh, the troupe's artistic director and choreographer, sought to create dances that local Chinese could relate to. He wove local customs and practices into dance styles and techniques that he had studied in Taiwan and Hong Kong. He incorporated, for instance, local street opera into dances where the performers danced barefoot, reflecting the difference between Malaysian and mainland Chinese.

Basic techniques of Chinese dance

Shen Yun literally means the rhythmic melody of the body. It outlines the principles of Chinese dance moves and is the foundation of almost all folk and classical dances. The four quintessential elements are (1) tilt, (2) twist, (3) curve and circle, and are prevalent in the shape, moves, flows and traits of Chinese dance. The aesthetics of Chinese dance are developed on these four elements, executed with an energy field that always leads back to the self, contrasted by the (4) punctuation of eye focus, breathing and minute moves.

❶ ❷ ❸ ❹

His dances won the hearts of many in the late 1970s and early 1980s. Among his more famous works are a dance drama *Kong Que Dong Nan Fei* (The Peacocks Flew Separate Ways), and short pieces entitled *Feng Nian* (Fruitful Harvest), *Si Jun Zhi* (The Four Gentlemen–Plum, Orchid, Bamboo, Chrysanthemum) and *Niao Yu* (Words of the Birds). These works were either based on Chinese classics, folktales, and legends or developed from the values, customs and aesthetics of the Chinese people. With his outstanding talent in stage décor and costume, sensitivity to music and the ability to empower the performers with a strong stage presence and performance skills, Koh's productions have inspired many dedicated dancers and choreographers.

In 1991, the production of *Hang Li Po* marked a new phase in Malaysian Chinese dance. This full-length four-act dance drama was a melting pot of Chinese and Malay dance and music. Instead of taking inspiration from Chinese folklore and literature, it tells of the love between two famous characters in Malaysian history—the Chinese princess Hang Li Po and the Sultan of Melaka, Mansur Shah, whom she married. The script allowed the four choreographers—Wong Fook Choon, Lee Len Yau, Wong Kit Yaw and Mew Chang Tsing—to include classical Chinese and Malay dances in scenes as well as create dramatic sequences that combine Chinese dance, ballet, kung fu and Malay silat movements. This production toured the country from 1991 to 1994 and was also performed for royalty.

From ribbon to selendang

The word *wu* (dance) carries the connotation of people manipulating props in their hands while moving to music and rhythms during rituals or gatherings. Chinese dance has a long history of mastery of hand props such as fans, cloth or long sleeves. Choreographers have explored dancing with cloth of various sizes and lengths. *Selendang* (shawl) are extended into metres and come to life effortlessly in the hands of dancing maidens. The use of sheer georgette is a departure from the norm of traditional silk.

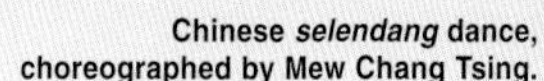

Chinese *selendang* dance, choreographed by Mew Chang Tsing.

The old and the new

Attempts to create 'local' Chinese dances are an ongoing effort. The works of Wong Kit Yaw, who later focused on developing children's dance, often reflect the experience of children growing up in mixed cultural environments. His dance series *Kik Kik Kok Kok* features children wearing wooden clogs and sarongs, singing local rhymes and waving pyjama pants on their arms, imitating Chinese opera performers. His works reveal the beauty and joy of cross-cultural interaction in the innocent creative play of children.

While modern Chinese dance has gone beyond mere replication, one personality promoting and preserving it in its original form is Cheong Ling Poo, the first Malaysian to be trained professionally abroad in Chinese classical and folk dance. Upon her return in 1991, Cheong continued the development that Koh had initiated, but unlike Koh, her focus has been on preserving Chinese dance in its original form. She traverses the country, instructing at various schools. With her vast stage experience and sound training, Cheong has succeeded in delivering the philosophy, soul and techniques of Chinese dance. Her choreography performed by teenagers and mature dancers alike has won awards in the National Chinese Dance Festival held annually since 1978. This festival has provided opportunities for Chinese dancers throughout Malaysia to gather and share their work.

Besides preserving the original form of Chinese dances, local choreographers continuously draw on elements from various Southeast Asian cultures. Their works reflect attempts to create a Malaysian identity either by developing new dance techniques, improvising in costume or even commissioning new music. This has engendered an appeal that transcends race, creed and colour, allowing contemporary Chinese dance to find a place in the nation's multi-cultural identity.

Wong Kit Yaw gives Chinese dance a contemporary treatment.

LEFT TOP: *Passage to the South*, choreographed by Cheong Lin Poo.

LEFT BOTTOM: *Spring* by classical dance specialist Cheong Lin Poo.

Indian folk and classical dances

Indian classical and folk dances were brought to Malaysia by immigrants from the sub-continent in the early 20th century. Folk dances, associated with religious ceremonies, temple festivals and marriages, came with the indentured labourers who worked in rubber estates under British rule around the 1930s. Classical dance forms, in particular Bharata Natyam and Odissi, were introduced in the mid-1950s and early 1980s, respectively, by Indian dancers.

Indian folk dance repertoire in Malaysia has been given a local flavour through stylized treatment and innovative choreography.

Swan Lake, a dance drama adapted from the ballet, produced by teachers and students at the Temple of Fine Arts.

Folk traditions

Indian folk dances all have rural origins. They are performed by ordinary people rather than professionals. They include dances such as Karagattam, associated with temple deities. Other dances, such as Kumi, are performed during religious festivals, at weddings and other social events. These dances, which do not have fixed forms, exist till today. Folk dances may be either spontaneous expressions of those untrained in any dance discipline, or choreographed work taught by dance schools.

Types of Indian folk dances in Malaysia

Folk dances are mainly associated with the major Indian festivals, such as Thaipusam, during which trance sometimes occurs. Dances staged during religious festivals include the Kolattam, a lively dance usually performed by young boys and girls. The dancers strike pairs of sticks with partners at cross-rhythms with their feet to the beat of drums. The boys are dressed in *jippa* and *dhoti*, with a shawl tied around their waist while the girls don saris or long skirts (*pavadai*) with bells fastened around their ankles.

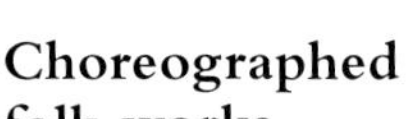

Choreographed folk works

Since its establishment in 1981, the Temple of Fine Arts in Kuala Lumpur has taken the lead in choreographing Indian folk dances and dance dramas in Malaysia. Borrowing movements from the South Indian classical traditions, local teachers have developed stylized versions of village folk dances, such as the fisherman's dance, harvest dance, and the Kuratti or gypsy dance.

The late V. K. Sivadas, one of the institution's pioneer dance directors, initiated the folk dance choreographing efforts. Another dance exponent and director at the institution, the late Gopal Shetty, choreographed the famous Peacock Dance drama, which combined both folk and classical movements, and has become unique in the Indian dance repertoire of Malaysia.

There are other institutions in Penang and Johor Bahru that have also taken initiatives to teach and present Indian dances. Students at vernacular schools are taught folk dances as a part of efforts to preserve Indian culture. Performances are held during festivals and at temples.

The classical tradition

The classical dances, Bharata Natyam and Odissi, have received wide recognition and popularity in Malaysia. Performances are staged regularly in urban centres. A third form, Kathakali, enjoys less popularity

Karagattam

Karagattam (pot dance, pictured right) is performed in conjunction with the festival of the Hindu goddess Mariamma. *Karagam* is an earthen pot decorated with flowers and mango leaves. The goddess is invoked in the karagam and dancers balance the pots on their heads while dancing in a trance-like state. The dance begins in slow tempo and becomes progressively faster, culminating in fast whirling movements with dancers performing acrobatic–like sequences while balancing the pots on their heads.

Kavadi and movement

The kavadi is part of the Thaipusam and Panguni Utthiram festivals. During the early hours of the festival morning, devotees carry the kavadi, some with physical mortification such as piercing their tongues and cheeks with skewers (*vel*). They invoke the deity Lord Muruga in trance, moving with spontaneous movements. The kavadi bearers dress in clothes dyed in turmeric as a symbol of austerity, and bells are fastened around their ankles to create rhythm. The Indian drum (*urumi mela*) is played in accompaniment. In recent years a newly developed dance called Kavadi Attam (kavadi dance) has been performed.

Bhangra

Bhangra, the harvest festival dance of the Punjabi community, is a vibrant and colourful folk dance (left), accompanied by a medley of folk songs and vigorous rhythms beaten out on big drums. As a communal dance that involves all age groups in the village, bhangra is a spontaneous expression. Over the years, however, it has developed into a stylized dance performed by groups of men or women, incorporating stunts and requiring dexterity. Bhangra is also performed to celebrate Vasakhi, the birth of Sikhism, and at cultural shows. Its popularity in Malaysia is reflected by the participation of other communities.

and is performed only on cultural occasions.

Bharata Natyam originates from South India. Its style is elegant, classical, angular and symmetrical. Its gestures, music and rhythm have been described as a language of poetry. Dance sequences are made up of basic steps called *adavus* accompanied by hand gestures and facial expressions known as *abhinaya*. Bharata Natyam is often viewed as an art that gives spiritual beauty to the flesh and lifts one from temporal to eternal values. Many exponents regard it as a form of yoga, in which the dancer attempts to achieve bliss of oneness with the divine. Musical accompaniment is provided by the *nattuvangam* and *mridangam* drums, stringed instruments as in the *veena* and violin, and the flute.

Bharata Natyam dancers are dressed in silk saris and bedecked in ornamental jewellery.

Odissi, which originated from the eastern India state of Orissa, is a tradition that reflects a balance of both the lyrical (*lasya*) and vigorous (*tandava*) aspects of dance. Its dance forms have more curves, making it a more sensual dance than Bharata Natyam.

Development of classical dance

Among the first people to teach Bharata Natyam in pre-independent Malaya was Sivadas, who founded his dance school called the Sivadas-Vatsala Dance Troupe in 1953, and who trained hundreds of students. In 1954, Shetty started dance classes at the Sangeetha Abhivirdhi Sabha Association in Brickfields, Kuala Lumpur. He was responsible for introducing dance dramas, such as Ramayana and Life and Light, to Malaysian audiences. Both Sivadas and Shetty experimented with various dance forms and were noted for choreographing dances with a Malaysian flavour by blending Indian and Malay styles and forms. Among such works are Sivadas's Eagle and Snake, and Shetty's Dyana. The Thiruchendur sisters, Shrimathi Malayajadevi and Usha Prema, were also among the earliest teachers of classical dance in Malaysia.

The next generation of teachers and dancers include Chandrabanu and Ramli Ibrahim, who made their debut in the 1980s. Ramli, who is also trained in classical ballet and modern dance, is credited with grooming some of the finest exponents of Indian classical dance in the country (see 'Arts organizations and their contributions'). Other prominent teachers and dancers include Krishna Kumari, an alumnus of India's famed Kalakshetra dance school; Sri Ganesan, a dancer of international repute; and Shrimati Indra Manickam.

Innovations

Although Indian classical dance is traditionally a solo performance, local choreographers often present it as a group dance featuring Malaysians of all races. They have also blended various classical forms to create a more contemporary form. In addition, they have modified the traditional Bharata Natyam repertoire by adding new compositions, and so widening the dance vocabulary.

Hand gestures

There are 28 single hand gestures (*hastas*) and 24 double hand gestures that symbolize a multitude of ideas or objects in Indian classical dance. They complement body movements and facial expressions to convey the meaning of a dance. Some of the gestures are shown here.

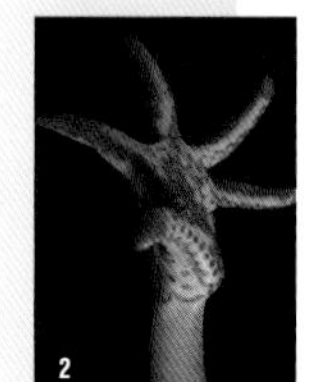

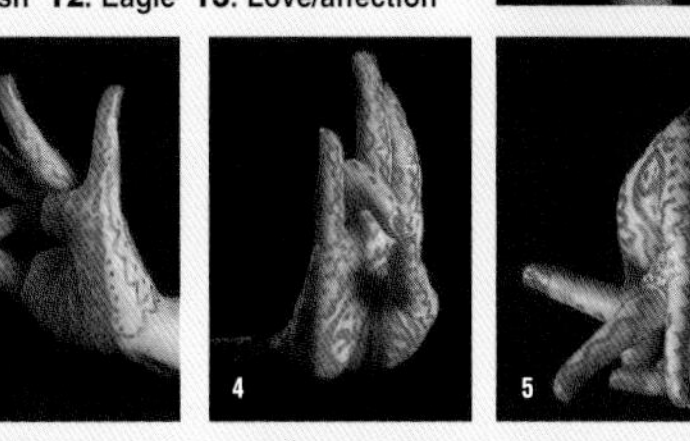

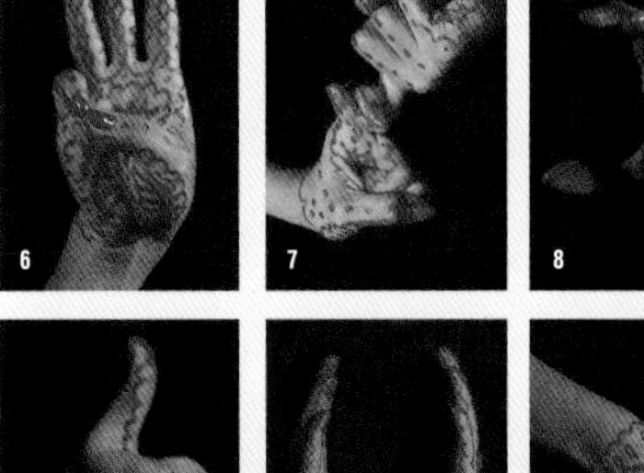

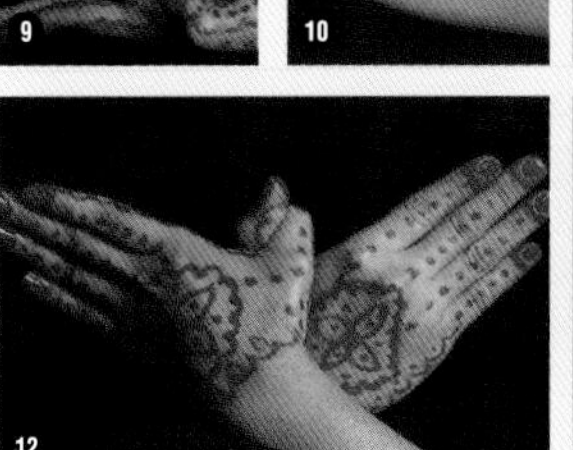

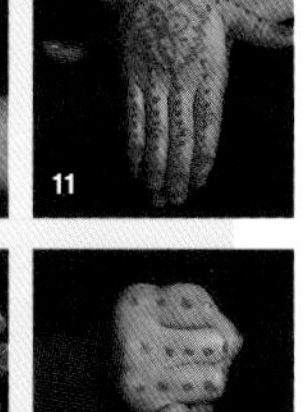

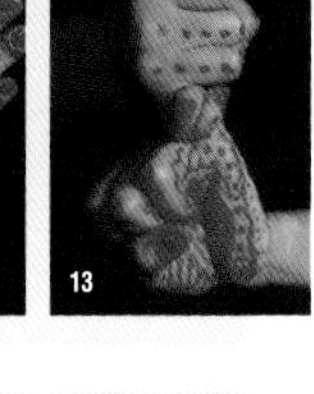

1. Respectful **2.** Lotus in bloom **3.** Swan **4.** Peacock **5.** Holding a lotus **6.** Trident **7.** Hatred/enmity **8.** Tiger **9.** Symbol of Siva **10.** Crocodile **11.** Fish **12.** Eagle **13.** Love/affection

Kathakali

This dance drama (above) originated from South India, and is based on the Hindu epics *Mahabharata* and *Ramayana*. The most striking element of Kathakali is its dramatic quality—the portrayal of mythological beings and demons; elaborate costumes and highly exaggerated facial paint.

Odissi

The dance style of Odissi (below) follows the tradition of *Natyasastra*, the oldest treatise on dance and drama, and is characterized by three body bends called *tribhangi*—involving deflection of the head, torso and hips. A variety of hand gestures are used as in Bharata Natyam. The subject of dance pieces is usually worship of Lord Vishnu or Lord Krishna, depicting man's yearning for God.

Music for the Odissi dance is provided by the *pakhawaj* (a north Indian version of the *mridangam* drum), flute, metal cymbals (*manjira*), and stringed instruments such as the *sitar* and *tambura*.

1. Chinese opera—the grandest form of Chinese street theatre—is performed during major festive months.

2. A 1970s Jikey performance. Jikey is said to be linked to the Thai opera genre of Likay.

3. Bangsawan has been revived and reinvented for contemporary Malaysia.

4. Bangsawan productions were often adapted from films or based on local legends, as this 1977 poster indicates.

OPERATIC GENRES

Deities in Chinese opera are often represented by painted faces.

Opera is a Western term used to describe sung and spoken drama primarily based upon romantic and melodramatic themes. The term has also come to be loosely applied to several Asian theatre genres even if these do not exactly parallel the concept of opera in the West.

Two major strands of the opera are found in Malaysia: the Malaysian and the Chinese. The Malaysian tradition which finally found its form as Bangsawan developed through a circuitous route from the Urdu or Hindustani Parsi theatre, this genre itself having been inspired, in the first place, by the Italian Commedia Del'arte and Renaissance theatre.

The characteristic features of the opera—scenarios rather than scripts for its extensive and highly varied repertoire of stories borrowed from Asia and Europe, eclectic music, painted scenery, wings and borders, improvised dialogue, stereotyped characters and stylized acting—may also be encountered in several other forms stylistically similar to Bangsawan. Some of these, such as Hamdolok performed in Johor or Hadrah Noge active in Kedah, have obvious Middle East origins; on the other hand Jikey, active in Kedah, reflects a stronger Thai influence. Jikey, in fact, may be a linking or transitional form between Bangsawan and Likay, the Thai opera. In the local Malaysian context, however, the various manifestations of the opera have been reshaped in varying degrees to suit the Malay ethos. Of all these, Bangsawan remains the most important for cultural and nationalistic reasons.

The second example of the opera genre, the Chinese opera, is performed primarily during Chinese religious festivals, on temporary stages built to face the entrances to temples or in open spaces. The performances are much reduced in duration, with opera being staged for only a day or two, before giving way to concerts of popular music. There are no real commercial performances of Chinese opera, and neither have efforts been made in its Malaysian history to perform this genre in any other way than the traditional. Despite its existence for more than a century, there has been no localization or adaptation to make Chinese opera more Malaysian in character.

Although several of the operatic genres continue to be performed in the country, this theatre style, despite its past importance, is struggling to find a place in contemporary Malaysia. Its future lies only in its revival, and may eventually be taken over by musical drama, possibly based on the same romantic themes that in the past made opera attractive. For this kind of performances, made contemporary by increasingly sophisticated staging possibilities, there may still be an audience.

Chinese opera and the lesser genres of Malay opera have their own problems, with the Malay genres in fact facing potential extinction. The situation is slightly different for Bangsawan. Given its current state, it is clear that serious, timely efforts at preservation and popularization with some adaptation of this genre have a chance of success, particularly in view of the status of Bangsawan as a form of 'national' theatre in Malaysia.

4

Bangsawan and Jikey operatic theatre

Bangsawan and Jikey are two forms of operatic theatre derived from genres that entered Malaya in the 19th century. Both are distinct from traditional theatre but Bangsawan, being the more modern of the two, fused Western and Asian elements. It comprised plays with spectacular settings, popular stage personalities, orchestral music, vaudeville and the latest modern dances. As a popular theatre form, Bangsawan laid the foundation for the local cinema industry.

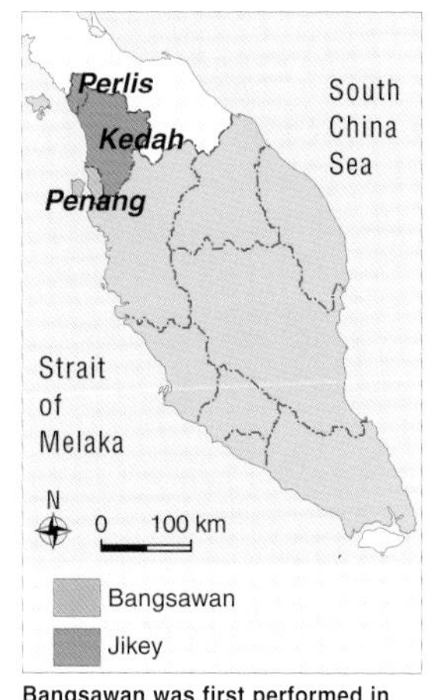

Bangsawan was first performed in Penang, while Jikey is found in Kedah and Perlis.

Origins of Bangsawan

It is believed that Bangsawan was first performed in Penang in the 1870s as an adaptation of the Gujerati Parsi theatre which toured Malaya. The term *Wayang Parsi tiruan*, or imitation Wayang Parsi, was used to describe local troupes performing Parsi plays in the Malay language. In the mid-1890s, the term Bangsawan came to be used as the plays centred on royalty and royal characters. In the early 1900s, 'opera' was also employed in imitation of visiting foreign troupes. Troupes called themselves Opera Yap Chow Thong, Nooran Opera, Star Opera Co. or Dean's Opera. By the turn of the 20th century, Bangsawan had become established as the local popular theatre in Malaya and was staged in both major towns and rural districts.

Bangsawan engendered the first Malay orchestra and created a market for locally produced popular music. By the 1920s and 1930s, Bangsawan had created its own 'culture' in terms of stars, fashion, music and dances. It was the new medium of cultural expression for Malaya's urban dwellers.

Characteristics

Bangsawan featured characteristics that were distinct from traditional Malay theatre. It was highly commercial, heterogeneous, versatile and performed purely for entertainment. It emphasized variety in the plays and novelty in its staging. It was promoted through advertisements in the media, had a paying audience and used a modern proscenium stage.

The Nooran Opera troupe from the 1940s posing on an elaborate stage.

Current Bangsawan performances feature mostly Malay stories.

Performances included a mixture of drama, dance, music, comedy and magical elements. A typical performance would comprise a full-length play (or three or four short plays) with songs, instrumental music plus interludes called 'extra turns' inserted between acts. Extra turns consisted of orchestral music, songs, dances, comedy and novelty acts from a variety of sources including Western theatre and vaudeville.

New musical themes and melodies were constantly being created by Bangsawan bandmasters, who adapted popular music of other parts of the world. The latest dances were also featured, such as the tango, charleston, foxtrot and waltz.

Stories performed were diverse. A performance could constitute Hindustani and Arabian fairy tales, a Shakespearean tragedy, a Chinese romance, a Malay story, or an Indonesian play. As the plays were not scripted, audiences relied on stock characters and linear story lines to follow the play.

Decline and revival

Bangsawan declined after 1945 when audiences were lured away by the cinema. In the 1990s, however, it enjoyed a revival of sorts. Bangsawan performances are sometimes staged for government functions and at festivals. Malay stories such as *Puteri Gunung Ledang* (Princess of Mount Ledang) or *Hang Tuah* make up most of the repertoire. Efforts have been made to revive Bangsawan at institutions of higher learning such as Universiti Sains Malaysia.

Jikey

This operatic theatre is performed by Thai and Malay communities in Kedah and Perlis. It is believed that Jikey developed from the Islamic religious chanting known as *zikir*. There is a dearth of written evidence about Jikey's origins, but performers claim that the genre was derived from India and introduced by Bengali traders in the Malay Peninsula. A turbaned Indian gentleman is an important comic character in Jikey, lending credence to this theory.

Jikey is maintained by a small number of troupes, each comprising 12 to 16 people. Performances take place in a simple traditional style *panggung* on the floor. Sets used are minimal. Principal roles are that of the king (*raja*), prince (*putera*), princess (*puteri*), an old sage (*mahaguru* or *maharisi*), the turbaned 'Bengali', male and female comic characters known respectively as *peran* and *inang*, and ogres.

The dramatic repertoire is made up of stories derived mostly from Malay and Thai folk tales and legends. The orchestra consists of instruments used in traditional theatre genres: *serunai*, gongs, *rebana* drums and wooden clappers. Sometimes, modern instruments are added.

Performances begin with theatre opening rituals, a few preliminary musical pieces, and the Bengali's greetings leading to the story proper. Closing rituals end the performance.

Left: The 'Bengali' character wears Malay clothes, but has a beard and a turban.

Above: A scene from a Jikey performance.

Elements of Bangsawan

Orchestra

The number or types of instruments in the musical ensemble or orchestra varied from troupe to troupe. New instruments could be added if the bandmaster so wished. By the 1930s, the Bangsawan orchestra consisted of Western instruments such as the violin, trumpet, trombone, saxophone, flute, clarinet, piano, guitar, drums and maracas. Non-Western instruments included the Malay *rebana* and the Indian harmonium and *tabla*, which were first used in the Parsi theatre.

Musical repertoire

The bandmaster relied on a repertoire of musical pieces or *lagu* to evoke mood, establish characters, convey ideas, or accompany action in the plot of the story. The songs comprised popular musical genres which accompanied social dancing among the various ethnic groups in Malaya. In Malay stories, Asli music was used in sad songs, Inang in the garden scenes and Joget in fighting scenes. In Western stories, the slow waltz was played during sad scenes; the quick waltz, foxtrot, and quickstep in garden scenes; and the march in fighting scenes.

Characters and costumes

Stock characters in Bangsawan plays consisted of fine (*halus*) characters such as the heroine (*seri panggung*), hero (*orang muda*) and king (*raja*); and rough (*kasar*) characters such as the villain, pirate or clown.

Staging and settings

Bangsawan was the first indigenous theatre to use the proscenium stage. It separated the performers from the audience who sat in seats arranged in rows. The stage setting was of the drop and wing variety. Performances were held in closed-door rented theatres, make-shift tents or in amusement parks. Scene types used in plot building included the palace (*istana*) for court audience; garden (*taman*) for love scenes; sea (*laut*) for warfare and sailing scenes; forest (*hutan*) for hunting and fighting scenes; village (*kampung*) for ordinary village scenes; heaven (*kayangan*) for heavenly scenes; and sand (*pasir*) for desert scenes.

Side-wings for various scenes in Bangsawan performances, circa 1920–30.

Opera tent, circa 1920–30.

People in Bangsawan

As commercial urban theatre, Bangsawan attracted multi-ethnic performers, patrons, audiences and theatre owners. Performers were professionals who were lured by the glamour of the stage, worked exclusively as entertainers and were known for particular roles. Entrepreneurial and competitive in their outlook, they were the precursors of modern Malaysian cinema stars.

Above: Poster of a production staged by a Bangsawan company in the 1960s. Bangsawan often adapted stories from films.

Right: Scene from a 1970 play *Megat Teraweh* starring (clockwise from left) Rahim B, A. Bakar M., Kasminah B. and Rahman B.

Women at centre stage

Women performers were afforded the unprecedented opportunity to achieve prominence in cultural life and gain self-expression in public. They were independent in all respects. Bangsawan women could choose their spouses and initiate separation or divorce if the marriage soured. They were also financially independent, and could support themselves and their children. However, as performing women they were viewed with disdain by traditionalists and the religious-minded. They bore the traditional stigma of women who performed for a mixed audience, and who worked at night to earn a living.

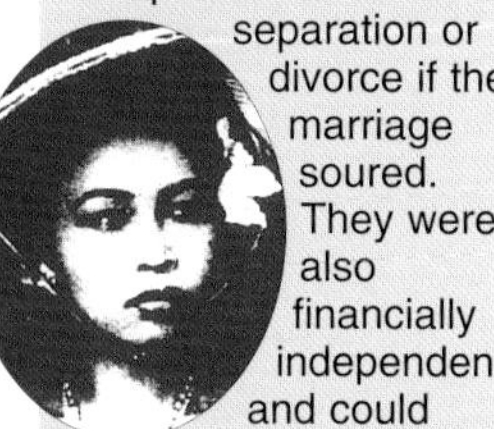

Siput Sarawak, a famous 20th-century star.

Learning the trade

Acting was a full-time occupation for the Bangsawan performer. All those who joined Bangsawan companies were attracted by the stardom, fame and adventure which the travelling troupes offered. The Bangsawan newcomer was drawn gradually into the life of the troupe, initially playing small roles.

Young children were apprenticed and given children's or other minor parts, and child stars were promoted as novelties. Children also sang or danced in the extra turns. Most apprentices had to play the role of court attendants, referred to as 'holding the spear' (*pegang tombak*). They learnt by observing the more experienced performers from the side-wings. They had to familiarize themselves with all the roles, songs and dances. Apprentices also had to help out with the daily chores such as cleaning and distributing posters in the towns and villages.

Once they became stars (*bintang*), performers had to constantly improve their skills in singing, dancing and the art of self-defence. They had to accommodate the changing tastes of audiences and learn the latest songs and dances. Life as stars meant having to give up much personal freedom and observe strict codes of conduct on stage and off. Women could not go out during the day or go near a window lest they were seen by outsiders. They were told that if people could see their faces in the daytime, they would not come and see them perform in the evening.

As Bangsawan troupes proliferated, performers became entrepreneurial; when another troupe offered them bigger roles and higher salaries, they would move.

Extended family network

Bangsawan performers of the early 20th century regarded the troupe as a substitute family. This extended family network embraced members of all races, and a camaraderie was fostered within the community. They were mutually dependent on one another for survival. Mutual help and fellow-feeling arose because they were away from their families in the *kampung* (village). Having to travel long and sometimes hazardous journeys by sea also brought them closer.

Living in a *rumah kongsi* (shared house), they

Stars of Bangsawan

Ainon Chik
Famous *seri panggung* (heroine), dubbed Greta Garbo of Malaya. Joined Genani Star Opera when she was orphaned at eight. Her father was a Bugis while her mother was Sarawakian Chinese.

Minah Alias
Her parents were Nani bin Haji Omar, the manager and *orang muda* (hero) of Genani Star Opera, and Catharine de Brish, an actress. Started singing at the age of four.

I was to play the role of the jungle child in 'Ginnufifa'. To my dismay, the leaves with which I was covered were full of ants. I was feeling so itchy that I forgot my part. Instead of pulling the antelope's tail, I pulled his horns.'
(*Star*, 15 December 1984)

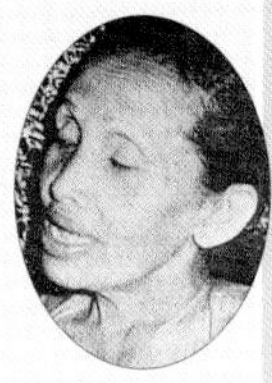

Mahmud Jun
Well-known *orang muda* (hero). Ran away from home in Alor Star to join Grand Jubilee Opera in Ipoh at the age of 14. Became a famous actor in Malay movies in the 1950s and 1960s.

Mat Arab
Famous comedian. Joined Bangsawan after his parents died. His father was an Arab while his mother was Malay.

Aman Belon
Known as the Charlie Chaplin of the East. He obtained permission from the Japanese in 1942 to start a troupe in Singapore.

Alias Manan
Joined Ruby's Grand Opera in his teens, later formed his own troupe, Sri Timur Bangsawan. Instructed Bangsawan at Universiti Sains Malaysia in the late 1970s and 1980s.

Rahman B.
Well-known *orang muda* (hero) of Rahman Star Opera. Grew up in the midst of Bangsawan activity in his father's (Bakar M) troupe.

'When the rain came, the roof would leak, the stage would leak, we had to run hither and thither. Still, we were satisfied with our lives.'
(Tan Sooi Beng, 1997)

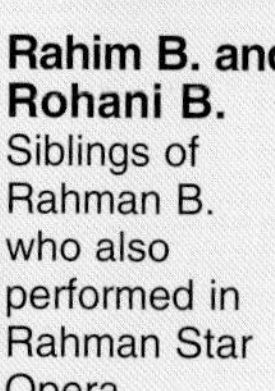

Rahim B. and Rohani B.
Siblings of Rahman B. who also performed in Rahman Star Opera.

cooked and ate together. They addressed each other as *mak* (mother), *pak* (father), *kak* (older sister), *abang* (older brother) or *adik* (younger brother or sister). New recruits were adopted as *anak angkat* (adopted children). The practice of adoptive parenthood ensured that the children were adequately taken care of. This family unit was able to socialize younger members, cushioning the transition of new recruits from a rural to an urban setting, while ensuring they were not alienated from their cultural roots.

By living together and learning one another's culture, performers of different ethnic origins contributed directly to cultural and musical interaction, absorption and synthesis, which is typical of Bangsawan theatre.

Audiences and patrons

Bangsawan performances of the early 20th century attracted multi-ethnic audiences. Besides Malays, locally born Babas and Nyonyas, Jawi Peranakan, Chinese, Indians, Arabs and Europeans were drawn to it. In fact, the Babas and Nyonyas were such great fans of Bangsawan that they set up their own amateur Bangsawan groups.

Audiences were made up of various social strata. Special box seats were reserved for members of royalty who were keen followers of Bangsawan. British officials and the socially prominent—rich Chinese, Indian businessmen and Malay professionals—were often invited to be the patrons. The first-class seats were usually occupied by middle-income earners—Chinese shopkeepers, Malay schoolteachers, Indian traders and clerks—while second-class seats were taken by the less well-off. Labourers, peasants and servants watched from outside.

To show their appreciation, socially prominent members of the audience presented gold medals or silver and gold cups to the actors, actresses and managers of the troupes. Certificates of merit and letters of praise were also awarded to opera troupes by royalty. It was reported that individuals in the audience would fall in love with the performers and shower gifts on them.

Multi-ethnic performers

Well-known performers of varied ethnic backgrounds in the early 20th century included Tan Tjeng Bok, a Chinese actor; Sheik Omar, an Arab singer; Dora van Smith, a European prima donna; Suki, a hero who hailed from Padang, Sumatra; Ainon Chik, an actress of Chinese-Bugis descent; Siput Sarawak; and Alfonso Soliano, a Filipino musician.

Current context

Due to competition from Malay films and the preference for more realistic stories associated with independence and nationalism, the popularity of Bangsawan faded in the 1950s and 1960s. Famous Bangsawan performers such as Mahmud Jun, Suki, Shariff Medan and Ainon Chik joined film companies as actors and actresses, choreographers or musicians. Those who could not make it in the film world began to turn to other forms of entertainment such as the Ronggeng or Joget groups. Accomplished musicians such as Alfonso Soliano played in nightclubs.

By the 1970s, professional Bangsawan troupes that travelled from place to place ceased to exist. Sporadic performances were staged by Sri Timur Bangsawan (belonging to the late Alias Manan and Minah Alias) in Penang and the Pertubuhan Seni Bangsawan Negara (set up by two brothers Rahman B. and Rahim B.) in Kuala Lumpur. These groups were mainly made up of factory workers, students and family members. Rahman B. continues to pass on his knowledge to students of the Akademi Seni Kebangsaan. In Penang, Bahroodin bin Ahmad, who acted in the Sri Timur Bangsawan, has attempted to present Bangsawan in its multi-cultural form performed by a multi-ethnic cast in stories such as *Sam Pek Eng Tye*, *Butterfly Lovers* and *Rama and Sita*. The amateur performers rehearse intensively before each performance. Scripts are often memorized by the younger performers who are not trained in improvisation.

By the 1920s and 1930s chorus girls were performing the latest modern dances as a regular feature called 'extra turns'. Seen here are chorus girls from the Bintang Timur company in a 1952 Bangsawan performance.

Advertisement that appeared in the *Straits Echo* on 23 December 1931, of *The Silver Mask*, a 1931 Bangsawan adaptation of the film *The Mark of Zoro*.

Charity! Charity!! Charity!!!
IN AID OF
China Flood Relief Fund
THE
Dean's Star Opera
OF SINGAPORE WILL STAGE
UNDER THE DISTINGUISHED PATRONAGE OF
The Chinese Consul and Mrs. Hsieh Hsiang
"THE SILVER MASK"
A romantic, gripping and thrilling play adapted from the screen production, "THE MARK OF ZORO" in which Douglas Fairbanks, the film star, played his role to such perfection.
AT
THEATRE ROYAL
On THURSDAY NIGHT (X'MAS EVE)
DECEMBER 24th.

"SILVER MASK" will be supported during intervals between the acts by specially got up Vaudeville Extra Turns, both in Quality and Quantity unparalleled before. The choice and novel numbers with suitably enlivening music to harmonise include:

(1) Spanish Tambourine
By Miss Tijah & Mr. Dean supported by the Chorus Girls.

(2) Pucca Chinese Songs
By the Versatile Artiste, K. Deen.

(3) Hindustani Combined Numbers
By Miss Tijah and Che Saadiah.

(4) Malayan Memories [Typical Malay Songs]
By Miss Tijah and Miss Salma the non-record singers.

HERE'S A RARE OPPORTUNITY TO ENJOY AN EVENING'S PERFECT ENTERTAINMENT AND THEREBY CONTRIBUTE TO A MOST DESERVING C A U S E—T H E CHINA FLOOD RELIEF FUND.
Every cent thus spent is spent for the saving of lives.

Prices of Admission $3-00, $2-00, $1-00, 50cts.
Show Begins at 9 p.m. & Ends at 1 a.m.

Chinese opera

Chinese opera, commonly known as Wayang Cina, *was brought to Malaysia by Chinese immigrants in the late 19th century. It is performed in the Cantonese, Teochew, Hokkien and Hainanese dialects. Staged as commercial entertainment or as ritual offering to the gods, it enjoyed popularity in the early 20th century, but has since lost out to more modern forms of entertainment. Since the 1990s, Chinese opera is staged primarily for religious festivals rather than for entertainment. Like Chinese puppet theatre,* Wayang Cina *is urban-based.*

Painted faces of opera actors

Characters in Chinese opera are depicted by painted faces (above) and colours having specific meanings (below).

- crafty/cunning
- good character
- courageous/enterprising
- intelligent
- obstinate/stubborn
- honest, upright character
- suggests ghostly quality
- spirits of higher order/gods

Source: Elizabeth Halson

The performance

Opera performances are mostly held on makeshift stages set up in temple grounds or in open spaces. Performances staged for religious festivals are divided into two sections—one in the afternoon which features second-rank actors and actresses, and another at night which showcases the star performers. The staging of opera is as much an occasion for social gathering as it is an offering. During the performance, people move about freely, chat with their friends, or even eat at the side stalls.

The opera begins with a prologue. The Eight Immortals (known for their supernatural powers) first pay their respects, offer birthday greetings and congratulate the deity on his/her long life in the introductory piece called 'A Birthday Greeting from the Eight Immortals' (*Baxian Hesou*). The Eight Immortals also wish the audience long life, prosperity and honour.

This sequence is followed by a thanksgiving ceremony, Tiaojiaguan, performed by the character Jiaguan who wears a white mask and red robes. He walks across the stage carrying two red scrolls with Chinese characters painted on them. He wishes the audience peace and prosperity and thanks the deity for his/her blessings.

The 'Presenting the Prince' (*Songtaizi*) segment is then acted out. One of the seven immortal daughters of the Jade King presents Lu Mong Ceng, her mortal husband, with their son. The princess praises Lu for his success and his filial piety. Lu has now become an important official. In this segment, the performers express the desire that the audience would have talented sons. As the legend goes, the child later became famous as the chief scholar of the empire.

Chinese opera forms an important ritual during religious occasions especially during the *Phor Tor* or Hungry Ghost festival, which is widely observed by Chinese communities in Malaysia.

Teochew and Cantonese operas additionally perform the segment 'Six Ministers Invest a Chancellor' (*Liuguo Fengxiang*). This is an opportunity for the troupe to show off its riches in actors, actresses, costumes and techniques.

All the actors and actresses then descend the stage to the temple to pay their respects to the temple deity. Lu and the princess offer their son (in the form of a wooden puppet) together with a red scholar's hat to the temple deity. The hat is symbolic of success. The temple representative then returns the puppet and hat to the troupe together with biscuits and a red packet. Only then does the actual story for the night begin.

Roles in Chinese opera

Role	Opera term	Role types
Male	*Sheng*	Old male (*laosheng*), young male (*xiaosheng*), military male (*wusheng*) or civilian male (*wensheng*).
Female	*Dan*	Virtuous tragic heroine (*chingyi*), flirtatious lady (*huadan*), old female (*laodan*) and female warrior (*daomadan*).
Clown	*Chou*	Male servant, shopkeeper, merchant.
Painted face	*Jing*	Powerful characters, either good or evil, such as the Monkey King, a judge, and the Ox King.

Repertoire

Opera stories focus on the life and deeds of emperors, generals and the aristocracy, romantic love between the scholar and the beauty, fairies and demons and the conquests of barbaric tribes. Some of the popular stories are drawn from Chinese classics such as 'Romance of the Three Kingdoms', 'The Water's Edge' or folk tales such as 'Sam Pek Eng Tai' and 'Madame White Snake'. Standards of social behaviour such as refinement, patience, bravery, devotion to duty and moral virtue are extolled in these stories.

Musical ensemble

The musical ensemble is divided into the civil (*wen*) ensemble comprising wind and string instruments, and military (*wu*) ensemble comprising gongs, drums and other percussion instruments. The civil section

accompanies singing and provides background music whenever needed. Percussion instruments play when there is a change of scene, when performers appear or leave the stage and during dramatic situations such as fighting sequences.

The instruments used in Teochew, Cantonese, Hokkien and Hainanese operas vary. For instance, the civil section of the Teochew opera comprises the dulcimer (*yangqin*), two-stringed fiddle (*erhu*) and the wind instrument (*sona*), while that of the Cantonese opera consists of the *erhu*, *yangqin*, three-stringed guitar (*sanxian*), flute (*dizi*) and *suona*. The military section of both operas comprises drums, gongs, cymbals, wood blocks, clappers, bells and cymbals.

Current context

Since the 1970s, Chinese opera groups have introduced changes to attract the younger generation. The Hokkien opera offers two-hour renditions of Chinese and Western popular songs before the opera proper begins. Electric guitar bands or karaoke machines accompany the singers while they sing and dance on stage. Other changes include the use of colloquial dialect and the expansion of the humorous sequences with contemporary references like 'going to town by taxi' or 'eating curry'. Western instruments such as the violin and cello have been added to the Teochew opera while the saxophone, violin and guitar have been introduced in the Cantonese opera.

Amateur groups have tried to Malaysianize Chinese opera through the performances of local stories such as 'Puteri Hang Li Po Tiba di Melaka' and the use of Malay costumes and language in some performances. English translations of the script are often projected on a screen for the benefit of those who do not understand the language.

Headdress and costumes

The colour and decorations of costumes define the type, rank and status of the character. Red is worn by good characters of high rank while blue is worn by both good and bad characters of high rank. Yellow is reserved for royalty, green for highly virtuous men and white for the very old or the very young or for occasions of mourning. Black implies violent and aggressive male characters. Pink and turquoise imply the youthfulness of the characters.

Important characters such as emperors wear elaborate headdresses. A scholar puts on a blue double crowned cap with two long flaps or wings and decorated with a small rosette of woollen fabric and a pearl in the centre. Attendants and servants wear soft, black hats.

The female performer's elaborate hairdressing technique shown in sequence.

Stylized movements

In Chinese opera, stylized movements take the place of stage props. A character is riding a horse when he lifts his hairy-cane and moves it around the stage. The actor walks around the stage to show that he has travelled a long distance or to show that time has passed. Actors running around the stage waving black flags indicate that a storm is coming. When a performer stands on a chair, he is standing on an elevation such as a hill or wall. When he walks in between two silk flags embroidered with wheels, he is travelling in a wagon. A swing of the leg shows that a character is leaving a building.

This opera performer from the turn of 19th century illustrates that costuming in Chinese opera has remained elaborate and spectacular.

1. Performers executing the movements of the *menghadap rebab* in Mak Yong theatre.

2. Initiating the *rebab* prior to a ritual performance.

3. An actor playing the role of a clown in a Mak Yong performance.

4. Ritualistic Mak Yong theatre is a series of rituals and stories, including comic scenes.

5. *Balai tiang empat puluh* (40-pillar structure of bamboo) bearing offerings at ritual performances.

6. Offerings for a special Mak Yong performance done for *semah angin* (wind blandishment).

7. A dance in a Mak Yong ritual performance.

8. In Main Puteri healing rituals 'patients' enter a state of trance to be 'cured' by shamans.

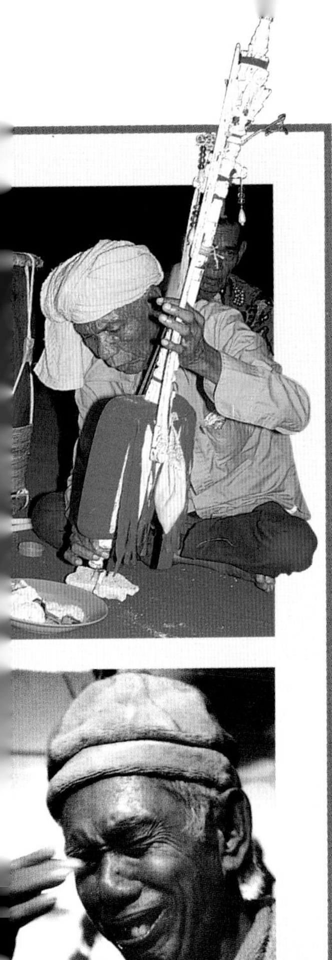

THEATRE AS RITUAL, RITUAL AS THEATRE

In traditional Malay society the principal function of theatre is to provide entertainment. At the same time, however, in the older genres of theatre such as Mak Yong and Wayang Kulit, ritual activity constitutes an important part of a performance.

The ritual activity in these genres takes the form of theatre opening and closing rituals. The opening ceremony is essentially meant to appease the invisible powers, in particular environmental spirits, and to seek their cooperation to avoid mishaps during a performance. Such appeasement of the spirits is essential, firstly, because the physical theatre structure stands on the ground and near localities, such as hills or rivers, in which such spirits have their homes. Secondly, the stories in the repertoire of traditional theatre usually have gods or supernatural heroes as principal characters. This makes traditional theatre a sacred art form that requires proper performance, and all possible care. This is to some extent ensured by a qualified *bomoh* who conducts the rituals. The closing rituals are done upon the completion of a performance as a means of thanking the spirits for their cooperation.

Theatre as ritual exists when specific genres, such as Mak Yong or Wayang Kulit, which are ordinarily performed for entertainment, are staged with the intention of serving more serious functions, including that of healing through wind blandishment (*semah angin*), strengthening of a soul or spirit (*semangat*) that has been weakened or the recall of semangat that has been lost. *Angin* represents a particularly strong urge or desire for something. In theatre one may have such a desire for a particular genre. An artiste of traditional theatre, be he a puppeteer, dancer, actor or musician, who has not performed for an extended period of time may suffer from depression or some other malady, which may manifest itself in various ways such as inability to eat or sleep, lethargy and lack of interest. Thus the more important of the older theatre forms continue to play a role as therapeutic agents.

Then there are performance genres that are in fact purely healing rituals, their sole purpose being that of healing illnesses of the mind or spirit. These styles of theatre are never staged for entertainment. They involve healers (*bomoh*), but unlike the bomoh who heal physical illnesses, these healers enter into a state of trance, through which they come into contact with the particular spirit believed to be responsible for the disease. Cure is achieved by driving away a malicious spirit or persuading it to leave the body of the patient.

These healing rituals have the essential qualities of theatre, such as basic character changes and the use of music. The bomoh in these rituals are in fact true shamans, and Main Puteri is by far the most significant and most complex of all therapeutic theatre styles active among the Malays.

Pak Yong, the lead role in Mak Yong theatre, is generally played by a female.

Healing performances

Malay shamanistic theatre exists as a means of ritualistic healing. Of such forms of theatre found in Malaysia, Main Puteri is the most elaborate, sophisticated and complex. Bagih is a less dramatic healing ritual, without the theatrical elements of Main Puteri. Two other healing rituals, Gebiah and Belian, are no longer performed by the Malays, but are still kept alive by the Orang Asli.

A patient in a Main Puteri session being consoled by a relative.

Healing rituals

Traditional Malay healing rituals are based upon an ancient Malay belief system. Essentially animistic, it attributes non-physical illnesses to possession by spirits, to the weakening or loss of a person's soul-energy (*semangat*), or to *angin*, literally meaning wind (see 'Belief systems of traditional theatre').

Main Puteri and Bagih are basically simple healing ceremonies conducted in the sitting area of a *kampung* (village) home. For more elaborate performances, a simple wooden and thatch structure (*panggung*) is constructed near the patient's house. The panggung is constructed at ground level and is open on all sides. The more complex form of ritual healing theatre, called *berjamu*, is enacted for the fulfilment of vows, or the initiation of a Main Puteri performer (*sembah guru*). It involves feting the spirits and gods over three nights of performance.

Main Puteri trance sessions are also used as a means of establishing contact with spiritual beings during ritualistic performances of Mak Yong and Wayang Kulit Siam. It is mostly found in the eastern state of Kelantan and the Malay areas of southern Thailand.

A form of healing theatre found only in Terengganu is Ulik Mayang, an animistic trance dance performed exclusively by maidens, and accompanied by singing and music. Performances are accompanied by drums, gongs, violin and accordion. Its origins remain unknown, but traditionally this dance is associated with healing. It is said to be connected with harvest rituals, and some opinions indicate that it is done in honour of sea spirits.

Trance dance

The main theatrical element of Main Puteri lies in the trance (*lupa*) sessions, where the *tok puteri*, the patient and sometimes audience members enter trance states. A series of dances are performed. The arrival of the spirit is marked by physical and psychological changes in the dancer, accompanied with intensely dramatic movements.

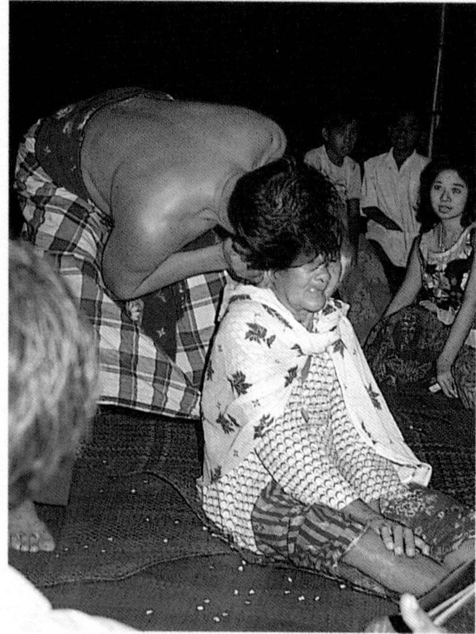

A shaman 'sucking' a spirit from a patient (seated) said to have been possessed.

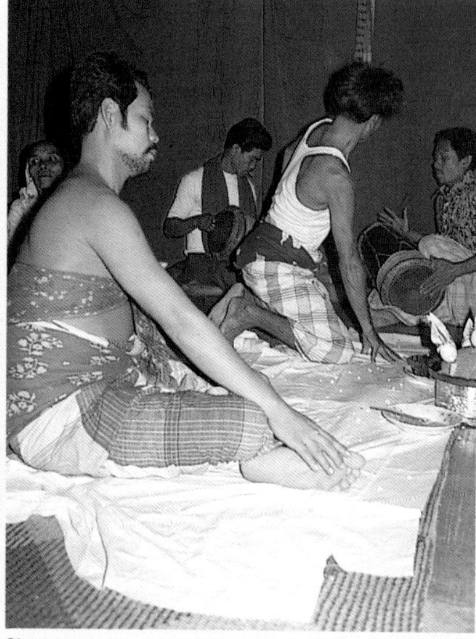

Shamans go into trance before they commence a healing session.

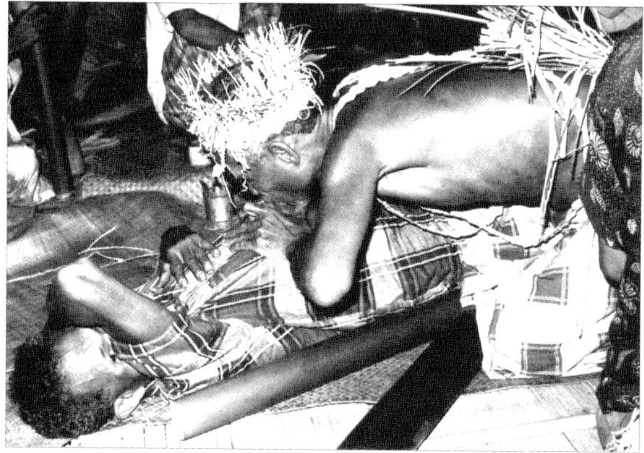

The Orang Asli's healing ceremony is similar to Main Puteri and Bagih, rooted in animistic beliefs.

Composition of a Main Puteri troupe

A Main Puteri troupe comprises a shaman (*bomoh puteri* or *tok puteri*) and an interrogator of spirits (*tok minduk*). The tok minduk serves as the tok puteri's assistant and is usually a qualified bomoh himself. Traditional Malay shamans—alternatively called bomoh, *dukun* and *pawang*—figure extensively in Main Puteri.

The tok puteri, either a man or a woman, acts as a conduit for spirits that are summoned or which voluntarily descend from the spirit world. The tok minduk's role is to interrogate the entranced tok puteri who becomes, during trance sessions, the vehicle for the spirits. Each possession is manifested in altered behaviour patterns on the part of the tok puteri as he assumes the characteristics of the visiting spirit. Physical changes and alterations in voice are often noticeable. In the state of trance, the tok puteri is said to plunge into the invisible world, thereby coming into contact with a range of spirits.

The tok minduk also acts as the principal musician, playing the three-stringed lute (*rebab*). In any single performance, usually lasting between one and three nights, several shamans officiate, assuming the roles of tok puteri or tok minduk in turn.

Music for the performance is provided by a troupe of musicians. A basic Mak Yong orchestra is used, comprising the rebab, a pair of bossed gongs (*tetawak*) and a pair of double-headed barrel drums (*gendang*) and, sometimes, cymbals (*kesi*) and a pair of inverted gongs (*canang*), beaten with sticks. Much of the musical repertoire derives from Mak Yong.

The performance

A Main Puteri performance begins with the theatre opening rituals (*buka panggung*). Following an opening musical piece (*lagu bertabuh*) and several preliminary pieces, the bomoh sings the salutation song (*lagu bertabik*). This leads to the trance (*lupa*) sessions. These are the most exciting in terms of drama, visual effects and music. While singing and dancing, the tok puteri enters a trance, violently swaying his head. He assumes the characteristics of a succession of spirits as he attempts to 'bring down' the one that is causing illness. When the spirit is found, the tok minduk begins negotiating with it. Promises are extracted from the spirit to cease harassing the patient, and the spirit is promised food or other offerings. Music is then played, and the spirit departs.

The highly elaborate ritual (berjamu) for a shaman initiation or for fulfilling vows involves the removal of the spiritual paraphernalia at this point. A bathing ceremony (*bersiram*) for the patient is conducted. A feast is held for the human participants, and a ritual closing ceremony (*tutup panggung*) ends the performance.

Bagih

The Bagih healing ritual is believed to be at least 500 years old and is likely to have developed from the Orang Asli's Belian ceremony. Bagih does not cure loss of semangat (soul) or angin; instead, it focuses on spirit possession by ancient holy persons (*keramat*) or warriors from ancient myths. A performance involves three persons—the healer/shaman (*tok bagih*), the interrogator/shaman's assistant (tok minduk), and the patient. No musical instruments are used. The only accessory is a bunch of rattan leaves held by the tok bagih.

Performances usually take place in a patient's house. Offerings (*kenduri*) are made. With the patient lying or sitting on the floor, the tok bagih reads the invocations (*mantera*). He smokes a bunch of rattan leaves over a censer, and the onset of a trance or possession is indicated by the violent shaking of the leaves. He throws fistfuls of turmeric-coloured rice in different directions. The possessing spirit is interrogated by the tok minduk and driven off. To do this, the tok bagih may literally pull the spirit from the patient's big toe, or suck it from his head. Thread is passed along the length of the patient's body to indicate a path to the spirit world, and he/she is given blessed lime to squeeze into a bath (*mandi limau*) for spiritual cleansing.

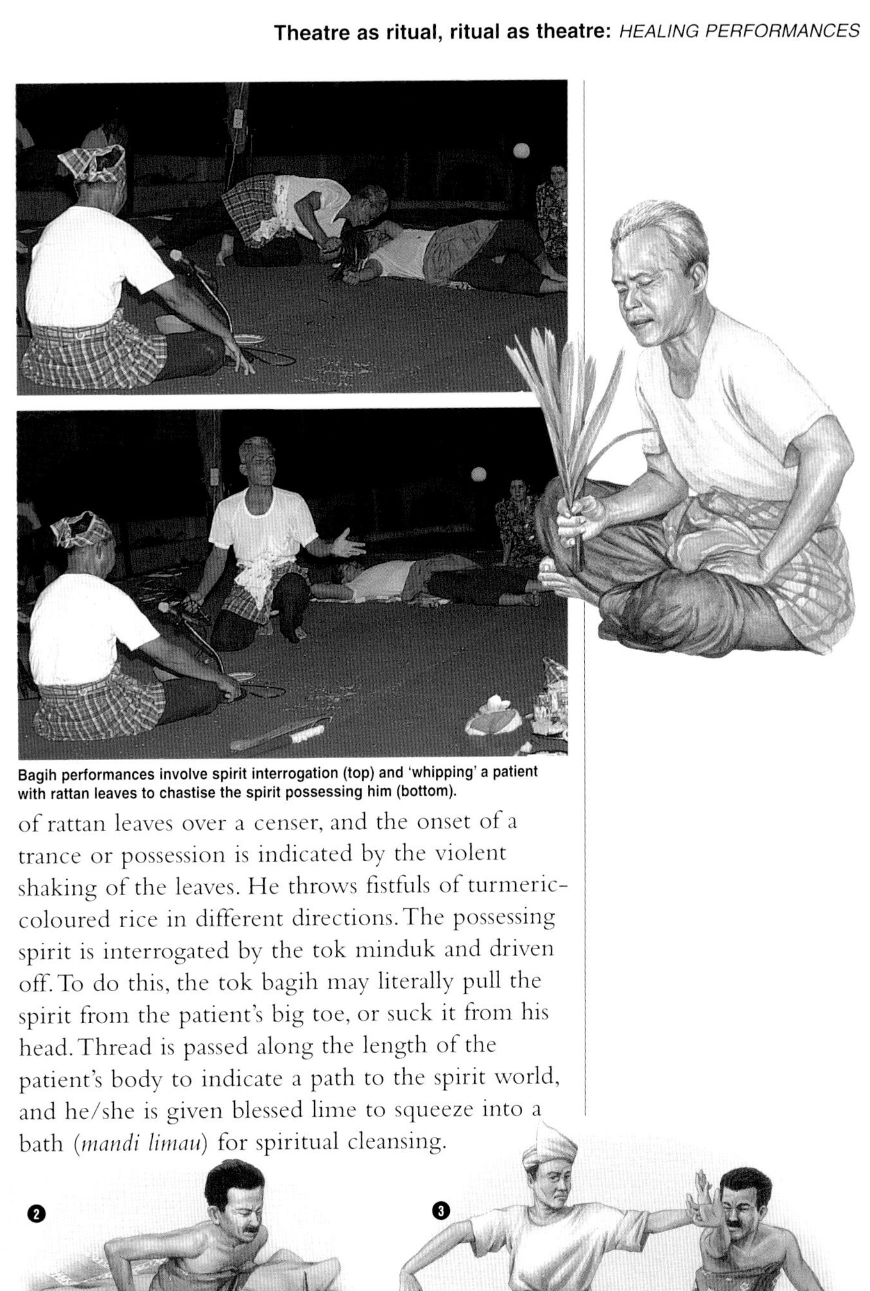

Bagih performances involve spirit interrogation (top) and 'whipping' a patient with rattan leaves to chastise the spirit possessing him (bottom).

Therapeutic theatre

The idea behind Main Puteri is that disease derives from spirits. It is associated with the concept of soul-energy (*semangat*) which may be weakened or stolen by spirits. Through healing rituals such as this, the semangat is restored and replenished. The basic elements of Main Puteri are illustrated here.

1 Offerings are made, the patient takes his place, and the Main Puteri session begins.

2 The *tok puteri* dances himself into a trance. The *tok minduk*, his assistant, is in the foreground playing the *rebab*.

3 The entranced tok puteri dances and duels with the patient. This is the crux of Main Puteri.

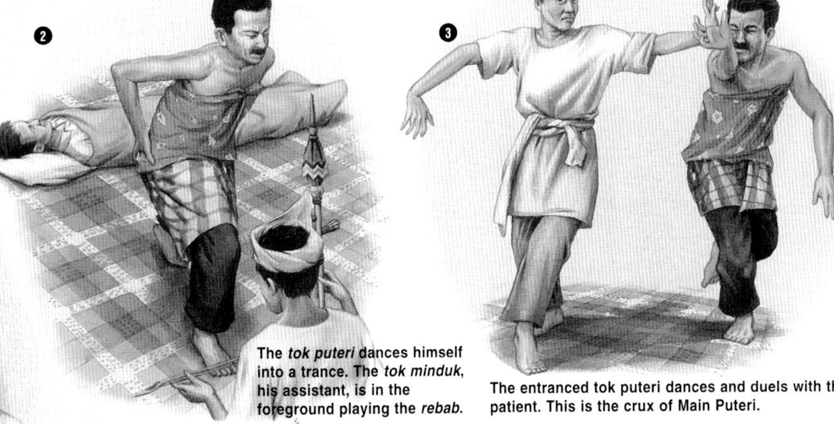

4 The negotiations are over, the offending spirit is evicted, and the patient is cured.

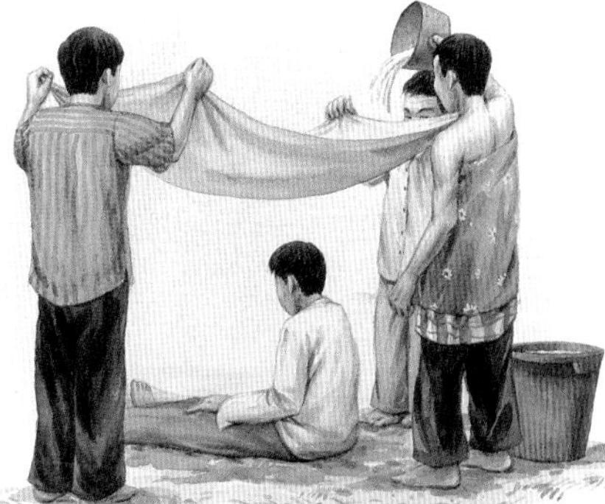

5 The patient is ritually bathed to rid him of remaining negative influences.

Mak Yong as ritual

A ritual Mak Yong performance is more elaborate than that staged for entertainment, combining shamanism, feasting the spirits and dance theatre. It reflects the deep, mystical significance of Mak Yong's stories and dances, and its original aim to serve as a conduit to the spirit world. Ritual performances are enacted for spiritual healing, to pay homage to a teacher and for the graduation of a performer.

Performers are cleansed in a ceremony upon completion of a Mak Yong ritual to get rid of any lingering negative influences.

The spiritual performance

While a ritual (*berjamu*) Mak Yong performance shares many features of that staged purely for entertainment, it demands a host of additional activities. These include the preparation of certain ritual items, trance sessions with the Main Puteri shaman (*bomoh*), and elaborate offerings.

The graduation of a Mak Yong performer, who may be either male or female, is the most dramatic manifestation of a ritual ceremony. It combines 'wind' blandishment (*semah angin*) and saluting the Mak Yong teacher (*sembah guru*), and is a series of ceremonies, ritual observances and Mak Yong stories. It is, in effect, a graduation ceremony during which the teaching acquired by a student from a teacher is ritually transferred to that student. The ceremony includes Main Puteri trance sessions. The series of ritual activities and theatre lasts three nights. The first two nights' performances begin at nine o'clock following the final evening prayer (*isyak*), and end at about midnight. The activities of the highly important third night go on until well after sunrise on the fourth day.

A Mak Yong graduation ceremony

A graduating lead performer has to fete the spirits, pay respect to the teacher and please his/her own spirit. This involves considerable ritual and much activity by shamans. Conducting *semah angin* will prepare the performer spiritually, emotionally and psychologically for the formal graduation ceremony. It is conducted in tandem with the *sembah guru* rite, which salutes the Mak Yong teacher.

A dancer must complete his/her practical training in dance, vocal music and acting, besides mastering the literary and spiritual aspects. The time for the sembah guru performance is set by the trainee in consultation with the teacher. In the event of a teacher's demise, the trainee must enrol with another teacher before the sembah guru can take place.

The spirits' feast

It is believed that from the moment a Mak Yong student's training begins, the spirits eagerly watch and await its completion, their objective being the ritual feasting. Ritual activities have to be conducted with great care and skill. Mistakes in the ceremony, delay or its non-performance are believed to provoke attacks by spirits, requiring Main Puteri healing.

After several years of training, a Mak Yong student's graduation is marked by a ritual that recognizes the student as a performer.

Malaysia's best-known Mak Yong performer, the late Khatijah Awang (in red) in a 1975 ritual performance.

Ritual Mak Yong performances are rare, given the small number of active Mak Yong troupes currently in existence. Such performances still occur in Terengganu and Kelantan despite disapproval by the authorities for religious reasons.

Opening night

A ritualistic performance commences with a theatre opening ritual conducted by a shaman, a more elaborate form than that prepared for regular Mak Yong. The identity of the sponsor (*tuan kerja*), usually the trainee, is announced, along with his/her lineage, and the fact that the performer is inheriting the mantle of Mak Yong. This also serves the purpose of blandishing the 'wind' (*memujuk angin*) of the sponsor.

The fact that the ritual performance is being held for the purpose of sembah guru is also indicated in the invocations (*mantera*), in which it is made clear to the spirits that the covenant made with them at the beginning of the training is about to be fulfilled. The spirits are asked to protect the performers, and not to make any unnecessary future demands once they have been properly entertained, both by the performance and through the feast offered to them. Finally, before the opening ceremony takes place, the shaman hands over the offerings (*kenduri*) to the invisible host. The shaman now conducts the Main Puteri sessions, during which the spirits are interrogated and placated.

The performance then begins, continuing until about midnight. The second night's performance is almost identical with the first night but involves some Main Puteri sessions. The 'Dewa Muda' story is performed on both nights.

Culmination of the performance

The crucial final night consists of the *menghadap rebab* ritualistic dance and preliminary dances, and a portion of the 'Dewa Pechil' story. It stops at the banishment of the prince from the palace, and separation from his wife, Tuan Puteri Chemara

Bermas. Main Puteri sessions are then held to further strengthen the performers' spiritual energy, and to inform any remaining spirits of the feast.

The second phase of the final night's performance, lasting from one o'clock to four o'clock, is the most significant spiritually. The 'Dewa Pechil' story is completed with the return of the prince. This is followed by the fulfilment of the vow (*pelepas niat*). The gods and spirits descend into the *balai* (a bamboo structure bearing offerings) and the mythical garden, Taman Banjaran Sari. They examine the offerings of the palace tray and regale themselves in the garden. At this point the performers are in a trance. This dramatic palm blossom trance (*upacara lupa mayang*) completes the second phase. A break follows to make way for the dawn (*subuh*) prayers.

The performance then continues with more Main Puteri sessions, followed by the release ceremony (*pelepas*). Any malicious or negative influences (*badi*) present are driven away, and the area is spiritually cleansed. The ritual paraphernalia is removed. The visiting spirits are sent off through the ripping of the sky-cloth (*kain langit*) draped across the theatre ceiling, and the theatre is closed.

Following a bath and other preparations, the Mak Yong trainee prepares for the sembah guru. The teacher symbolically hands over the knowledge taught to his/her charge. The performer is now a qualified Mak Yong, and may both perform and teach others. The Mak Yong is then ritually bathed (*bersiram*) to the strains of 'Lagu Sedayung Pak Yong' played by the orchestra. A communal feast follows.

Convention dictates that a Mak Yong performer conducts only one sembah guru performance during his/her lifetime. A performer may conduct a less elaborate berjamu performance for the purpose of semah angin.

Menghadap rebab: An ancient legacy

This ritualistic dance is the most important and impressive in Mak Yong. It involves the Pak Yong (lead role) and the female performers. They salute the three-stringed lute (*rebab*) and the spirits inhabiting it. It is also an opportunity for the actresses to prepare themselves, ritually, for the roles they are about to enact. This is especially crucial in a ritual performance, with its intense spirituality. For the Pak Yong, this sequence continues the process that had previously commenced offstage in secret ancient rituals—the symbolic and ritualistic transformation from actress to god-king.

The actresses, led by the Pak Yong, enter the acting area (*gelenggang*) to the tune of 'Sang Pak Yong turun'. Sitting cross-legged and with the pak yong in front, they face the rebab player and also the direction of the rising sun. The actresses then make a salutation gesture (*sembah*) and the dance begins, accompanied with song.

The late Cik Ning (left) was a leading Mak Yong performer in the 1980s.

'Dewa Muda': The tale of the magic kite

Regarded as the first Mak Yong story, 'Dewa Muda' must be performed on the first night. A central symbol of a kite represents the human soul and the shaman in flight. It has a death and revival theme. The kite symbolically melds the earth and sky, an important association in the ancient Malay culture of the region.

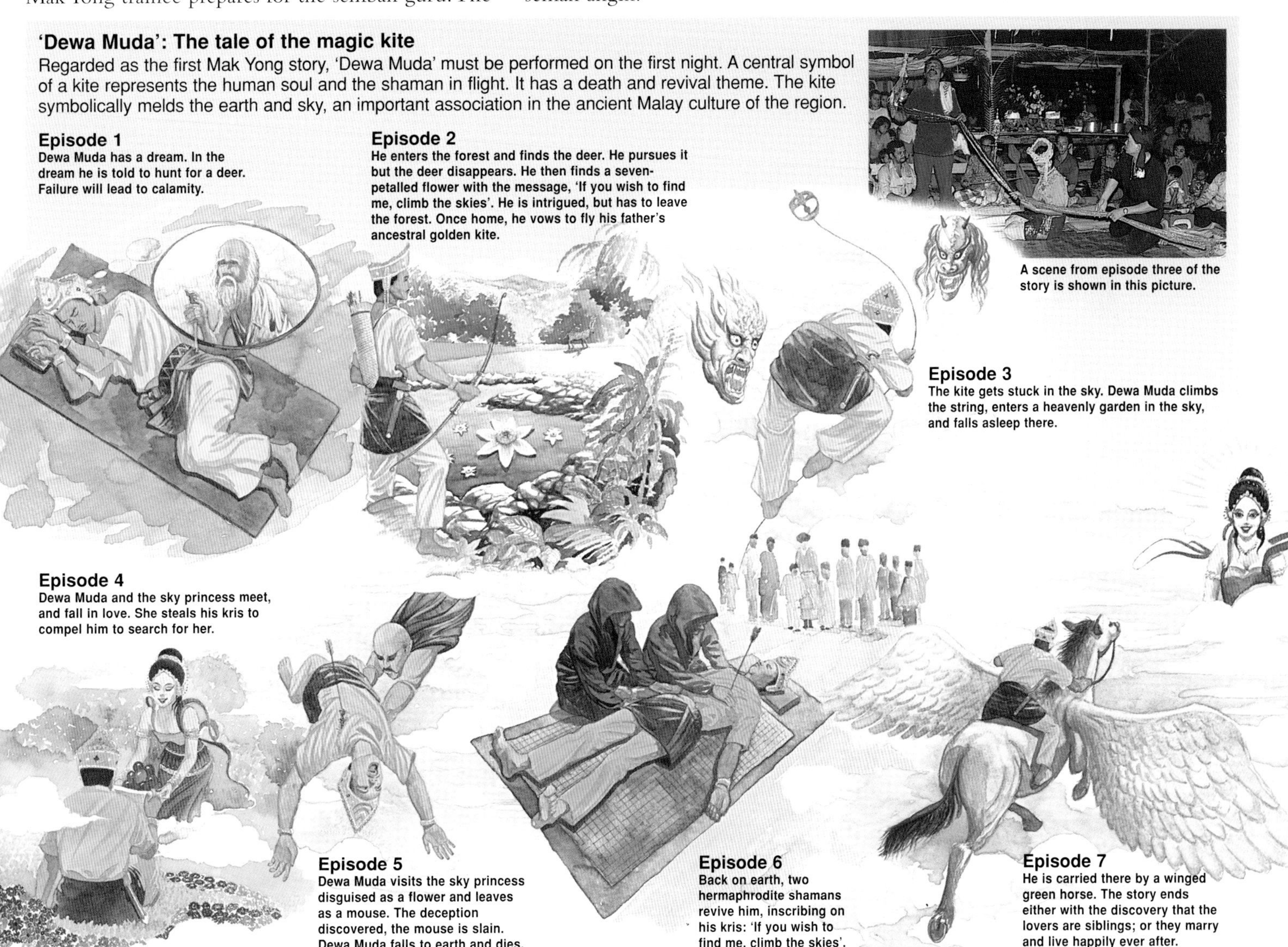

Episode 1
Dewa Muda has a dream. In the dream he is told to hunt for a deer. Failure will lead to calamity.

Episode 2
He enters the forest and finds the deer. He pursues it but the deer disappears. He then finds a seven-petalled flower with the message, 'If you wish to find me, climb the skies'. He is intrigued, but has to leave the forest. Once home, he vows to fly his father's ancestral golden kite.

A scene from episode three of the story is shown in this picture.

Episode 3
The kite gets stuck in the sky. Dewa Muda climbs the string, enters a heavenly garden in the sky, and falls asleep there.

Episode 4
Dewa Muda and the sky princess meet, and fall in love. She steals his kris to compel him to search for her.

Episode 5
Dewa Muda visits the sky princess disguised as a flower and leaves as a mouse. The deception discovered, the mouse is slain. Dewa Muda falls to earth and dies.

Episode 6
Back on earth, two hermaphrodite shamans revive him, inscribing on his kris: 'If you wish to find me, climb the skies'.

Episode 7
He is carried there by a winged green horse. The story ends either with the discovery that the lovers are siblings; or they marry and live happily ever after.

Wayang Kulit Siam as ritual

In the ritual performance of Wayang Kulit Siam, staging of the story is combined with elaborate offerings and shamanistic activity through which the spirits are contacted by the puppeteer and feasted. Enacted for specific purposes, such as a puppeteer's graduation or to fulfil a vow, such performances are not intended for entertainment.

Sita Dewi is believed to be the mother of all puppeteers. Offerings made to her are often delicately constructed.

Occasions of the ritual performance

Ritual (*berjamu*) performances of Wayang Kulit Siam take place to mark a puppeteer's graduation (*sembah guru*), for the opening of a new theatre, to fulfil a vow (*pelepas niat*), or to cure an ailing puppeteer (*semah angin*).

These performances usually take place at a specially constructed theatre (*panggung*) close to the puppeteer's home. A ritual performance lasts three nights, ending on the morning of the fourth day. The first two nights follow the pattern of non-ritual performances. During the third night, ritual activities intensify significantly.

There are only a few puppeteers left who are able to conduct a berjamu Wayang Kulit as it is structurally complex. Such performances are rare even in the genre's home state of Kelantan.

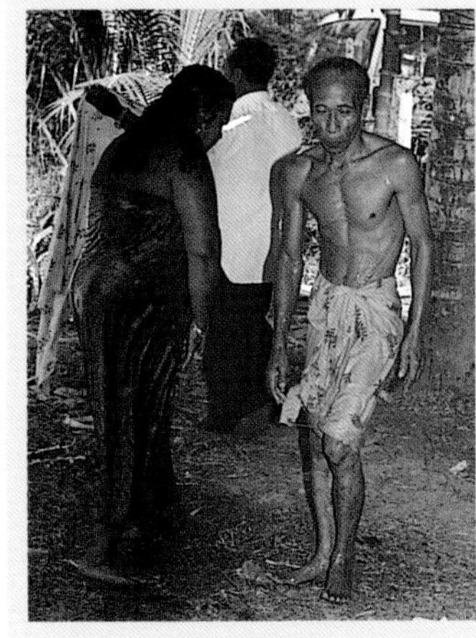

Cleansing ritual
After a Wayang Kulit Siam ritual, the *dalang* bathes (left) to the strains of 'Lagu Bersiram' (bathing song). Prior to this, he and members of his family as well as anyone else may drink the water in three pots containing croton leaves and other offerings to drive away lingering malicious influences as a result of contact with the supernatural.

The performance

The third night commences with the recitation of ritual formulae (*mantera*). The offerings are also enumerated for the benefit of the recipient spirits.

The orchestra, with lighted candles placed on the instruments to placate the spirits residing in them, plays the opening signal piece (*bertabuh*), and a selection of other pieces. An invitation (*memadah*) is then extended to the invisible beings—spirits, ogres, gods and mythical characters from the *Ramayana* epic. The 'lagu guru' is sung, providing the invisible beings with details of the person sponsoring the performance and its intended purpose.

Players and paraphernalia

1. The flag pole or *tiang candi* is a 'spirit conductor'. It marks the site of the feast, guiding invisible beings to it.
2. The *panggung* (theatre) is sacred. It houses the spirits invited to the feast. When the screen is removed on the third night, this sanctified area is symbolically extended to take in the entire surroundings.
3. The *kain langit* is a piece of cloth strung with betel leaves, betel nuts and other items. It becomes a spiritual avenue for the gods to descend to earth. At the end of the ceremony, it is ripped down, opening a passageway for the spirits to ascend.
4. The puppeteer (*dalang*) is the representative of the Hindu god Shiva. In performance, he is believed to be re-enacting the universe's creation.
5. Each dalang has his own control spirit. Here, the dalang is shown possessed by the spirit of Hanuman (Monkey General). When possessed by this spirit, the dalang simulates the movements of a monkey. He acts with much drama, devouring the offerings with relish.
6. The *balai tiang empat puluh* is a palace structure that rests on 40 pillars. Constructed of bamboo and swathed in colourful paper, it holds offerings of food for different categories of invisible beings.
7. The musicians play pieces that have the power to repel ferocious spirits and to induce trance states. The instruments are also believed to host spirits.
8. The *buyung* is a pot of water with croton leaves and palm blossoms. The water is a powerful tool for repelling evil spirits, and is drunk by all present for spiritual cleansing.
9. The *sakak*, made from bamboo, is a food tray.
10. The *jung suluk kapal ulana* is a special offering to placate and flatter the King of the Nagas, a powerful spirit who inhabits and rules the world of water.

From his position behind the screen (*kelir*), the puppeteer (*dalang*) waves the *pohon beringin* puppet. Sometimes he may even go into a state of semi-trance. Negative influences in the theatre are neutralized, cleansing of the theatre being effected by scattering turmeric-coloured rice. The Pak Dogol and Wak Long puppets are flattered at this point by the dalang. Pak Dogol symbolizes the mythical original teacher of all dalang, while Wak Long has a dual role in the berjamu performance. He is the dalang's messenger to the spirits, and possesses the body of the human dalang when he, entranced, invites the spirits to the feast.

An apprentice dalang (*dalang muda*) then performs the *bahagian dalang muda*, which has two parts, the first featuring the Wak Peran Hutan (Forest Clown) episode, in which the sage Maharisi is invited to the berjamu. The second features the Betara Kala (God of Time) episode, which explains the mysticism of Wayang Kulit. The play breaks for *subuh* (dawn) prayers. For the morning session, the screen is rolled up, and the entire area is cordoned off with a length of string. The musicians, wearing cotton headcloths, take their positions. The dalang, too, takes his position. The orchestra plays a musical interlude. The Betara Guru (Shiva) puppet is placed on a ritual offering consisting of rice placed on a cushion. The dalang absorbs the Betara Guru's energy and assumes his character.

Feasting the gods

The invitation to the invisible spirit host now takes place in earnest. All important spirits have to be contacted and invited to the feast. This is done by the dalang through Wak Long. Holding the Wak Long puppet, the dalang enters a trance. He becomes possessed by Wak Long's spirit, and sets off to the heavens (*kayangan*) to issue invitations to *Ramayana* characters. The spirit descends to earth and the dalang is possessed by this spirit-visitor. Through the dalang, it consumes the food offering before it departs. The dalang comes out of trance and is soon on another mission to issue more invitations to the ritual feasting.

Finale

Following the feasting, the sage Maharisi, Pak Dogol and Wak Long puppets are dipped in three pots of water and croton leaves for the release (*pelepas*) ceremony. The paraphernalia are removed to music and placed in an isolated spot to prevent their desecration by the spirits. In a final ceremony that also marks the end of the activities, the participating spirits are sent off. A pot of water is smashed while the word *lepas*, meaning release, is uttered thrice. The yellow cloth suspended from the ceiling (*kain langit*) is torn down in a symbolic ripping of the sky for the spirits to return.

Preceding the invitations to the spirits in a ritual performance, the mysticism of Wayang Kulit is explained. The episode features Betara Kala, an evil form of the Hindu god, Shiva (bottom). Betara Kala pursues a beautiful young damsel (top). He chances upon a *wayang* play, and is beguiled by its spiritual wisdom.

Ritual placement of instruments

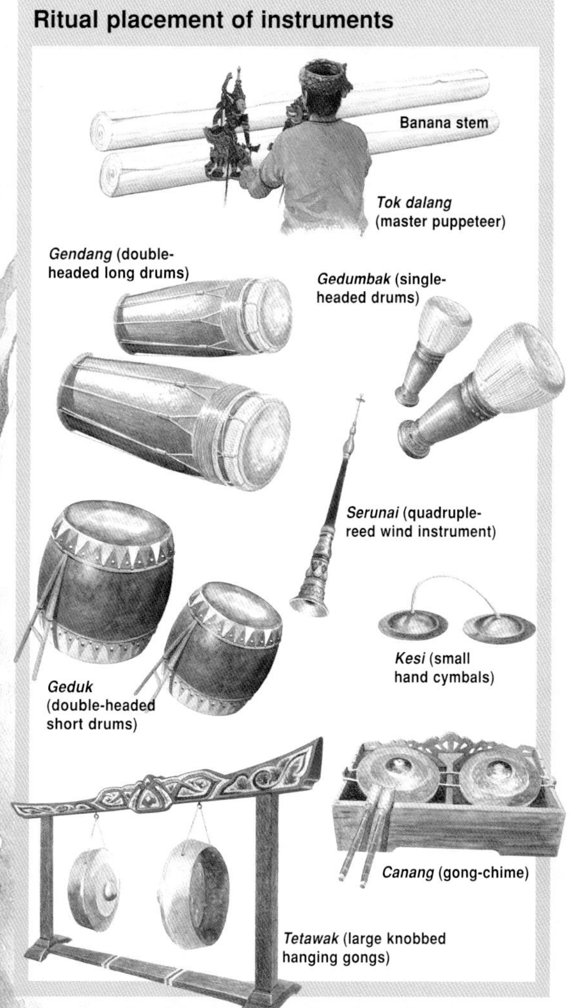

In a Wayang Kulit ritual performance important spirits are invited to a feast, and through the *dalang* consume the food offerings.

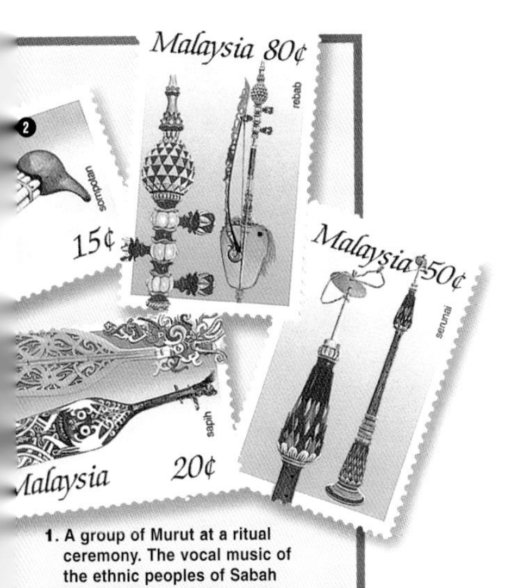

1. A group of Murut at a ritual ceremony. The vocal music of the ethnic peoples of Sabah and Sarawak includes ritual chants performed by high priestesses for healing and honouring spirits.

2. Stamps issued by the postal authorities in 1987 commemorating traditional Malaysian musical instruments such as the *sapeh, serunai, rebab* and *sompotan.*

3. Music for Malay shadow puppet theatre has changed little over the centuries and remains largely a oral tradition.

4. Indian folk and classical music is played in its original traditional style in Malaysia, but is sometimes combined with elements from other cultures for a local flavour.

5. A group of Orang Asli with drums, zithers and flutes, circa 1906. The aboriginal people sometimes borrowed Malay instruments.

FOLK AND SYNCRETIC MUSIC

Folk and syncretic music is distinguished from other types of music by the fact that folk songs and music are a product of the common man who usually lives in a world dictated and ordered by an oral tradition. Here a writing system may or may not exist, but the principal means of transmitting knowledge is by word of mouth and by rote teaching.

In Malaysia, many types of music have existed and evolved for centuries in this oral tradition, passed down from one generation to the next by example and other means of outward expression. In such a tradition change in a musical style occurs very slowly because the community which produces the music takes great care to preserve the main characteristics and how it is produced. A good example is the music for the shadow puppet play as well as dance drama in the Malay theatrical arts.

Wayang Kulit Siam, Mak Yong, Mek Mulung, Rodat, Hadrah, Gendang Tarinai and other arts have existed for several centuries within an oral tradition, with no written scores, song lyrics, scripts or other documents. These forms are found primarily in the rural areas of the country, particularly in the northern peninsular states. It is only in the last two decades of the 20th century that the music of some of these forms has been notated, most notably Wayang Kulit Siam, Mak Yong and Hadrah. Although musical instruments may have been borrowed and absorbed into these genres from outside sources (such as the Middle East or India) many centuries ago, the method of using the instruments and the musical material have changed and evolved into a uniquely Malay musical tradition with little or no connection to past usage in their original cultures.

In contrast, syncretic (or acculturated) music is found in both the urban and rural areas. It combines elements of folk and classical music of a given culture group with outside elements. In Malaysia, some aspects of folk and classical music have combined with Arabic, Persian, Indian, Chinese and Western musical elements. In most cases, the outside elements are borrowed, but are still recognizable as to their place or culture of origin, and in some cases there is little true synthesis of these elements into the root culture.

Early syncretic musical forms in Malaya were originally disseminated through the Bangsawan theatre and the dance halls (*pentas joget*) where Arabic, Hindustani, Chinese, Javanese, Western and Malay pop tunes were heard. Bangsawan music was the first popular music in Malaya. Ghazal, Dondang Sayang, Lagu Melayu Asli, Keroncong, Zapin, Inang and Joget are examples of music which combine native and foreign musical elements, and which developed along with other syncretic music forms during the past two centuries and longer to project a rich and varied expression of a multicultural society.

The *gendang* drum is a basic instrument in traditional Malay music.

Orang Asli music

The Orang Asli maintain an intimate relationship with the natural environment and their music culture takes inspiration from this. Musical instruments are made from forest materials, while the music itself echoes sounds of the forest. Music is performed for pleasure or for ceremonial purposes rooted in animistic beliefs which revere the mountains, forests, seas and rivers.

An Orang Asli boy with a single-headed, waisted drum.

Rainforest music

The Orang Asli live in close contact with their natural environment—the rainforests, rivers, hills, foothills and mountainous terrain. Their houses are constructed of bamboo, rattan, wood and thatch from the forest. The natural environment has been a strong influence in shaping their music as well. Musical instruments are made from forest materials such as wood, bamboo, vines and leaves, while the musical sound often imitates sounds of the forest, from crackling branches to warbling birds and chirping insects.

Music of wood and bamboo

The types of musical instruments found among most Orang Asli groups are tube zithers, stamping tubes, flutes and the jaw's harp (also called 'jew's harp' or 'mouth harp'). Some Orang Asli, especially the Senoi group, have borrowed musical instruments from neighbouring Malay communities. These instruments include the quadruple-reed oboe (*serunai*), the small knobbed gong struck with a wood or padded beater (*tetawak*), and the frame drum (*rebana*, sometimes called *berano* or *batak*).

A favourite stringed instrument played by Orang Asli children is a ground zither called *gendang kebatak*. A hole is dug in the ground and covered with a layer of bark. A taut string runs over the bark and is attached to two short sticks placed in the ground at opposite ends. A third stick, placed on the bark, supports the string which is divided into two uneven sections, producing two different pitches. The two lengths of the string are struck with a stick in various rhythmic patterns. Although Orang Asli music is produced by simple instruments, it is delicate and melodious, and often serves an important function in their community.

A Temiar at a Sewang ritual.

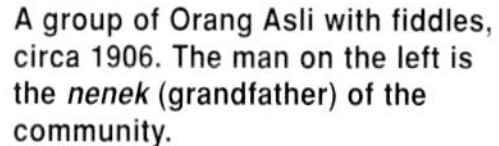

A group of Orang Asli with fiddles, circa 1906. The man on the left is the *nenek* (grandfather) of the community.

Ceremonial music

Ceremonial music takes many forms and is performed for many different purposes—to cure an illness, for mourning the deceased, to celebrate specific times in the harvest cycle, for the building of a new house, to welcome a returned traveller or arriving guest, or simply for general enjoyment.

Orang Asli playing on a nose flute and a stick zither.

A proto-Malay ensemble of *biola* (violin), *rebana* drum and gong.

Dreamsongs

Among the Temiar, songs are derived from dreams and are believed to have the power to cure illness. The shaman receives his songs from a spirit source and re-enacts them during a healing ceremony known as the Sewang ritual. The songs are usually performed in 'call-and-response' style in which the male shaman sings a line of text which is then repeated in unison by the female chorus. Chorus members also play the stamping tubes.

These elaborate healing ceremonies require a full night's performance with continuous singing, instrumental music and trance-dancing. The degree of complexity and detail in a given ceremony depends on its purpose, and the power of the song stems from the relationship between the shaman and its spirit source.

Songs for lost souls

Among the Jah Hut people, sacred songs are a means to maintain good relations with their gods. Communication with these beings is through shamanistic trance and singing sessions during which the shaman searches for lost souls. He and his assistant sing in call-and-response style while a chorus repeats the words sung by the shaman.

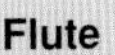

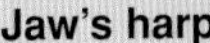

Orang Asli musical instruments

	Zither	Stamping tube	Flute	Jaw's harp

Material	Bamboo, but the strings are made of either vine, root or nylon.	Bamboo	Bamboo	Bamboo (*ginggong*), metal (*genggon*) or the rib of a palm leaf (*ranggon*).
Characteristics	Tubal in construction, it is 40–50 centimetres long, 10–12 centimetres in diameter, and with 2–4 strings stretched and attached at each end of the tube. Called *kereb* or *krem* among the Senoi. Sometimes the strings are cut from the cortex of the bamboo tube itself.The strings remain attached at each end of the tube and small wood bridges are inserted beneath the strings to tune the instrument.	A pair of tubes (one long and one short called 'father' and 'mother' respectively) 60–70 centimetres in length. The tube is closed at the bottom by the natural node and opened at the top end.	A tubal aerophone varying in diameter and length. 	A flat-bodied mouth harp which is about 7–10 centimetres high with a tongue (*lamella*) cut in the middle.
Music motif	Short repeated two- or three-note melodies are played to imitate work activities, the sounds of birds or insects.	Short identical repeated beats in a specific rhythmic pattern.	Short contrasting motifs which are repeated or combined to produce long compositions.	Repeated melodies crafted to imitate speech sounds.
Performance	Usually played by women, it is used among the Jah Hut in healing ceremonies. In other contexts and among other groups, it is usually played for personal entertainment.	Played to accompany singing during night-time ritual ceremonies.	Associated with the spirit world, the melancholy flute melodies express sadness and yearning. The delicate and sweet sounds are also used for courting, and for general entertainment.	Played exclusively by men for personal enjoyment. 
Method of play	The strings are usually plucked by the fingers, but they may also be struck or bowed. On the *pergam* zither of the Jah Hut people, the top end of the tube is struck by one hand producing a percussive rhythmic accompaniment to the melody of the plucked strings.	A percussion instrument which is held in the hand as a pair and struck onto a wooden board or bamboo pole. Called *goh* by the Temiar and *ding galung* by the Jah Hut.	Blown from the side (transverse) or the end (vertical) by mouth, the flute is variously called *siloy*, *begut*, *suling*. Nose flutes are called *pensol* or *suling*.	Placed between the lips and one end is plucked, causing the lamella to vibrate. The player's mouth is the resonator, producing a fundamental tone and several overtones, depending on the size of the mouth cavity and placement of the player's tongue in the mouth.

Malay instrumental music

The instrumental music originating among the Malays of Peninsular Malaysia, Sabah and Sarawak is played by ensembles that are essentially percussive in nature. These ensembles incorporate instruments such as drums, bronze gongs, wood slabs and coconut shells. Some types of Malay instrumental music are found throughout the country; others are regional. The various kinds of music are performed for marriages and religious celebrations, at festivals, competitions and official events.

Gendang silat ensembles comprise *serunai* players, knobbed gong players and drummers, and provide accompaniment for *silat* competitions.

Drum ensembles

Probably the most ubiquitous drum ensemble found in Malaysia is the *kompang* ensemble. Kompang music features in processions at marriages and circumcisions and sometimes accompanies the singing of Islamic verses such as the *marhaban, zikir* and *selawat*. It is also found in more secular situations such as drumming competitions, to welcome important visitors to state functions and to provide lively rhythms at festivals.

Children playing the *gendang silat*, a drum and wind ensemble found in the north-eastern states of Kelantan and Terengganu.

The kompang drum is related to the *rebana* found in Indonesia and the *dufuf* in the Middle East.

It is not uncommon to hear large kompang ensembles beating out their interlocking rhythmic patterns as they walk in processions such as the National Day parade. This music is truly a communal effort, for there is no single person who plays the complete rhythmic pattern by himself. Kompang ensembles typically produce thundering and highly resonant precision drumming, and create a festive and vibrant ambience at any occasion.

Another group comprising only drums is the *rebana ubi* ensemble, found mainly in Kelantan. This ensemble performs music during the harvest season in villages and at festivals in larger towns. Many villages in Kelantan have their own set of rebana ubi. An ensemble may be heard from afar, and provides fast-paced, thunderous interlocking rhythms that contribute to the liveliness of festivals.

This music requires precision drumming. The skill and creativity of the solo drummer usually determines the winner of competitions among rebana ubi teams from different villages.

Drum and wind ensembles

Two ensembles consisting of percussion and wind instruments are found in the Malay communities of northern Peninsular Malaysia. These are the *gendang tarinai* in Kedah and Perlis and the *gendang silat* in Kelantan and Terengganu.

The gendang tarinai traditionally provides music to accompany dances for the entertainment of guests at a wedding, during the ceremony of staining the bride's hands and feet with henna—hence, the name *tari* (dance) *inai* (henna dye), or *tarinai*. The ensemble is also referred to as the *gendang* (drums) *keling* (Indian) because of the use of the double-headed drums believed to have been brought to Malaysia by Indian Muslims. It is said that this ensemble and its music originated in the Middle East during the time of the Prophet Moses, and was played to prepare soldiers for battle, with each of about 12 pieces (many of which are still played today) signalling a given action to be carried out by the soldiers. New repertory has been composed for dance and other purposes over the decades.

Even though it developed as a village tradition, at one time trained dancers and musicians performed the tarinai in the palace for the entertainment of royalty. Today it is also heard at official state functions.

Sounds of the *kompang*

The *kompang* musical repertory consists of percussive rhythmic patterns (there is no melody). Each of the three groups of drummers in the ensemble (left), called *melalu*, *menyelang* and *menganak*, plays a distinctive rhythm. When all three groups play simultaneously, the combination of timbres produces a complete rhythmic pattern. The *melalu* group provides the basic rhythm, while the *menyelang* and *menganak* drummers play different rhythms that interlock with the basic pattern. Sometimes a fourth group may be added, called the *mengocok*, which plays yet another pattern to lend variety and greater density to the main pattern.

Malay Musical Ensembles

Type of ensemble	Characteristics & ensemble size	Method of play & music motif
Drum Ensembles		
Kompang	Frame drum with a diameter of 20–30 or more centimetres. Small village ensembles are made up of 7–8 players; larger ensembles for parades, processions or festivals may have 20 or more.	Player holds kompang with one hand and strikes the drumhead with the other hand in specific ways, sometimes vocalizing the timbres using sounds such as '*tak*' and '*dung*'.
Rebana ubi	Drum weighing about 100 kilograms with a thick drumhead of water buffalo hide. 6–8 drums with two players on each drum.	Two players beat simultaneously on one drumhead. One group beats on the downbeat, the second plays on the upbeat, creating a steady, running beat. A third group beats out a different pattern, superimposing a contrasting rhythm.
Drum and Wind Ensembles		
Gendang tarinai	Small quadruple-reed wind instrument (*serunai*), about 30 cm long; two shallow-rimmed, knobbed gongs (30–40 centimetres in diameter); and two double-headed drums (about 45–48 centimetres long), one slightly larger than the other, played in an interlocking style by two players.	Player holds drum horizontally and hits it with his hand and with a lightweight rattan beater to provide a lively, sometimes syncopated rhythmic pattern. The gongs, when struck with a padded beater, emit two pitches that punctuate the phrases of the drum rhythms. The serunai is used to play long, melodic phrases that flow above the percussive parts.
Gendang silat	Large serunai, about 45 centimetres long; two barrel-shaped, double-headed drums (50–55 centimetres long); and a large knobbed gong (over 60 centimetres in diameter).	Two drummers hold their drums horizontally (or the drums may be supported on wooden racks) and hit the drumheads with their hands and with a thick wooden stick, producing patterns to accompany the sparring *silat* performers' movements. The single pitch of the gong punctuates the drum patterns, and the serunai player spins out a seemingly never-ending melodic line using the circular breathing technique.
Struck Coconut Ensemble		
Kertuk kelapa	A coconut shell attached to a wooden supporting stand, with a slat of wood attached over the open top of the coconut. Several of these comprise a set (one player to a coconut).	Players hit the wood with padded beaters in interlocking rhythmic patterns, producing variety by using slightly different pitches on the keys. Different timbres result from alternately striking the key with the wood part and then the padded part of the beater.

Colourfully decorated with geometric designs, the *rebana ubi* sometimes carries the name of the village with which it is associated. It is either hung vertically from the rafters of a roofed, unwalled shelter or set on the ground with the drumhead in a vertical position for playing.

In contrast, a different folk village percussion and wind ensemble, the *gendang silat*, is found in Kelantan and Terengganu to accompany the sparring of competitors in the traditional Malay art of self-defence called *silat*. The silat competitions may occur in the village or be staged as part of a state festival. Whatever the occasion, there is always a large audience along with the dramatic and dynamic music of the gendang silat. As the participants' actions and movements in the silat competition increase in speed and become more aggressive, the tempo of the music, too, picks up speed.

Struck wood and coconut ensembles

Ensembles of percussion instruments made of materials from the environment proliferate throughout the country, and in the Kelantanese Malay community two instruments are made of wood and coconut shell: the *kertuk kayu* (struck wood) and *kertuk kelapa* (struck coconut).

In the decades before World War II and probably earlier, the kertuk kayu was popularly played as entertainment in the villages of Kelantan. Today, the kertuk kayu is extinct, and another percussion instrument, the kertuk kelapa, has taken its place and played during the harvest season or at festivals. The kertuk kelapa is like a single-keyed xylophone, the rhythms sometimes imitating those from other music genres, namely shadow play music, while other patterns are newly composed. Teams of kertuk kelapa players from different villagers compete at state festivals with their instruments colourfully painted and decorated.

Making of the *rebab*

The *rebab* is a two- or three-stringed lute with an almost heart-shaped body made from the wood of a jackfruit tree, and covered with a thin layer of skin taken from a cow's stomach. Unlike other Southeast Asian fiddles, the Malay rebab has short tuning pegs.

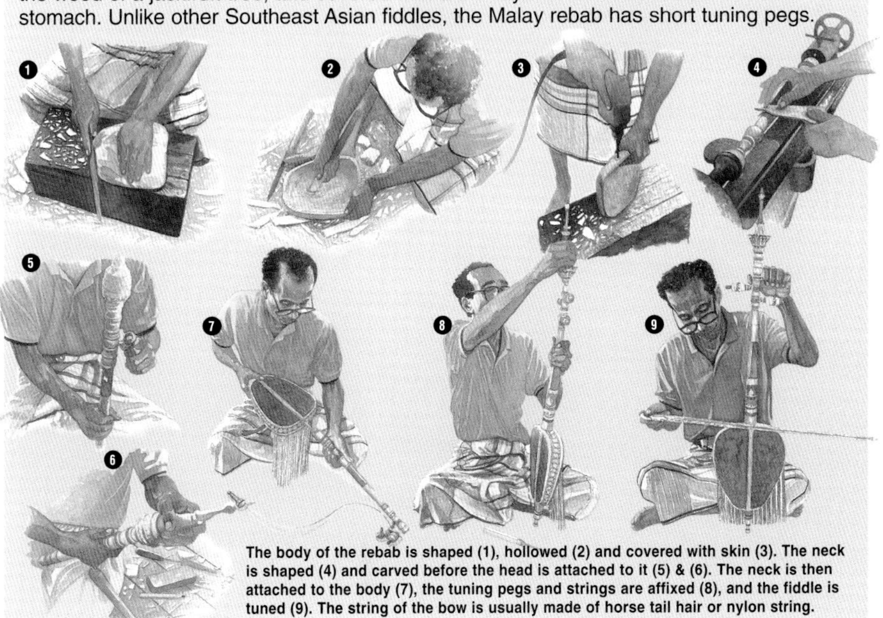

The body of the rebab is shaped (1), hollowed (2) and covered with skin (3). The neck is shaped (4) and carved before the head is attached to it (5) & (6). The neck is then attached to the body (7), the tuning pegs and strings are affixed (8), and the fiddle is tuned (9). The string of the bow is usually made of horse tail hair or nylon string.

Top: *Kertuk kelapa* (struck coconut) instruments are a popular means of entertainment in Kelantan.

Bottom: *Gendang tarinai* ensembles used to perform in the royal courts of Kedah and Perlis. Like the *gendang silat* these ensembles are made up of the *serunai*, knobbed gong and drums.

Vocal music of Sabah and Sarawak

The vocal music among the many ethnic groups in Sabah and Sarawak takes many forms, ranging from love songs to ritual chanting, from elaborately styled performances to extemporaneous compositions. These vocal music genres are the main means by which the oral literature of the folk culture in Sabah and Sarawak is spread and sustained.

Singing

The singing of songs is a very wide category of non-ritual vocal music that is found in some form in virtually every culture in Sabah and Sarawak. It includes non-ritual songs—such as traditional love songs, drinking songs, ballads and other genres such as Christian songs and contemporary popular songs —as well as ritual songs for healing purposes.

Amongst the Kadazandusun, Sabah's largest indigenous ethnic group, singing is known as *sinding* in Tambunan (*lonsoi* in Kampung Sunsuron, Tambunan) and *humozou* in Penampang. Traditional songs are often sung by one or two skilled performers (either men or women) for entertainment at village feasts and other gatherings. Some of the verses are very old, having been passed down through generations.

With the development of pop music since the 1960s, many traditional songs with pentatonic melodies have been accompanied by diatonic harmonies played by electric bands.

Kayan woman chieftain singing a *parap* during a wedding ceremony in Sarawak.

Solo singer of the wa narrative genre in Sarawak's upper Rajang river.

Call-and-response genres

There are many genres of vocal music based on call-and-response patterns between individuals or groups. These are often composed spontaneously and may or may not have a *pantun*-like four-line verse structure with a particular rhyming and semantic scheme. For example, in Sabah, *sudawil* is a type of Kadazandusun singing from Tambunan, composed of four-line verses. Two groups of people (often men and women) sing alternate verses. It is said to have originated from shouted messages communicated across a distance.

The Orang Ulu of Sarawak's Baram and upper Rajang rivers have a well-developed musical tradition. A verse is sung by a man or woman soloist, and repeated by the chorus. This song can express intention, praise of a certain person, sorrow for an absent or deceased one, love and other emotions. Musically the pentatonic melodies are repetitive and the chorus provides a drone-like accompaniment.

Other poetic forms with a specific rhyming scheme can also take the form of repartee between two people, such as the forms *jawang* and *ganu* among the Iban of Sarawak. A wide range of topics, such as welcoming visitors, praising spirits and relating genealogies, offers a broad repertory for entertainment in the longhouse. Other songs known simply as *lagu tusut* also relate genealogy among the interior ethnic groups such as the Kajang peoples.

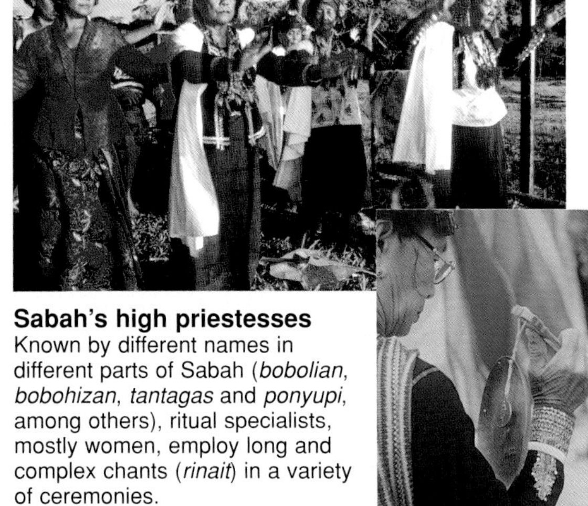

Sabah's high priestesses

Known by different names in different parts of Sabah (*bobolian, bobohizan, tantagas* and *ponyupi*, among others), ritual specialists, mostly women, employ long and complex chants (*rinait*) in a variety of ceremonies.

It takes many years for a woman to become a ritual specialist. From girlhood she must memorize all the rinait and recite them only during the appropriate ceremony. Some types can only be learnt after a woman is married, or after she becomes a grandmother. Girls often learn the rinait from their mothers, while others pay senior practitioners to teach them. In many cultures, the learning and practice of reciting the rinait requires the practitioner to have a familiar spirit and sometimes to be able to enter trance.

TOP: Kadazandusun *bobohizan* in a ceremony to honour the rice spirits. **INSET:** A *tantagas* shaking her *tutubik* rattler during rituals.

Ritual chanting

Ritual chanting is another important category of vocal music in both Sabah and Sarawak. Amongst most of the Dusunic, Murutic and Paitanic groups of Sabah, ritual specialists and spirit mediums perform ceremonies for healing, rice cultivation and harvesting, and honouring spirits. The practitioners are usually women, known by different names in different cultures, although men may also be ritual specialists. Ritual ceremonies can take several days and, depending on type and context, sometimes occur in cycles over weeks or months.

The act of ritual chanting in Sabah is described by various names in different cultures, but the verses chanted are nearly always referred to as *rinait*. The rinait are very long and complex, consisting of hundreds of couplets of stanzas; each couplet contains one stanza in normal language and the other in an ancient ritual language. Rinait are an important source of oral literature in Sabah, describing everything in the traditional belief systems, from the creation of the

High priestesses (*tantagas*) at a *mangahau-rumaha* ceremony of the Lotud Dusun in Sabah.

world, rice and mankind, to activities and adventures of spirits, instructions regarding correct behaviour, house building and ritual performance. Performance styles vary according to ceremony, context and culture, from soft mumbling to loud melodic chanting.

The major sacred, ceremonial chants of the Iban of Sarawak, known as *timang* or *pengap*, are sung at special and important festivals (*gawai*) to invite the spirits to participate in the celebration and feasting. Amongst the main types of chants in Iban culture are those for man's welfare and safety (*timang beintu-intu*), for good fortune (*timang tuah*), for bountiful padi seed (*timang benih*) or for a ritual of very high significance (*timang gawai amat*). Although regional variations exist in the presentation of the chant, in general the main stanzas are vocalized by a male singer and his assistant, interspersed with choral refrains from a small group of males. This can go on for several hours or days. Sometimes the singers accompany the chanting by beating wooden staffs on the floor of the longhouse in regular, duple rhythm.

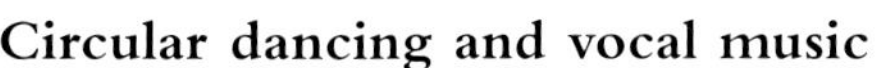

A Kadazandusun high priestess chanting *rinait* and dancing during *moginakan* ceremonies.

Recitations

The oral literature of the peoples of Sabah and Sarawak is also conveyed through vocal music. The *dsair* or *edsair* of the Iranun of Sabah is a type of vocal music in which the performer tells a long story in poetic form using stylized phrases and linking passages to connect different sections. Subject matter may be drawn from past historical or even mythical events, and used to either entertain or instruct. This type of performance usually takes place at night at important social gatherings such as weddings. Great skill and practice are required before one can become a proficient performer, especially in the recitation of poetic stories from the *Darangen*, the epic poem of the Iranun, which recounts the fantastic feats and exploits of the mythical hero Bantogen.

In Sarawak, epics called *ensera*, sung in both poetry and prose, relate the adventures of the various local culture heroes, while legends called *sugi*, conducted entirely in poetical language, focus mainly upon a single hero called Keling. Among many interior peoples of Sarawak the *wa*, a long narrative piece usually sung by a female group consisting of a soloist and a chorus, is often used to close a particular event or happening in the longhouse. Its text can express thanks, greeting, history or genealogy. While the soloist sings the main text of the wa, the chorus periodically interjects a refrain on the single syllable, é, using a long descending melodic line.

TOP: Kadazandusun *bobohizan* chanting *rinait* during *adat babalai* ceremonies at Papar, Sabah.

BOTTOM: Members of Sarawak's Kayan community singing.

Circular dancing and vocal music

Various communities in Sabah perform different types of circular dances accompanied by spontaneous vocal music. In the northern and southern parts of Tambunan, elderly people move slowly in a circle, their bodies swaying from side to side as they chant verses in a call-and-response pattern, punctuated by the refrain *andayayang* (or *indayayang*). The spontaneous verses, humorous and entertaining, refer to people as well as past and present events. The dance usually takes place at night during the rice harvest. When performing the Bajau/Sama runsay, men (and sometimes women), rapidly stamp their feet to the rhythm of the chanting to signal the resolution of a topic. This stamping dance usually takes place at weddings and other social gatherings as a form of matchmaking when young people are present.

Popular Kadazandusun drinking song

'Jambatan do Tomporuli' by Justin Lusah

Pak pak kangkundo
Sumunsui do jambatan
Jambatan do Tomporuli
Bakasut tinggi oku.

Sumunsui do jambatan
Jambatan do Tomporuli
Pak pak kangkundo
Bakasut tinggi oku.

Silaka nodi kasut ku
Naratu id jambatan
Tinggal po do sutakin
Nowit ku ginumuli

Ontok di hari tiga
Tomu id Tomporuli
Mingusuk po hilo'd kadai
Moginum do kasut tinggi

(My shoes) Will say "pak pak"
While walking (carefully) on the bridge
The Tamparuli bridge (a hanging bridge)
I'm wearing high heeled shoes.

While walking (carefully) on the bridge
The Tamparuli bridge
(My shoes) will say "pak pak"
I'm wearing high heeled shoes.

Damn my shoes!
They fell off the bridge
All I have left are my socks
Which I took back.

On that Wednesday
It was market day in Tamparuli
I went to every shop
Looking for high heeled shoes.

Translated by Laurentius Kitingan

Stylized crying

Very intense and loud stylized crying is a form of mourning in most cultures in Sabah and Sarawak. Amongst the Kadazandusun from Tambunan, the deceased is laid out in the house for a day and a night prior to burial, during which time relatives and friends come to pay their last respects. A genre of stylized melodic crying, called *pogigiad*, is performed by skilled women. The words and melodies vary according to the age and sex of the deceased: *Oroi idi!* is cried for a mother, *Oroi ama!* for a father and *Oroi otou!* for a child. In Sarawak, a ceremonial chant called *sabak* is sung by an Iban woman at funerals. The chant tells of the life and deeds of the deceased, his relationship to those still living, and the journey of his soul.

TOP: Lotud *tantangas* chanting *rinait* in the *monidong* ceremony of the *mangahau* at Tuaran, Sabah.

BOTTOM: A *libabou* (spirit medium) and a group of *tantagas* performing ritual dancing during a ceremony to chase the rain away during a season of heavy rain and floods in Sabah in 1996.

Musical instruments of Sabah and Sarawak

Sabah and Sarawak have a rich instrumental music tradition, reflective of the many different ethnic groups living in the states. Solo instruments are usually played for personal entertainment, while group ensembles are used during rituals and celebrations. Instruments may be played by either men or women although this can vary according to culture, context and instrument.

Gong ensembles in Sabah often include the *kulintangan*, a single row of six to nine kettle gongs. Its parallel in Sarawak is the *engkerumong* ensemble, which includes hanging knobbed gongs (*tawak* and *bandai*) and a single-headed drum (*ketebong*) or a double-headed drum (*dumbak*).

Top: Hanging gongs used by the Kadazandusun have various names, such as (from left) *tagung tatahis, kuribadon* and *bobogon.*

Bottom: Some ensembles in Sabah comprise a wooden *gabang* xylophone and two slit-gongs (*kantung*).

Gongs and xylophones

Each community has its own characteristic gong ensemble and gong music, although gongs were not traditionally made locally but were traded in from Brunei and the southern Philippines. Each village has its own set of instruments, the gongs usually owned by individuals. Gongs often have both generic names as single objects and musical names when included in a set, the latter referring to the musical parts they play. Gong ensembles from the interior tend to contain more instruments than those on the coast. For example, gong ensembles of the Murutic groups in the interior of Sabah can include 12 or more gongs and sometimes a drum to accompanying dancing, whereas those of the Kadazandusun contain six or seven hanging gongs and a drum.

In Sarawak, gong ensembles are most notable among the Bidayuh people who use seven or more gongs, while smaller ensembles are found among the other ethnic groups. The Iban play the *engkerumong* ensemble—named after the main melody instrument, the gong-chime—which includes hanging gongs and drums, at specific ceremonies and as accompaniment to dance.

The gong music of Sabah and Sarawak features interlocking rhythmic patterns played by pairs or sets of gongs within the ensemble; in effect, several interlocking sets or parts are played simultaneously. In former times gong music was played to accompany dance during rituals and on other ceremonial occasions, and to propitiate or invoke the spirits, but today it is played for processions, for dance in secular contexts, or for general entertainment.

Xylophones are also found in certain areas. The small metal-keyed *salun* is sometimes played in ritual gong music of the Lotud Dusun from Tuaran in Sabah, while a larger, wooden-keyed *gabang* xylophone is found in eastern Sabah. If a gong ensemble is unavailable, a set of struck bamboo idiophones can be used instead. Each individual bamboo idiophone is pitched and named according to the gong part it copies.

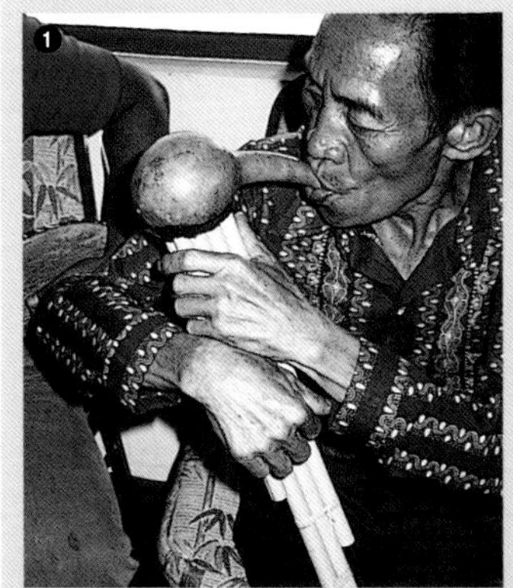

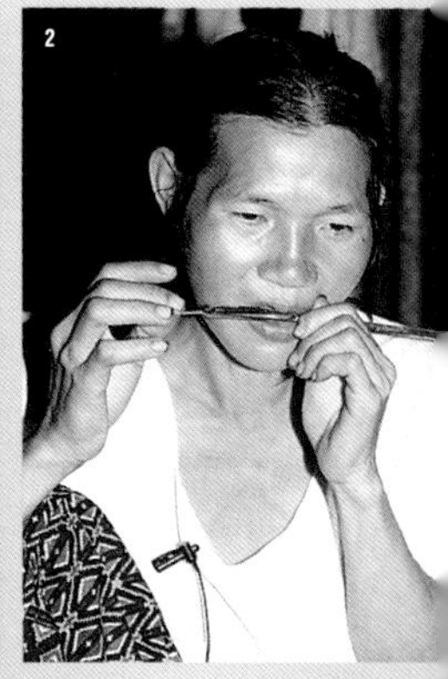

Among some Kenyah and Kayan groups in Sarawak, a wooden xylophone called *jatung utang* is added to a small ensemble of two plucked lutes (*sapeh*) to accompany dance. The jatung utang duplicates the melody played by one of the sapeh.

Drums

Various drums are found in Sabah and Sarawak, and most gong ensembles include a drum to emphasize the main rhythmic pattern of their music. Traditional native drums in Sabah may be single-headed, such as the *karatung* from Tambunan and the Rungus *tontog*, or double-headed, as in the Lotud *gandang*. Frame drums are used by some coastal communities of Sabah, but are not part of the indigenous traditions of the interior. A single Spanish military drum called *tambol* usually accompanies gong ensemble music of the east coast Bajau and Suluk. Coastal groups, such as the Iranun, west coast Bajau and Brunei, use double-headed barrel-shaped drums, which are struck with the hands.

Zithers and lutes

Indigenous tube zithers and strummed lutes, as well as plucked and bowed lutes of Arabic origin, are part of the instrumental music tradition of Sabah and Sarawak. In Sabah, the *tongkungon* is a plucked zither that imitates gong music. Played as a solo instrument for personal entertainment mainly among Dusunic communities, it is made from a single node of bamboo with strips cut in its surface to form its strings, and a hole cut in the back or top for resonance. The Sarawak version, called *satong*, is made similarly. Its melodies are short and often imitate the sounds of work action, clucking insects, or the noises of small animals in the forest. When

1. The *sompoton* mouth organ of the Kadazandusun of Sabah; 2. Jaw's harps are made from palmwood in Sabah, and from both palmwood and bamboo in Sarawak; 3. *Tongkungon*, a plucked zither that imitates gong music; 4. An ancient *sundatang* (double-stringed lute) from Tambunan, Sabah; 5. A Penan *engkerurai* player and 6. Nose flute.

played in ensemble, the zither provides the melody. The *sundatang*, a long-necked strummed lute, is played mainly in Dusunic communities in Sabah. Often imitating dance music, sundatang music can also copy the tunes of traditional songs and chants.

The most popular stringed instrument in Sarawak is the sapeh of the Kenyah people, but today played by many other upriver peoples. The sapeh may appear as a solo instrument, or two sapeh are often played together to accompany dance. Because the sound is rather soft, an electronic amplifier is often attached to the instrument.

The *gambus*, a plucked lute of Arabic origin, is sometimes found amongst Muslims in Sabah and Sarawak. It is played mainly for entertainment, when its music draws on the rhythms of Malay dances. Bowed lutes of Arabic origin are also found in some Muslim communities, such as the Iranun *biula*, a three-stringed violin.

Flutes, jaw's harps and mouth organs

Both Sabah and Sarawak have a variety of traditional aerophones, including the ubiquitous short bamboo flute blown by air from the mouth (known as *suling* in both states), the longer flute blown by air from the nose (known as *turali* in Sabah and *selengut* in Sarawak), the jaw's harp and the mouth organ. They are all solo instruments played for personal expression, performance styles varying according to the musical norms of a given culture.

Flute melodies are improvisatory in nature and tend to be highly florid. Suling melodies are played for courting or for general entertainment. In Sabah, the nose flute can be played for happy personal entertainment. In some parts of the state, however, the instrument is associated with melancholy and is played to express personal grief following a death. In Sarawak, the nose flute is often played softly during resting times in the longhouse.

Although short melodies or patterns imitating speech are occasionally played on the jaw's harp, some ethnic groups play different styles for different occasions. For example, the Kadazandusun of Tambunan have five different styles of playing: early in the morning to attract edible lizards from bamboo; as a form of remembrance when a relative or friend is leaving; for relaxation after the rice harvest; and for imitating gong music to accompany dancing. Other groups imitate the tunes of traditional songs and chants.

Perhaps the best-known aerophone from Sabah and Sarawak is the mouth organ. It consists of a double raft of eight bamboo pipes with palmwood reeds (*sompoton*) in Sabah, or a circular bundle of seven pipes in Sarawak (*engkerurai*, *keluri* or *keledi*), embedded in a gourd windchamber. Mouth organs are usually played solo though occasionally several are played with a small gong to accompany dancing.

Keeping traditional music alive

Various efforts are being made in both Sabah and Sarawak to keep traditional music alive and to expose it to people outside the states. For example, the annual Rainforest World Music Festival, held in Kuching since 1998, features the best in traditional music from Sarawak, Sabah and Peninsular Malaysia as well as from other parts of the world. Musicians from longhouses deep in the rainforest perform on a range of gongs, drums, flutes, lutes and mouth organs alongside other traditional musical ensembles at the Sarawak Cultural Village.

The *sapeh* is a traditional lute of the upriver peoples of Sarawak, especially the Kenyah, Kayan and Kelabit. The shape of the body resembles a sampan and it is often called 'the boat lute' in the West.

The making of the *sapeh*

The *sapeh* has an elongated body which is hollowed out and functions as a resonator. The carver, usually a musician, uses similar tools to those used in boat-building to make and carve the sapeh which is over a metre long, and approximately 40 centimetres wide. It is made from a single bole of *tebuloh* (a dipterocarp) wood. The frets are carved from palm stalk, and held on by a gum made by the *kelulut* bee.

1. A tree is selected. 2. Its trunk is cut to the required size. 3. After it is shaped and planed, one side of the trunk is marked where it is to be hollowed to provide for the soundbox. 4, 5 and 6. Using an adze, the sapeh maker starts cutting the wood, switching to a spear-like chisel to chip and hollow out the inside of the soundbox, a difficult and tedious process. 7. The top part of the sapeh is then carved. 8 & 9. The tuning pegs are inserted and the frets are affixed before the strings are attached and the sapeh is tuned.

Music of the Malay shadow play

Music is an integral element of shadow play theatre. It brings to life the epics, puppets and spirit of the shadow play. The 'Lagu Bertabik', or introductory piece of the Wayang Kulit musical ensemble, is probably the most powerful of all traditional Malay music. It is ancient, melodious and hypnotic, and like most musical pieces for the Wayang Kulit, is played by an ensemble of drums, gongs and a quadruple-reed oboe.

Watercolour paintings by artist Shafie Hj. Hassan of craftsmen making traditional instruments: the *gendang* drum (top) and the *serunai* oboe (bottom).

The music

The loud, vigorous sounds emanating from an ensemble of drums, gongs and a reed wind instrument best exemplify the music for the most popular Malay shadow play, the Wayang Kulit Siam.

Other styles of Wayang Kulit also feature distinctive types of music ensembles. For example, the Javanese Wayang Kulit Purwa, found in the southern state of Johor, is accompanied by the gamelan (ensemble of bronze instruments). In contrast, the Thai influenced Wayang Kulit Gedek, performed in the northwest states of Malaysia, features an ensemble of drums, gongs, a reed pipe and, sometimes, Thai fiddles. A fourth type, performed in the northern Malay courts in the 19th and early 20th centuries, is known as Wayang Kulit Melayu (or Wayang Kulit Java).

Whilst Wayang Kulit Purwa and Wayang Kulit Gedek are from Javanese and Thai cultures, Wayang Kulit Siam and Wayang Kulit Melayu are, in substance, indigenous. They are the best examples of Malay Wayang Kulit music.

The principal characters of the Indian *Ramayana*, Seri Rama and Sita Dewi. The repertoire of most of the Malay shadow play styles in Malaysia is derived from the epics *Ramayana* and *Mahabharata*.

The music of Wayang Kulit Melayu

The music and instruments of Wayang Kulit Melayu are strongly influenced by the Javanese Wayang Kulit Purwa. This is attributed to the fact that puppeteers (*dalang*) of Wayang Kulit Melayu were often sent to Java to improve their skills and to learn new stories. Despite this, it adapted strains of local influences, becoming an important court-based form. It was staged for the entertainment of the sultan and for palace rituals in Kedah and Kelantan.

Wayang Kulit Melayu has a specific repertoire of musical pieces, with each piece fulfilling a specific function in the performance of a story. Although the repertoire may have been quite large at one time, only a few pieces are still performed. The piece (*lagu*) entitled 'Seri Panggung' usually opens the performance. When played in a very slow tempo, it serves as a time-filler. In a fast tempo, it accompanies the action of battle and scenes in which warriors and the minister appear before the king.

Music underscores the puppets' movements. When the general movement of the puppets and pace of the drama is slow, the tempo of the music is equally slow. Movement by characters of high social status is usually accompanied by the 'Gemutu' piece, while the walking piece for nearly any type of character is called 'Kelayung Embun Tiga'. The lagu 'Jubang Embun Satu' is most often heard when a refined female character appears in a story, while the piece 'Mangu' is heard whenever the clown-servants Semar and Turas pay homage to the king.

The music of Wayang Kulit Siam

In contrast to the courtly Wayang Kulit Melayu, the music of Wayang Kulit Siam is fast paced, and accompanies puppet movements and actions which are quick, energetic and often comical. The music is

Wayang Kulit Melayu ensemble

This ensemble consists of two double-headed barrel drums (*gendang*), a three-stringed bowed lute (*rebab*), a gong-chime consisting of at least six small knobbed gongs placed horizontally in a wooden rack (*canang*), two large hanging bronze gongs (*tetawak*), a medium-sized knobbed gong placed horizontally on a wooden stand (*mong*) and a pair of small hand cymbals (*kesi*). The ensemble provides the music which accompanies specific kinds of scenes, actions and puppet movements in a performance. While the rebab provides melody to accompany the dalang's singing, the canang musicians play short, repeated melodic motifs. The other knobbed gongs serve as markers of time-units in the music, much like the gongs in the Javanese gamelan. The gendang player beats out the percussive rhythmic patterns, which also underscore the movements of the puppets.

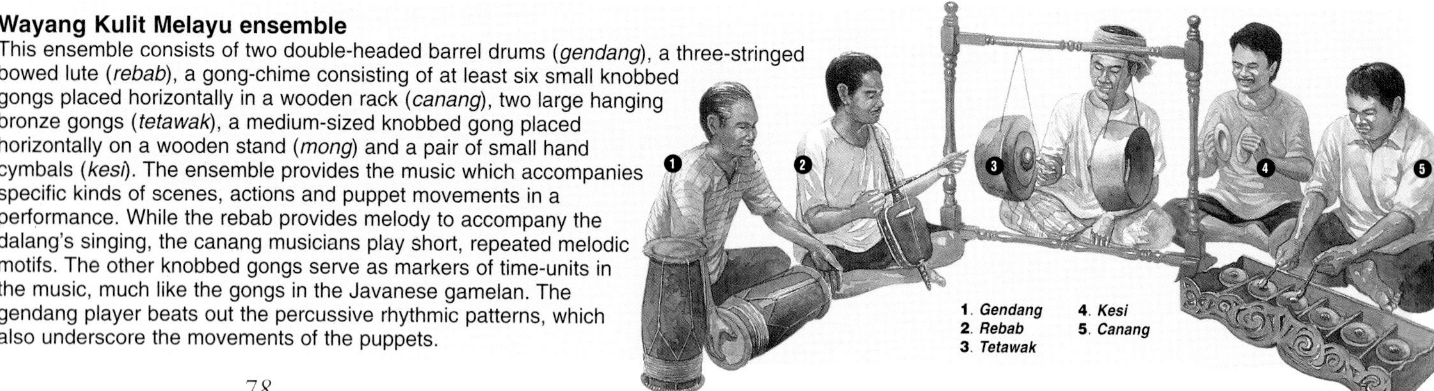

Wayang Kulit Siam ensemble

The ensemble consists of pairs of instruments, each in a large and small size, called mother (*ibu*) and child (*anak*) respectively. The main melody instrument is a quadruple-reed wind instrument called the *serunai*. The larger version of this instrument, the loud-sounding *serunai ibu*, is used for all purely instrumental pieces, while the smaller and softer sounding *serunai anak* accompanies the sung pieces. The percussive rhythmic patterns are played on pairs of drums. These are the *gedumbak* (a single-headed, goblet-shaped drum), the *gendang* (a double-headed, long barrel drum) and the *geduk* (a double-headed, short barrel drum beaten with sticks).

The gedumbak provides the rhythmic patterns for nearly all the pieces. The gendang usually accompanies the sung pieces, and the rhythmic patterns played on the geduk usually depict violent action in the story. The time-marking (colotomic) instruments are the *kesi* (small hand cymbals), the *canang* (gong-chime) and the *tetawak* (hanging gong).

An archive image of Wayang Kulit musicians (below) in contrast to more modern players (above). The attire is modernized, but the music and repertoire have barely changed.

The musicians

The musicians are known as the *panjak*. The number of musicians varies between seven and 10. Musicians often play a number of instruments, and also double as the puppeteer's assistant. The troupe tends to be exclusively male, though there is no taboo against a woman performing music. The musicians are versatile and highly skilled in performing for other genres such as Mak Yong, Menora and silat. However, performing music alone is not economically sustaining for these professionals, and most have primary jobs as farmers or fishermen. Musicians are generally attached to one puppeteer, but may temporarily move between troupes. Training for musicians begins at an early age as apprentices to established musicians, with the student usually first learning the parts on the idiophones (*canang, kesi, tetawak*), membranophones (*geduk, gedumbak, gendang*), and aerophone (*serunai*). A musician is considered properly trained when he is able to play all instruments and to perform all pieces in the repertoire. He then picks his favourite instrument to play professionally.

1. *Gedumbak* 2. *Canang* 3. *Gendang* 4. *Kesi* 5. *Geduk* 6. *Serunai* 7. *Tetawak*

part of the folk music found in the northern states of Peninsular Malaysia. Although this musical tradition has absorbed many elements from diverse cultures over the centuries, it has evolved into a style which is unique unto itself.

The Wayang Kulit Siam musical repertoire comprises about 30 different pieces. Each has a specific function in relating the story in a performance. The music itself is often loud and robust. The melody is highly florid with many melodic ornaments and fast-running notes played on the *serunai*.

This melody, whether sung by the dalang or played on the serunai, is underscored by a repeated time unit (repeated colotomic unit) which is measured and played on the bronze instruments (*kesi, canang* and *tetawak*). The given time unit in a piece is also the basic form in the music which is repeated throughout a given tune in a cyclical manner. The drummers in the ensemble play specific rhythmic patterns that match the length of the colotomic unit. The drumming patterns are distinctive for each piece in the repertoire; however, the same or similar melodies may be used for different pieces. In effect, it is the drum rhythmic patterns that define the specific pieces and not the melodies.

Songs

The sung pieces such as 'Lagu Berkabar', 'Kabar dan Dayang', 'Menyanyi' and 'Mengulit' are accompanied by the *serunai anak* which gives a softer sound and a slightly higher pitch than the *serunai ibu*. These songs are always accompanied by percussive rhythmic patterns played in interlocking style on the two *gendang* drums as in Mak Yong theatre music (see 'Music of Mak Yong, Mek Mulung and Jikey').

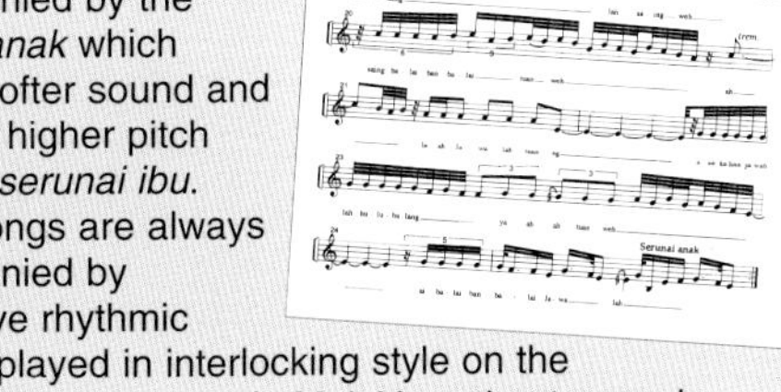

Slow tempo

Gendang anak:	c	.	|	c	.	c	.	c	.c	.c	.
Gendang ibu:	.	p	|	.	p	.	p	.	p	p	p
Tetawak:		g	|	.	.	.	.	.	.	.	G
Canang:		x	|	o	x	o	x	o	x	o	x
Kesi:		.	|	.o	x	.o	x	.o	x	.o	x

Fast tempo

Gendang anak:	.c	.c	.c	.c	.t	.c	.t	.c
Gendang ibu:	p	p	p	p	p	d	p	d
Tetawak:	.	.	.	.	.	.	.	g
Canang:	o	x	o	x	o	x	o	x
Kesi:	o	x	o	x	o	x	o	x

Source: Patricia Matusky and Hamzah Awang Amat, 1998

TOP: Western-style song score sheet.

ABOVE AND LEFT: Notation system locally developed for the study and documentation of Wayang Kulit music.

Puppet movement

Movement of the puppets always requires sound from the orchestra, either as a brief ad lib beating of the instruments (*gertak perkakas*) or as an actual song (*lagu*). The lagu sets the mood and accompanies specific movement. For example, there are pieces for violent action ('Lagu Berperang'), pieces for walking by types of characters ('Lagu Berjalan', 'Hulubalang', 'Orang Darat'), pieces for specific characters themselves ('Lagu Seri Rama', 'Maharisi', 'Maharaja Rawana') and music for certain kinds of events or for giving news, for example, 'Lagu Mengulit', 'Memburu', 'Menghindar' and 'Lagu Berkabar'.

Music of Mak Yong, Mek Mulung and Jikey

Northern Malaysian folk music comprises music for puppet theatre and theatricals that feature human actors, such as Mak Yong, Mek Mulung and Jikey. In these forms the music and vocals have specific functions in the relating of a story. Each of these three forms of traditional theatre, found in the northern states of Peninsular Malaysia, has its own musical repertoire and ensemble. The musicians sit on floor mats along the periphery of the stage, while acting takes place at centre stage.

Instruments in the Jikey ensemble (from left): *rebana* drums, *cerik*, hanging gong, violin, *kesi* and *pi*.

Music of Mak Yong

The Mak Yong musical repertory consists of many vocal pieces with instrumental accompaniment (*lagu nyanyian*) and the purely instrumental pieces (*lagu paluan-paluan* or *san gendang*, that is, the 'drummed' pieces). The vocal pieces far outnumber the instrumental tunes. Some of the vocal pieces include choral parts. While the opening song and dance piece ('Lagu Menghadap Rebab') has a special ritual function, other pieces convey a message, give news, or express an emotion or feeling. The entire repertoire comprises some 30 specific pieces.

Music of Mek Mulung and Jikey

Both the Mek Mulung and Jikey theatres present stories or comic episodes that are accompanied by a specific musical repertoire. In each theatrical genre the tunes carry a specific function in the drama. Mek Mulung, for example, uses pieces such as the 'Lagu Bertabik' (for greeting the audience), 'Lagu Puteri Nak Bangkit' (for the introductory song by the princess character), and 'Lagu Pak Mulung Nak Bangkit' (for the initial song by the Pak Mulung character). Some dance pieces are purely instrumental. However, the vocal pieces predominate in the musical repertoire of both theatrical genres.

When specific action is required, or whenever news and emotions need to be conveyed in a story, instrumental music, song and sometimes dance become important elements in Mek Mulung and Jikey. Songs are vocalized to the accompaniment of the *pi* (or *serunai*) wind instrument, or with the *biola* (violin) in the case of Jikey. The melodies are simple and are supported by percussive rhythmic patterns played on the *rebana* drums.

The main rhythmic pattern is usually played on the large rebana, while the running beat is played on the smaller drums. The main rhythm of a given piece, consisting of a specific number of beats or bars, is repeated with regularity throughout the piece. The temporal element in the music is played on the hanging gong and the pairs of *cerik* (bamboo clappers). The gong and cerik usually beat out a time unit (the colotomic unit) of a specific length throughout a piece.

The Mak Yong ensemble

The small ensemble that provides the instrumental accompaniment is percussion-dominated. It consists of one *rebab*, two elongated barrel drums called *gendang*, and two large, hanging, knobbed, bronze gongs known as *tetawak*. Although these three kinds of instruments constitute the basic Mak Yong orchestra (pictured, left), other instruments may be added from time to time to play certain dance pieces. The added instruments such as the *serunai* reed pipe, *geduk* drum and *kesi* cymbals are borrowed from Wayang Kulit Siam and the Menora ensembles of northern Malaysia.

Resembling the sound of the human voice, the rebab is the main melody instrument in Mak Yong. The rebab duplicates the melody of the vocal line in a given piece while simultaneously providing its own improvised variation of the melody. This instrument is given a special place in the Mak Yong tradition as seen in the opening ritual dance piece, 'Lagu Menghadap Rebab', which pays homage to the instrument and its sounds. The highly florid melodic lines of the pieces are accompanied by percussive rhythmic patterns played in interlocking performance style on the two gendang drums. The drummed rhythmic patterns are typically four or eight beats in length and are repeated in regular and systematic ways. Both the rebab and gendang parts are anchored by a repeated time unit (the colotomic unit) played on the two tetawak gongs.

The choral singers

The chorus, called *jong dondang* (below), usually sings in unison, or alternatively, each singer in the chorus vocalizes her own variation of the basic melody all at the same time, usually using only the word '*dondang*'. Just as in the solo pieces, the accompaniment for the choral parts includes the *rebab*, drums and hanging gongs.

The Mek Mulung ensemble

The Mek Mulung ensemble features the serunai as the main melody instrument, while the percussive rhythmic patterns are beaten by hand on pairs of large and small rebana. A small knobbed hanging gong and several pairs of cerik further complement the ensemble.

The Jikey ensemble

The Jikey ensemble is somewhat larger than the Mek Mulung ensemble, reflecting influence from the Thai Menora ensemble. The main melody instruments are the biola and the pi, a Thai reed wind instrument. The percussive rhythmic patterns are beaten by hand on several rebana in large, medium and small sizes. The instruments used to play the repeated time unit in the pieces include several pairs of cerik, kesi (hand cymbals, also referred to by the Thai name *ching*) and a hanging gong. A smaller version of this ensemble would comprise one melody instrument (either the biola or the pi), a few pairs of cerik and drums.

Mak Yong musical pieces

Type	Theatrical purpose	Piece titles
Instrumental pieces with vocals (*lagu nyanyian*)	Fulfils ritual functions. Also to convey a message, give news or express an emotion or a lullaby. Also performed for travelling or walking, for lamentation or for special activities by the craftsman.	'Lagu Menghadap Rebab', 'Mengulit Raja Nak Tidur', 'Timang Welu', 'Kijang Mas', 'Jembar', 'Mengambul', 'Tok Wak'.
Purely instrumental pieces (*lagu palu-paluan* or *san gendang*)	Signals the beginning and end of a performance. Marks the action of travelling or quick scene changes. Also accompanies a line dance in a figure-of-eight floor pattern.	'Lagu Pak Yong Turun', 'Lagu San Penyudah', 'Lagu Barat', 'Lagu Tari Ragam'.

Mek Mulung

Mek Mulung performances for ritual purposes feature entranced dancers (top), while those for entertainment include comic characters (above).

Mek Mulung is a dance theatre style active only in the village of Wang Tepus in Kedah. A single group has been performing Mek Mulung since the genre's inception. Elements in Mek Mulung comprise dance, music, singing and dialogue. Mek Mulung is related to Menora, with which it shares common sources, myths and shamanistic beliefs. Although Mek Mulung shares some features with Mak Yong dance theatre, there is antagonism between the two genres. A common belief is that if a spirit associated with Mak Yong were to possess a Mek Mulung performer, the performance would be disastrous with dire spiritual consequences for the troupe.

The traditional repertoire consists of 12 stories which feature motifs borrowed from other genres such as Wayang Kulit and Mak Yong. Principal roles consist of the lead male (*pak mulung*), lead female (*mek mulung*), the clown (*pengasuh*), female attendant (*inang*) and the negative character (*musuh*). All roles are traditionally performed by men.

Staging is done without a backdrop in a temporary ground-level wooden structure that is open on three sides and which faces east. Costumes are basic except for the male lead, who dresses in clothing which denotes royalty. Clowns wear a wooden half-mask.

Mek Mulung Instruments

1. ***Rebana ibu*** **2.** ***Cerik*** **3.** ***Rebana penganak dan peningkah*** **4. Gong 5.** ***Serunai***

Social popular music

Social popular music is said to have developed during the post-Portuguese period in17th-century Malaya. Comprising syncretic Malay-language songs that often accompanied social dancing, this music took various forms known as Ronggeng, Dondang Sayang, Keroncong, Joget, Asli and Inang. The music fused Malay and Western elements and incorporated Indian, Middle Eastern and Chinese musical elements as well. Performances are held to entertain guests at social occasions such as weddings.

The violin, *rebana* drum, accordion and gong usually accompany the Dondang Sayang singers.

Origins of social popular music

Although it has not been established when Ronggeng, Asli, Inang, Joget or Dondang Sayang originated, references to similar genres were made in Malay texts such as the *Hikayat Hang Tuah* and *Tuhfat al-Nafis*. The *Hikayat Hang Tuah*, which dates from the 17th or 18th century, describes the singing of *pantun* to the accompaniment of the *rebana*, gong and *kecapi* (a plucked string instrument). This ensemble

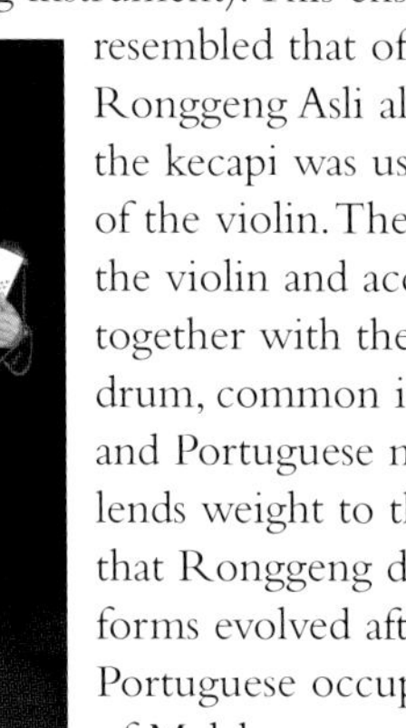

resembled that of the Ronggeng Asli although the kecapi was used instead of the violin. The use of the violin and accordion together with the frame drum, common in Spanish and Portuguese music, lends weight to the claim that Ronggeng dance forms evolved after the Portuguese occupation of Melaka.

A Ronggeng ensemble comprises the violin, accordion, *rebana* drum and gong. Modern ensembles also include the flute and guitar.

Ronggeng

This type of social dance performance features couples dancing and exchanging verses to the accompaniment of a violin or accordion, one or two frame drums, and a suspended gong.

The Ronggeng repertoire has always appealed to various ethnic groups because it is eclectic and flexible. Performers adapt to the changing tastes of the multi-ethnic audiences and to foreign popular music. In the early 20th century, Ronggeng songs evolved into a popular genre and were introduced through Bangsawan. The latest Anglo-American, Chinese, Middle Eastern and Thai popular songs were absorbed into the repertoire. Modern Western instruments such as trumpets, trombones and Western drums were added.

The new style of Ronggeng was also popularized through sessions called *pentas joget* (*joget* stage) held at amusement parks or travelling fun fairs. The Ronggeng dancers were professionals who danced for a fee. Male working-class patrons had to buy coupons to dance with the taxi dancers. The dancers were forbidden to touch their patrons as this was taboo at the time. Instead, they danced around and between the men, teasing them on stage.

Ronggeng troupes also performed at Malay and Baba weddings and other social functions outside entertainment parks. They travelled all over Malaysia and southern Thailand during the pre-World War II days. Ronggeng music also formed a major part of

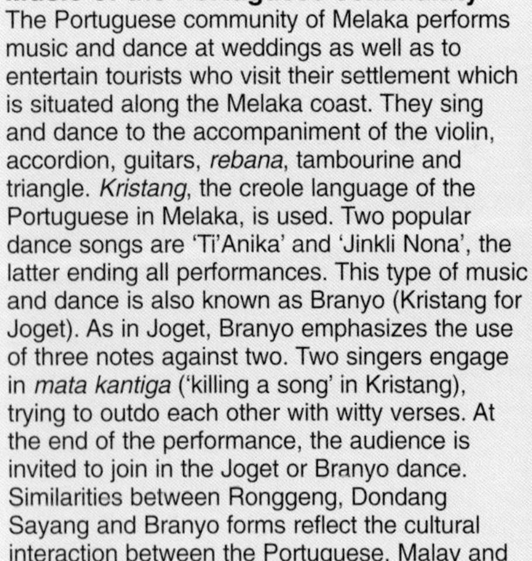

Music of the Portuguese community

The Portuguese community of Melaka performs music and dance at weddings as well as to entertain tourists who visit their settlement which is situated along the Melaka coast. They sing and dance to the accompaniment of the violin, accordion, guitars, *rebana*, tambourine and triangle. *Kristang*, the creole language of the Portuguese in Melaka, is used. Two popular dance songs are 'Ti'Anika' and 'Jinkli Nona', the latter ending all performances. This type of music and dance is also known as Branyo (Kristang for Joget). As in Joget, Branyo emphasizes the use of three notes against two. Two singers engage in *mata kantiga* ('killing a song' in Kristang), trying to outdo each other with witty verses. At the end of the performance, the audience is invited to join in the Joget or Branyo dance. Similarities between Ronggeng, Dondang Sayang and Branyo forms reflect the cultural interaction between the Portuguese, Malay and Baba communities in Melaka.

Portuguese songs such as 'Jinkli Nona' are sung in Kristang (left) to accompany folk dances (top). Performances end with the Branyo dance in which the audience is invited to participate (above).

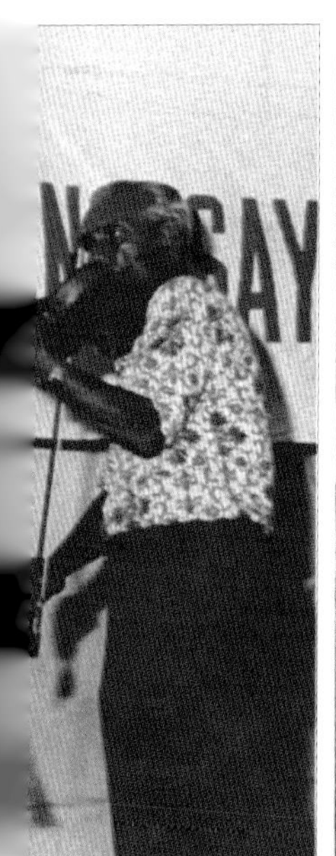

Female Dondang Sayang dancers wear the Malay *kebaya* and sarong.

local music recorded by gramophone companies during that period.

Various dance songs are staged during a Ronggeng performance, each having a characteristic rhythmic pattern played by the frame drums. The dance songs include Asli, Inang and Joget. Other social folk repertoire performed by the Ronggeng ensemble include Zapin, Masri, Dondang Sayang, Keroncong, Latin American dances such as mambo, rumba and cha-cha, Thai Ramvong, European waltz and Chinese songs.

Although the number of Ronggeng troupes and performers have decreased, Asli, Inang, Joget, Masri and Zapin songs are still very popular, and their rhythms are often incorporated into Chinese, Indian and Malay pop songs. Composers of all nationalities include the rhythms in their compositions for orchestras, drum ensembles and other traditional ensembles. The Masri rhythm is especially popular with pop *nasyid* groups because of its Middle Eastern qualities. Stylized versions of Asli, Inang, Joget, Masri and Zapin are performed by school children and state troupes at annual concerts and tourist shows. Since the 1990s, these social dance rhythms are featured in new arrangements of pop songs known as *Irama Malaysia* (Malaysian rhythm) where musicians mix the traditional Ronggeng ensemble with different traditional Malay drums as well as electric guitars and keyboards.

Ronggeng dance songs

Type	Characteristics/Rhythm	Examples of songs
Asli	Slow, sad dance song; eight-beat rhythm.	'Bunga Tanjung,' 'Tudung Periok', 'Seri Mersing', 'Mas Merah'
Inang	Lively, happy dance song; four-beat rhythm.	'Inang Cina', 'Inang Kelantan'
Joget	Happy dance song; alternating three notes against two.	'Hitam Manis', 'Tanjung Katong'

Dondang Sayang

Dondang Sayang (love songs) is an elaborate form of Malay poetry or *pantun* singing popular among the Babas of Melaka, Penang and Singapore. Two or more singers would try to outwit each other using pantun to debate varied topics ranging from love and business to animals and riddles. They are accompanied by a violin, an accordion, two rebana drums and a gong. The Babas used to get together to sing at the verandah of their houses or in the garden. Dondang Sayang was popularized throughout the peninsula in the early 20th century when singers were were invited to sing Dondang Sayang, Asli and joget songs at Bangsawan interludes and recorded by gramophone companies.

Asli music is characterized by unique vocalizations and specific rhythmic patterns.

Keroncong

Keroncong is made up of love songs that originated in the 16th-century music of the Portuguese colonies in the Moluccas and Batavia. These songs were first sung by Eurasians called 'crocodiles' who wandered around the towns of Batavia at night to serenade women, accompanied by the ukulele. Keroncong songs were later incorporated into popular theatre such as the Komedi Stambul.

Keroncong was popularized in Malaya by Indonesian singers such as Dinah, Amelia, Doli and Ahmad C. B. who performed in Bangsawan shows in the 1920s and 1930s (see 'People in Bangsawan'). By the 1930s, the modern idiom and instrumentation of Keroncong had become fixed. The ensemble comprises one or two singers, melodic instruments (violin, flute, guitar), rhythmic instruments (cello, ukulele and banjo or mandolin) and the double bass. Keroncong is recognizable from its instrumentation, unique rhythmic form and melody. The Keroncong repertoire in Malaysia includes original Keroncong Asli (such as 'Keroncong Moritsko' and 'Keroncong Sapu Lidi'); Keroncong Stambul performed in Komedi Stambul and Bangsawan (such as 'Stambul 1 Jampang' and 'Stambul II Baju Biru'); Keroncong Langgam or newer songs played in the Keroncong idiom (such as 'Bengawan Solo'); and Keroncong Malaysia or Malaysian melodies and lyrics sung to Keroncong-style accompaniment (such as 'Tanjung Bidara').

A Dondang Sayang performance usually comprises two or more singers to add flair to the exchange of *pantun*.

The influence of modern pop music is evident in the pop version of Keroncong played by groups using modern instrumentation.

Ghazal

Ghazal, the art of reciting romantic and religious verses in a singing style, was brought to Malaysia from the Middle East in the early 20th century. Over the years, local music traditions have influenced its form and style, transforming it from a simple reciting musical genre to one with a unique Malaysian flavour. Two strains are found in the country, the more popular variation being in the southern state of Johor.

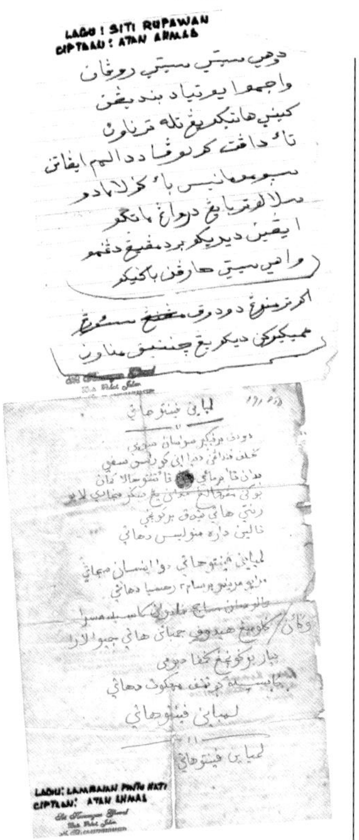

Old handwritten song sheets of Ghazal compositions by Atan Ahmad in Arabic script (Jawi).

Origins

Ghazal is found in many countries in Asia, especially in the Middle East whose citizens are mainly Muslims, such as Iran, Egypt, Iraq, Turkey, or in countries that were once ruled by Muslims as in the case of India and Pakistan. When Persia conquered countries in the Middle East and northern India, Ghazal spread to all the conquered lands.

One type of Ghazal (Ghazal party) was brought to the Malay Peninsula by Arab missionaries in the early 1900s and is still sung by groups performing *nasyid*, a form of Islamic religious music, played in the style of popular music of the Middle East. Many groups were formed all over the country, and a few still remain in Kedah, Penang, Sabah and Sarawak, usually accompanying nasyid singers or solo singers who render popular songs from the Middle East. This type of Ghazal includes musical accompaniment by modern instruments such as the accordion, violin, flute, guitar, double-bass, drums as well as the *o'ud* (plucked ukulele).

Ghazal Johor is believed to have been introduced by musicians from North India in the 1920s. A well-known musician, Haji Musa Yusof, nicknamed Pak Lomak, was credited with popularizing this strain of Ghazal in Johor. He was known to have been able to sing the Ghazal in Urdu, and learned to play the harmonium and tabla, the two main instruments in the Indian Ghazal.

He later modified the music to suit local taste by introducing local melodic and musical forms. He

also composed songs using the local language in lyrics in the popular Malay *pantun* (quatrain) form. He started by translating Urdu lyrics from the Indian Ghazal songs into the local dialect. Some of his songs are still popular today, such as 'Seri Mersing', 'Gunung Banang', and 'Pak Ngah Balik'. His works have become standard Ghazal songs and are included in the repertoire of all Ghazal groups.

Ghazal Johor ensemble

The ensemble (pictured, right) consists of the harmonium, tabla, violin, guitar, *gambus* and maracas. Occasionally the tambourine is added. The gambus is the local version of the Arabic *o'ud*, which was introduced in the 1950s to replace the original local *gambus kayu* that was much smaller and resembles the Chinese *pipa*. Gambus players in Johor preferred the o'ud because of its better sound and loudness. The maracas have replaced the bells that are sometimes used in the Indian Ghazal.

The violin and the harmonium are the main instruments that provide the melody, sometimes in unison with the singer. The gambus and guitar provide the accompaniment, and the maracas play the rhythm at regular beats, picking up tempo at the end of a passage. Occasionally the *rebana* drum and a gong are used when a local rhythm is being played. Another type of hand drum called *maruas* is also used to emphasize the drum beat in a particular rhythm.

Famous Ghazal singers and composers

Well-known Malaysian Ghazal singers: (1) Fadzil Ahmad, (2) Ahmad Jusoh and (3) S. A. Aishah. Other singers include Kamariah Noor, Zainurin Md. Dom, Fatimah Adan and Rosiah Chik. Talib Ahmad (4) was a famous composer whose songs are still popular today.

1

2

3

4

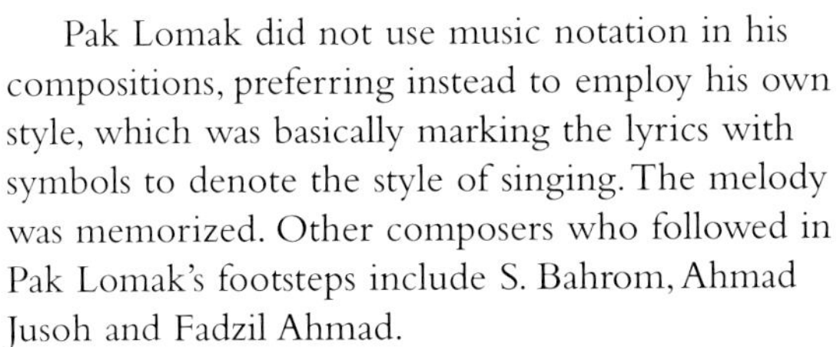

Above: Over the years Ghazal has developed a unique Malaysian identity by absorbing local musical traditions.

Left: Young Ghazal troupes in Johor pit their skills against each other in annual state-organized competitions.

Far left: There are about 30 active junior Ghazal groups in Johor known as Ghazal Remaja. The existence of these groups reflects the state government's success in keeping the music alive.

Pak Lomak did not use music notation in his compositions, preferring instead to employ his own style, which was basically marking the lyrics with symbols to denote the style of singing. The melody was memorized. Other composers who followed in Pak Lomak's footsteps include S. Bahrom, Ahmad Jusoh and Fadzil Ahmad.

Eventually Pak Lomak developed Ghazal Johor by expanding the original ensemble of harmonium and tabla to include the violin, guitar, *gambus* and maracas. The ensemble in this form remains to this day.

Ghazal songs were disseminated by Bangsawan singers and were recorded by gramophone companies in the early 1990s. Over the years Malay rhythms such as Joget, Inang, Zapin and Masri have been worked into the Ghazal musical repertoire. Many Ghazal songs composed in the original rhythm have been adapted by other musical genres and turned into folk songs with Asli eight-beat rhythms.

Ghazal Johor songs fall into two styles: Ghazal Asli and Ghazal Langgam. Ghazal Asli is the earlier style initiated by Pak Lomak. His compositions were based on the Asli form, where the melody is preceded by an introduction, and in between phrases there are musical interludes that must be observed. The Ghazal Langgam style follows the modern form found in other songs. An example of a Ghazal song in langgam form is 'Penawar Rindu'.

Decline and revival

At the height of Ghazal Johor's popularity in the 1950s, Ghazal groups were formed in almost all the districts and towns in the state. It was a popular pastime, and regular performances were held either in private houses or on open-air stages, especially at wedding receptions. A performance could last into the wee hours of the morning. However, in the following 30 years the appeal of Ghazal dissipated due to the growth of rock music. It was revived in the early 1990s.

Today, Ghazal is developed seriously in Johor, with the state government taking the lead by initiating several programmes, such as teaching the music in schools, formation of groups, research, and the production of recordings and reading materials related to the music. Ghazal singing and song-writing competitions are held annually and attract a large number of entrants. These efforts are paying off as an increasing number of young people in Johor, including schoolchildren, have shown an interest in the genre.

Recordings on compact discs are produced by the Yayasan Warisan Johor (Johor Heritage Trust) as part of the state government's efforts to develop Ghazal.

Singing style

Traditional Ghazal songs are sung at high pitch. This is probably because in earlier times, the violin or harmonium players could only play in one key which was E. A number of Ghazal songs are still played in that key. The other reason could be that loud singing was necessary in the days before the microphone was introduced, and singers had to literally shout to be heard. That singing style has remained till this day despite the presence of microphones. Another characteristic typical of the Ghazal singing style is the frequent use of ornamentations (*renek-renek*). Ornamentations are one or more notes considered an embellishment of a melody. There are three styles of such ornamentations—Malay, Hindu and Arabic—which are closely related to the melodic form used in the songs.

Indian music

Music is an integral element of celebrations and religious rituals among the Malaysian Indians. Over the centuries many types of folk, popular and classical music of India were carried to Malaysia by adventurers, merchants, immigrants and visitors. This music has influenced other styles and trends, notably in Malaysian popular music, and Indian musical instruments are also featured in contemporary jazz and art music.

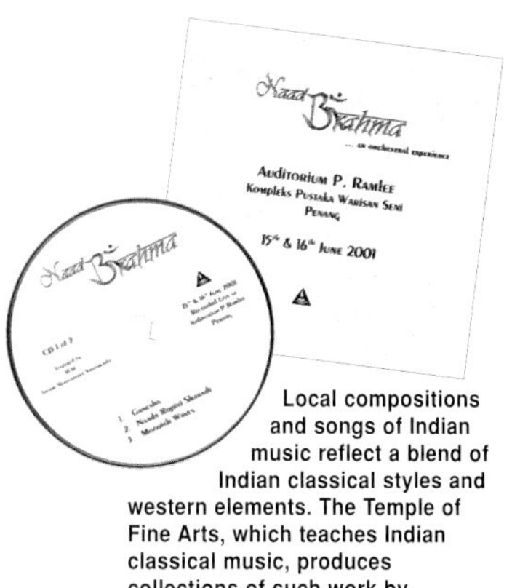

Local compositions and songs of Indian music reflect a blend of Indian classical styles and western elements. The Temple of Fine Arts, which teaches Indian classical music, produces collections of such work by Malaysian artistes.

Musical occasions

During Hindu religious celebrations in Malaysia, the temples vibrate with the sounds of the wind instrument *nagasvaram* and the double-headed drums *tavil*, while the subtle and refined strains of voice, *vina* and *sitar* lutes, and the *tabla* and *mridanga* drums grace the halls of private societies, academies of fine arts and concert halls in many urban areas.

Although the Indian music tradition in Malaysia basically maintains the major characteristics of Indian music from its homeland, some variations and stylistic differences have emerged in Malaysia.

Origins of Indian classical music

The Indian classical music tradition has its theoretical roots in the *Natyasastra*, a written manuscript that dates from 2nd BCE to 5th century CE. Nearly all the basic concepts in Indian classical music are to be found in this ancient manuscript including the musical elements of consonance, dissonance, pitch, scale, melody, *raga* (scale-like melody), rhythm and *tala* (time measure). As the Indian classical music tradition developed in India, two distinct styles and traditions of performance began to emerge around the 13th and 14th centuries. These were the Hindustani tradition based in the north of India and patronized by the Mogul sultanates, and the Carnatic tradition based in the south of India with its roots in ancient Hindu culture. Although the two traditions share the same basic theory—both recognize seven basic notes and five more variations on the seven—they exhibit differences in musical forms, terminology, performance of raga and tala, and the use of musical instruments.

The main instruments in the northern and southern Indian musical traditions include: **1.** sitar (plucked lute), **2.** *nagasvaram* (double-reed pipe), **3.** *tavil* and **4.** *mridanga* drums.

Musical traditions

In the Northern or Hindustani classical tradition the main melody instruments are the sitar, *surbahar* and *sarod* (plucked lutes), the *sarangi* (bowed lute), the *shahnai* (double-reed pipe), the *bamsri* (bamboo flute), the harmonium with keyboard and the *surmandal* (plucked zither). Among the important Hindustani percussion instruments are the *tabla/baya* (drums), the *pakhavaj* (double-headed drum), and the small *dukar-tikar* or *naghara* (kettle drums). The *tambura* (plucked lute) provides the drone.

Among the typical Carnatic musical instruments are the ancient *vina* (plucked lute), the *nagasvaram* (double-reed pipe) and its drone pipe accompaniment called the *ottu*, the violin, the *venu* (flute) and the *tambura*. The main percussion instruments in Carnatic music include the *mridanga* and *tavil* (drums), the *kanjira* (tambourine) and the *ghatam* (clay pot struck with the hands and fingers). The *sruti* (electronic box) is often used today to provide the drone pitch in the music.

In both traditions, compositions consist of improvisation of melody and rhythm and, hence, pieces are not written in score. Musicians use a particular *raga* (or *rag*) scale-like melody as the basis for the melody, and a particular *tala* (or *tal*) as the foundation for rhythm and time organization in a composition.

LEFT: Indian folk, classical and pop music in Malaysia retains many of its original elements although there is improvisation in contemporary works.

BELOW AND FAR LEFT: The orchestra of the Temple of Fine Arts as well as those of other institutions, are made up of musicians playing north and south Indian instruments as well as Western instruments, and produce a blend of Indian classical music as well as new music.

Malaysian context

While the Carnatic tradition is predominant in Malaysia and taught in the major institutions of Indian music learning, the Hindustani tradition is also performed and taught.

The development of Indian classical music in Malaysia can be traced to the 1950s and 1960s in institutions such as the Sangeetha Abhivirdhi Sabha (Association for the Propagation of Music) which was established in the Brickfields area of Kuala Lumpur in 1923. During that time performing artists from India including S. C. Nagasamy, Thangavelu and Yogeswary Nagalingam taught music in Malaysia privately. In 1981, the Temple of Fine Arts was set up, and the institution took on the task of nurturing not only Carnatic music, but also the Hindustani tradition. In fact, musicians from the two traditions come together at the Temple of Fine Arts to teach, rehearse and hold concerts, sometimes mixing both the Carnatic and Hindustani traditions.

The Temple of Fine Arts and other groups also promote light classical music as well as new music in order to attract all ethnic groups to their concerts. In new pieces the melodies tend to be shorter and the rhythms are fast and lively.

Today the new music from the Temple of Fine Arts and other institutions tends to feature many instruments in very large ensembles, often with 60 or more players. The performers also combine north and south Indian instruments and Western instruments in an attempt to find new tone colours, with the resulting nuances producing various flavours, and often combining these with vocal parts. As a means of reaching out to the general public the Temple of Fine Arts has also produced compact discs featuring new works by new Malaysian artistes. While Indian music attempts to find its own voice and space in the Malaysian performing arts, it has, over the years, influenced other styles and trends, particularly in popular music where Hindustani and Tamil film music have contributed to contemporary Malaysian pop through *Lagu Hindustan* in the 1950–60s and *Dangdut* in the 1980–90s. Some teachers and performers of Indian music are attempting to achieve a Malaysianized form of Indian music with the mixing of musical elements in the classical style with elements from other local cultures.

A drummer depicted in a painting, circa 1725 CE, at the Rajasthani School in India.

Bhangra

One of the notable genres of Indian folk music found in Malaysia is Bhangra. On the Indian sub-continent, Bhangra is a lively music and dance genre performed by Punjabi men wearing colourful costumes and turbans. In the Punjab, Bhangra is often a harvest festival event (*baisakhi*), and the female counterpart is called *giddha* when the women dance in a group. The dancing is usually accompanied by vigorous rhythms beaten out on the *dhol* (large cylindrical drum, left) or the double-headed *dholak* (barrel-shaped drum).

Bhangra music and dance have followed wherever South Asians, and especially Punjabis, have settled around the world, including Malaysia, the United Kingdom, the United States and Canada. In Malaysia it is performed to celebrate Vasakhi, the birth of Sikhism, and for entertainment at concerts. In Western countries Bhangra is performed not only in Indian communities but is also seen and heard in discos where it enjoys great popularity.

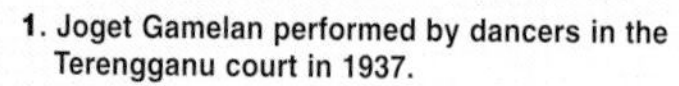

1. Joget Gamelan performed by dancers in the Terengganu court in 1937.

2. Once only performed for royalty, Terinai has developed into a popular dance.

3. The Terengganu royal orchestra of the late 19th century.

4. Archive image of a Malay gamelan ensemble, circa late 19th or early 20th century.

COURT PATRONAGE OF THE PERFORMING ARTS

The issue of court patronage for traditional Malay performing arts remains an intriguing one. Although popular imagination has it that the arts were always supported by royalty, available evidence does not support this view. Court support did exist, but it was very limited, unlike in Thailand, Cambodia and Java where court support for the arts has always been significant.

The most obvious early sources of any information regarding the Malay courts, the classical histories or legendary stories (*hikayat*), do not yield any clear evidence to indicate that the arts did indeed receive patronage. Nothing but incidental music receives any mention in these works. The *Hikayat Patani* is an exceptional work in this regard; however, no major genres of the traditional performing arts are mentioned, with the possible exception of Asyik.

Evidence of court patronage for the arts comes from relatively recent times. Puppeteers from Kelantan were sent to Java in the 1920s to learn and master the Javanese Wayang Kulit Gedog. This was performed in Kelantan as Wayang Kulit Melayu. Genres such as Asyik and Joget Gamelan served as entertainment for an educated elite. Joget Gamelan came to the Malay Peninsula through an early 19th-century intermarriage between the courts of Riau-Lingga and Pahang, and a subsequent marriage between the courts of Pahang and Terengganu. Thus what is called Gamelan Pahang or Joget Pahang came into being. Later, with the evolution of the unique Malay style of gamelan as well as the dance, these genres were named Gamelan Melayu and Joget Gamelan.

The *Hikayat Patani* confirms the possible existence of the Asyik dance and music in the Patani palace. In Kelantan, Asyik music and dance were performed for court entertainment by a retinue of dancers and musicians supported by the palace. This practice, however, seems to have died out by the beginning of the 20th century. And like Joget Gamelan, Asyik dance and its music have become part of popular rather than royal entertainment, although the style of performance remains unchanged. A similar situation prevailed over the Terinai dance of Perlis. It, too, was the beneficiary of court patronage which was subsequently lost. Today, Terinai is a popular dance both in Kelantan and in Perlis.

Two other important genres of music and dance deserve mention in connection with the role of the Malay courts: Nobat and Mak Yong. The Nobat orchestra was imported from the Middle East and possibly India some time before the 15th century. Unlike its original context, where the music served to inspire bravery among the soldiers, in the Malay sultanates where the Nobat was established, both the orchestra and its music took on a sacred aura, forming a part of the royal regalia. In the case of the Mak Yong dance theatre, evidence is lacking to connect it with any Malay court prior to the third decade of the 20th century when an attempt was made by a Kelantan nobleman to develop a court variety of Mak Yong. But the attempt did not bear fruit.

Mak Yong was briefly supported by the court in the 20th century.

Asyik and Joget Gamelan

The dances and music known as Asyik and Joget Gamelan were nurtured in the classical tradition in Malay palace culture. These art forms were given patronage by the courts of the Malay sultanates in the past and served as entertainment for an educated elite in traditional society. Today they survive outside the palace and are developing under the guidance of government agencies, universities and other private institutions. Trained musicians and dancers perform the music and dance, while works are composed by individuals, sometimes with inspiration from the folk tradition.

Stylized movements
Joget Gamelan dance movements represent stylized gestures of royal salutation, human behaviour and movements of birds and other animals. These movements are depicted in dance repertoires such as Timang Burung (dandling birds, pictured left), Sulang Arak (sharing of wine), Belanda Mabuk (drunken Dutchmen), Taman Sari (garden of essence; depicting gestures of picking and plucking of flowers in the royal garden), and Lambang Sari (waves of essence; depicting netting fish, rowing boats, throwing fishing nets and picking up the catch).

Joget Gamelan

Through an early 19th century royal marriage between the courts of Riau-Lingga in Indonesia and Pahang, and another in the early 20th century between the courts of Pahang and Terengganu, the Javanese musical instruments (gamelan), a specific musical repertory and dances were disseminated to the Malay Peninsula. In the mid-19th century this palace tradition was called Gamelan Pahang and Joget Pahang. Later its uniquely Malay style evolved into what is known today as Joget Gamelan and Gamelan Melayu, to distinguish it from its Indonesian parent. Many of the instruments from the Pahang gamelan of the 19th century may still be seen in the state museum.

A 19th-century Joget Gamelan performance by Terengganu court dancers.

During the 19th and early 20th centuries, this music and dance were entertainment only for royalty and was performed at engagements and weddings, royal birthdays, and to honour visiting state officials. Originally, Joget Gamelan had a repertoire of about 50 dances, but that has since dwindled. As entertainment, dances accompanied by specific musical pieces enacted episodes from the Panji stories, various epics and Malay folk tales. The dances are interpretative, and illustrate specific activities. Each dance has its own music. The Timang Burung dance, for instance, depicting the situation of a princess trying to catch a bird and her attendants who dance in imitation of movements of the bird, is accompanied by a particular piece of music of the same name. An entire performance can be based on such pieces.

Joget Gamelan is performed exclusively by females. The performers begin their dance by gesturing the *sembah* or salutation. There are three styles of the sembah: the premier royal salutation (*awal sembah*) where both hands are raised to the front of the body with the thumbs and index fingers touching; *sembah sulur buyung* (sprouting salutation), where the dancers raise their clasped hands in front of their bowed heads, tilting their hands forward; and *sembah kepak* (winged salutation), which is done by

Gamelan ensemble
The basic Gamelan Melayu consists of eight instruments: *gong agung* and *gong suwukan* (large, hanging knobbed gongs), *kenong* (a set of five large horizontally-placed gongs), *kerumong* (a set of 10 small horizontal knobbed gongs), *saron barung* and *peking* (medium and small sized bronze-keyed instruments), *gambang kayu* (wooden xylophone) and *gendang* (double-headed barrel drum beaten with the hands).

The hanging gongs and *kenong* serve as the time markers in the music. The stately and lowest-pitched gong agung always marks the end of a piece of music. The gendang provides the percussive rhythms.

The melody is prominent in all pieces of the repertory, for it is played by all of the xylophone and bronze-keyed instruments as well as the kerumong. The four- or eight-beat melodic phrases are balanced, often in the form of 'statement-and-answer'. The multi-layered melody is underscored by a repeated temporal unit (the colotomic unit, made up of a specific number of musical beats) played on the kenong and hanging gongs.

folding the left hand over the right index finger with the left thumb placed over the right thumb. The sembah kepak, however, is only performed after completing several dance motifs. The salutation dance motifs are performed several times—at the beginning, intermittently during the performance and at the end. The dancers use fans and scarves as dance properties to depict birds' wings or sleeping infants.

Decline and revival of the gamelan

During and after World War II the gamelan and its dancers of the Terengganu court became inactive. The gamelan instruments were put into storage, and the performers were no longer invited to the palace to practise and perform. This situation prevailed until 1969 when, at the urging and with the support of the late Tan Sri Mubin Sheppard, the surviving Joget Gamelan dancers and musicians from Terengganu played at a major conference on Malaysian arts in Kuala Lumpur. Since then the gamelan has seen a virtual rebirth with a distinctly Malaysian flair. The original instruments of the Terengganu gamelan have been retained and complemented with added instruments to make the ensemble larger and more flexible in performing a new repertory that is broader in style.

Today, surviving outside the palace, this music is performed for general entertainment in the public arena, for dance drama, and sometimes for official occasions. Universities and other institutions of higher learning as well as the Akademi Seni Kebangsaan (National Arts Academy) support the development of the Malaysian gamelan by offering courses in gamelan music and dance.

Asyik

Like the Joget Gamelan, the Asyik dance and its music were performed primarily for entertainment in the Kelantan court, and are believed to have originated from the palace of Patani in the 17th century. Occasions such as the sultan's birthday, weddings and other celebrations were enhanced by performances of the graceful Asyik dance. A retinue of dancers and musicians, supported by the palace, were trained to provide this form of entertainment.

Terinai

Terinai is an elegant court dance genre in Perlis, Kedah and Kelantan. Dances are mainly performed at weddings and have a distinctive narrative which tells of courtship and marriage. In the most popular of these dances, candles are held by the female performers. Other dances in the Terinai repertoire include Terinai Menghadap and Layang Mas (pictured, right), performed by women, and Ketam Bawa Anak and Dewa Raja, performed by men. All dances reflect connections with nature and natural imagery.

Originally Terinai dances featured a strong element of improvisation, but in recent decades the dances fit into specific patterns of movement. Layang Mas, for instance, is said to derive its movements from the swallow (*layang-layang*). The dance, obviously seductive and flirtatious in character, has clear shoulder and hip movements. The dancers also use a scarf secured to the waist, its ends held up with the thumb and forefinger, giving the appearance of wings. The ensemble (pictured above) accompanying the dance consists of a *serunai* (quadruple reed wind instrument), two *gendang keling* (Indian drums) and two *tetawak* (hanging gongs).

The Kelantan variety, usually performed at weddings, tends to be acrobatic in character, with the dancers, usually young children, bending backwards to pick up currency notes with the mouth. The musical ensemble, while maintaining the serunai, gendang and tetawak, also includes the *canang* (six small knobbed gongs arranged horizontally in a wooden rack) and *kesi* (small hand cymbals).

The Asyik dance was originally performed by a chorus of female dancers with a solo male dancer, accompanied by a female singer who sang the Asyik song while seated near the *rebana besar* (large drum). By the third quarter of the 20th century, however, this tradition had lost its court patronage. Today, the Asyik genre is rarely performed in its original form, having developed into a folk dance.

The dance is accompanied by an ensemble made of up *rebab* (stringed lute), *canang* (gong-chime), *tetawak* (hanging gongs), two *gendang* (drums), two or more *gendang asyik* (small, single-headed drums), and sometimes a *gambang* (wooden xylophone).

The word *asyik* means infatuated, and stylized gestures and motifs of the dance tell the story of a long-lost pet bird that once belonged to a princess, of it grooming and extending its beautiful wings and fluttering feathers. The dance begins with dancers gliding into the performance area in small steps while extending one arm to the side and placing the other in front of their body, and seating themselves to perform the paying of homage motif. This is followed by a series of stylized dance movements depicting grooming gestures and birds in flight. The dancers' movements are narrow and restrained, their hand gestures accentuated by the curling and flexing of fingers. The dance ends with the paying of homage motif.

LEFT: Two examples of Asyik dance performed in traditional court style.

The Nobat orchestra

The Nobat is an instrumental ensemble and repertoire of music that exists in the ancient classical music tradition of Malaysia. Introduced from the Middle East not later than the 15th century, the Nobat took on a sacred aura as it came to support the validity and authority of the ruling class, especially the sultans. The instruments of the Nobat form a treasured part of the royal regalia in a number of states in Malaysia where they are played on both joyful and sorrowful occasions.

The Selangor Nobat playing at the coronation of the state's ruler, Sultan Sharafuddin Idris Shah in 2003.

Unlike the Nobat drums of Kedah, Perak and Selangor, which are made from wood, the drums in the Terengganu Nobat are made of silver. A gift to the Sultan of Terengganu from the last Sultan of Riau-Lingga, who was forced to abdicate by the Dutch in 1911, the drums were executed by the finest Malay silversmiths in Batavia (Jakarta) and are covered with delicate, foliated designs. The drumheads are made from goatskin. The tone of these drums is said to be incomparably more melodious than that of their wooden prototypes.

Origins

It is believed that the Nobat comes from the Middle East where the music ensemble of the sultan, since at least the 9th century, was called the *naubah* or *naubat*. During the early history of Islam, the *naubat* was played to inspire bravery and a fighting spirit among soldiers who went into battle. The term naubat also referred to a suite of pieces played by a specific type of orchestra. In many societies in the Middle East and Islamic Africa, an ensemble of drums, a double-reed wind instrument and a long trumpet still make up the orchestra of the sultan.

In the Malay Archipelago, the Nobat's function was less martial, being instead an essential part of sacred royal regalia. It has been recorded that drums of sovereignty were in use in the Malay Sultanate of Patani and elsewhere in the region at least a century before the founding of Melaka, and no Malay raja was recognized as ruler in those kingdoms which possessed a Nobat unless he had been ceremonially 'drummed' during his installation.

The rulers of Melaka adopted the tradition early in the 15th century (although there is no Nobat ensemble extant in the state). At the end of the 15th century, the Melaka Sultan granted a Nobat to the newly established Sultan of Kedah to legitimize his position and install him as a ruler. The Portuguese captured Melaka in 1511. Seventeen years after that the eldest son of the former sultan moved north to Perak, taking a Nobat of the Melaka model with him. Around 1770, Selangor became the fourth state in the Peninsula to acquire a Nobat when the Sultan of Perak granted a Bugis prince authority to establish a new kingdom and installed him on the throne to the accompaniment of the Perak Nobat.

Performance occasions

Although the Nobat is played infrequently, it continues to be a vital part of the installation of a ruler, and is also heard at the wedding and funeral of a ruler, his royal consort and his children. In earlier times, it was played on a number of other occasions, such as during a son's circumcision, or when the ruler proceeded to a river for ceremonial ablutions and prayers, or at the beginning and end of the Muslim fasting month. It is still played in some states every evening during Ramadan at the time of breaking the fast.

The *Nobat* ensemble

The basic Nobat orchestra consists of three drums and two wind instruments. These are two double-headed barrel drums, one large (*gendang Nobat*) and the other smaller (called *gendang anak*), which are laid horizontally and hit with the hand and with an outward-bending wooden stick; a small kettledrum (variously referred to as *nehara* in Kedah, *nengkara* in Perak, *nengara* in Terengganu and *langkara* in Selangor), which is placed upright and hit with a pair of light sticks; a quadruple-reed wind instrument or oboe (*serunai*), and a long silver trumpet (*nafiri*) which produces only two or three different pitches.

In Kedah, Terengganu and Selangor, six instruments are now played, but in Perak only five. In Kedah, a small, narrow-rimmed hanging gong is included, and in Terengganu, a pair of cymbals called *kopok-kopok*. The Selangor Nobat includes two kettledrums.

1. Hanging gong
2. Long silver trumpet (*nafiri*)
3. Small double-headed barrel drum (*gendang anak*)
4. Pair of cymbals (*kopok-kopok*)
5. Kettledrum (*nengkara*)
6. Oboe (*serunai*)
7. Large double-headed barrel drum (*gendang Nobat*)

The musicians

Traditionally, the Nobat can only be played by royal command, and the instruments can only be handled by the ruler and members of his family, or by a select group of court musicians known as *orang kalur*. These musicians belong to certain families whose members have served the courts for generations and who pass down their musical tradition orally within the family. It was believed that illness would befall any unauthorized person who touched or even stepped over the instruments. The musicians are trained to play a specific repertoire of pieces known as *man*. In the Kedah court, for example, 19 pieces are known and still performed, and some are written down in a rudimentary notation system called *dai*, which is based on symbols taken from the Jawi (modified Arabic) script. This writing system notates only certain parts in the music and acts as a mnemonic device for the musicians. A specific music notation is not known among the other Nobat groups.

Nobat players from the court of Terengganu in the 1920s.

The repertoire

Each piece in the Nobat repertoire is given a name and performs a special function or use in the ceremonies and events in the palace, though these vary from one court to another. The piece entitled 'Raja Berangkat', for example, is played to accompany the procession of the sultan to or from the palace hall, while another piece, 'Raja Berlayar', accompanies the crowning or installation of a ruler.

The musical pieces themselves are distinguished by the rhythmic patterns played on the *gendang* and *nengkara* drums. The nengkara player is usually the leader of the ensemble. He introduces the rhythmic pattern and controls the tempo of a given piece. If the gong is part of the ensemble, it is used only on certain beats, often marking the end of a given rhythmic pattern. The *serunai* player provides a highly ornamented melody throughout a piece, while the sustained tones of the *nafiri* trumpet are played to mark the beginning and ending of sections in a piece of music. The fanfare-like motifs of the trumpet and the percussive rhythmic patterns of the drums are contrasted by the continually moving melody line of the serunai.

The tempo of most pieces is slow, reflecting the pace of the movements or actions in a particular ceremony. The majestic sound of this orchestra projects an aura of grandeur befitting the status and stateliness of the king or sultan.

Top: An excerpt from the song 'Raja Berlayar', played during the enthronement ceremony of a new ruler. The tempo is quite slow, reflecting the solemnity of the occasion.

Bottom: A few pieces of the Nobat repertoire are recorded in a rudimentary notation system based on symbols from the Jawi script.

Caring for the Nobat instruments

Storage conventions

In the states of Terengganu, Perak and Selangor, the instruments of the Nobat are kept in a special room within the palace complex, called Balai Nobat, which is linked to the main audience hall. The instruments are wrapped in yellow cloth (the colour denoting royalty in Malay society) and may be removed only for royal ceremonies.

In Alor Star, Kedah, the instruments are housed in a separate three-storey, octagonal-shaped tower next to the Royal Museum, the former palace of the Kedah sultanate. Built in 1912–13 in the Western Neoclassical style, the height of the tower allows the Nobat to be heard from afar. When the Nobat is required to be played at the present palace at Anak Bukit, a special ritual is conducted before the instruments can be transported.

Floor plan of Istana Sultan Mansur Shah, c. 1455

1. Reception hall
2. Main palace
3. Mosque
4. Ablution area
5. Procession hall
6. Nobat room
7. Waiting room on left
8. Waiting room on right
9. Audience hall

In the palace of Sultan Mansur Shah of Melaka, built around 1455, the Nobat was probably stored and played in a special room directly linked to the main procession hall of the palace.

Spiritual needs of the instruments

The royal Perak instruments are part of the original regalia of the state, and are closely associated with its guardian spirits. One of the chief duties of the state magician in Perak in bygone years was not only to 'keep alive' the state weapons, but also to conduct a feast for the royal musical instruments. At the annual ceremony held for this purpose, the state magician and his assistant paid obeisance to the regalia, offered delicacies to the guardian spirits and poured drink upon the royal drums and into the royal trumpets. The drink was said to have vanished miraculously.

The chief of the Nobat musicians in Perak also had the duty of airing the royal instruments from time to time. He would place them in an open-sided hut encircled with a line of fowl's feathers stuck in the ground over which no one was allowed to step.

The Balai Nobat in Alor Star, Kedah, is painted yellow, a colour associated with Malay royalty. The instruments stored inside are also wrapped in yellow cloth.

Mak Yong's court sojourn

The folk theatre of Mak Yong was briefly presented as court theatre early in the 20th century, when a Kelantan prince Long Abdul Ghaffar established Kampung Temenggung, a Kelantanese arts centre, in 1923. That effort to recreate the village art form as court dance theatre lasted 12 years. The legacy of courtly elegance and glamour was resurrected in 1971 with the creation of Kumpulan Seri Temenggung, which has become Malaysia's best-known Mak Yong troupe.

Modern Mak Yong performances retain some of the refinement that the original folk theatre went through during its brief association with the Kelantan court.

Long Abdul Ghaffar of Kelantan (1875–1935).

A village art

Controversy surrounds Mak Yong's original form. One view describes Mak Yong as court theatre performed for the Patani royalty of southern Thailand. There is no clear documented evidence to support this view. It is more likely that Mak Yong developed as a form of folk theatre with a strong ritual base. Its only link to Malay royalty appears to be the fact that Mak Yong, along with other art forms, was performed during important royal occasions such as the sultan's birthday. They were generally performed outside palace precincts, and hence cannot possibly be considered court theatre.

The status of Mak Yong as a folk art and its performance style changed for a short duration between 1923 and 1935. This was through the special interest taken in the genre by Long Abdul Ghaffar, the youngest son of Sultan Muhammad II of Kelantan. He established a cultural district in the palace grounds called Kampung Temenggung, intended to teach Mak Yong, Wayang Kulit, the big frame drum *(rebana besar)*, Asyik dance and *Pencak Silat*. With the recruitment of teachers from all over Kelantan, formal teaching of Mak Yong began in July 1923.

A performance by Kumpulan Seri Temenggung. The group claims to have adopted the style of court Mak Yong performance developed during the time of Long Abdul Ghaffar.

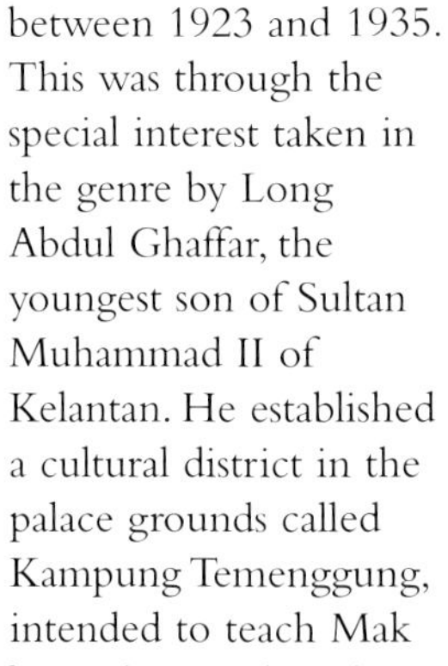

Long Abdul Ghaffar was particularly fond of Mak Yong. His ultimate aim was to create, using the village dancers and musicians, a refined version of courtly Mak Yong in the manner of the famous dance theatre styles in the palaces of Thailand, Cambodia and Indonesia. During Mak Yong's court sojourn, the convention requiring a lead female performer was established. The music, dance, costuming, make-up and staging of Mak Yong were refined to make it a style of theatre suitable for a sophisticated audience. At the same time, the folk style Mak Yong continued to be performed in villages by troupes from which the dancers and musicians were selected for Kampung Temenggung.

The support given to the performing arts by Long Abdul Ghaffar did not last. Towards the end of his life, the prince became a recluse and passed away in 1935. His demise, coupled with the beginning of World War II, ended the tradition of royal support for the arts in Kelantan. Kampung Temenggung faded into oblivion.

Kumpulan Seri Temenggung

The realization that younger Mak Yong performers should be found came about following an important conference on the traditional music and theatre of Southeast Asia held in Kuala Lumpur in August 1969. A Mak Yong group put together by the late Tan Sri Mubin Sheppard performed at that conference. The performers were elderly in appearance and compared unfavourably with the young and vibrant performers from Cambodia, Thailand and Indonesia. This led to the establishment of Kumpulan Seri Temenggung in 1970 by cultural policy makers. Khatijah Awang, a dancer at the Kompleks Budaya Negara at the time, was asked to start a new Mak Yong group of younger dancers. Kumpulan Seri Temenggung resurrected the elegant style that was developed in Kampung Temenggung. Strong links between the two were maintained; performers were trained by those who had previously been associated with Kampung

Mak Yong movements

In Kampung Temenggung, the highly elegant Mak Yong was seen as a symbolic expression of mystical Islamic ideas. Mak Yong's circular dances were believed to be the manifestation of Divine Unity or Totality of Being comparable to the famous circular dances of the Mevlevi Sufi whirling dervishes in Turkey. Long Abdul Ghaffar further believed that God's beauty (*jamal*) and strength (*jalal*) is exhibited in the female performer who plays the male lead role (*Pak Yong*). Some of the essential dance movements are represented here.

Temenggung. It led to the emergence of a glamorous and popular urban tradition of Mak Yong; in a sense, a resurrection of the elegant style which had faded into oblivion in 1935.

New directions, new challenges

With the establishment of Kumpulan Seri Temenggung, this ancient dance theatre style was given a new lease of life. The troupe's principal initial objectives were to revive the elegant court tradition that Long Abdul Ghaffar had envisioned. However, problems, mostly financial, beset the group following the death of its patron, Tan Sri Nik Ahmad Kamil, a member of the Kelantan royal family. It meant that Kumpulan Seri Temenggung had to accept compromises in quality and performance style in return for funding. These compromises have been at the expense of some essentials of the Mak Yong style. Performances for large audiences in urban auditoriums remove the intimacy of traditional theatre which is staged in-the-round—an essential in Mak Yong. Backdrops are used, and much of the beauty of both dance and music is sacrificed. Thus Mak Yong, as staged by Kumpulan Seri Temenggung, has evolved into a new kind of commercialized urban theatre, distinct from its original style.

Mak Yong entered a new phase with the introduction of the genre as a required subject for theatre, dance and music majors in the Akademi Seni Kebangsaan (National Arts Academy), which was established in 1994. Khatijah Awang was the first Mak Yong instructor at the academy, teaching from 1995 until her death in 2001. She imparted her expertise to the academy's students in the style manifested in court, with some adaptation for modern proscenium staging and urban audiences. Following her demise her legacy continues, with her family members taking over her role as instructor both at the academy as well as in Kelantan.

Susun sirih

Sawa mengorak tingkaran

Longlai

Keeping a tradition alive

1923 Several personalities formed the bridge between Kampung Temenggung and Kumpulan Seri Temenggung. The most important of these were Zainab binti Samad, Cik Kemala binti Muhammad and Abdullah Supang. By passing on their knowledge to new performers in the 1970s, several of the most important strands in court Mak Yong came propitiously together to produce a new and vibrant strain of Mak Yong.

ABOVE LEFT: An artist's recreation of the gateway to Kampung Temenggung.
ABOVE RIGHT: Kampung Temenggung was located in Tumpat, Kelantan.

1923–1935

Doyen of Kampung Temenggung, Cik Kemala, also Khatijah Awang's mother-in-law.

Abdullah Supang (left) was known for his effective portrayal of the Mak Yong clown, Peran Tua.

Zainab binti Samad, wife of Long Abdul Ghaffar, trained the new dancers of Kumpulan Seri Temenggung.

1971–2001

FAR LEFT: Khatijah Awang (1941–2001), the principal performer in Kumpulan Seri Temenggung.

LEFT: Khatijah Awang (as Pak Yong) and a clown at Kumpulan Seri Temenggung's maiden performance in 1971.

Present

Mak Yong is performed in the original village setting or in urban centres in Malaysia. While criticism has been directed at their modern staging methods, Kumpulan Seri Temenggung remains the most well-known troupe in the urban performance context.

A recent performance by Kumpulan Seri Temenggung.

1. A Sepoy regiment in the mid-19th century. Members of the regiment were the earliest performers of Borea.

2. The hobbyhorse dance of Kuda Kepang is a re-enactment of early Islamic battles.

3. Dikir Labah is a musical tradition connected with the praise of Prophet Muhammad on his birthday.

4. Dikir Barat is a modified and secularized version of *zikir* (Islamic religious chanting).

5. Zapin, derived from the Arabic *zaffan*, has evolved into a popular dance.

ISLAM AND THE PERFORMING ARTS

Islam constitutes one of the most important cultural influences on traditional Malay performing arts. Art forms associated with Islamic cultures in other countries have been imported directly into the Malay Peninsula, or through third countries. Others have been developed or shaped as a result of Middle Eastern or Islamic influences.

The impact of Islamic influences on Malay traditional music has been much stronger than on theatre or dance. The Ghazal vocal and instrumental style of Johor, for instance, has Middle Eastern as well as Indo-Pakistani elements, although performance techniques have changed. The spiked fiddle (*rebab*) appears in many variations in the Middle East, South Asia and Southeast Asia. In Malaysia it is best manifested in Mak Yong dance, in which it serves as the lead instrument.

Islamic elements are to be found in many other ways in traditional Malay performing arts, such as the singing of songs in Arabic-Persian styles, seen in religious or quasi-religious genres, including *qasidah* and *berzanji,* and in the many forms of *zikir* (religious chanting). The original form of zikir continues in Malaysia, but at the same time it has been transformed beyond recognition. The kind of transformation from religious to secular activity that has taken place in the case of zikir is paralleled in Borea.

The impact of Islam is also seen in theatre opening and closing ceremonies. Incantations in these ceremonies contain selections from the Qur'an as well as Islamic supplications (*doa*); in certain instances influences from indigenous and Hindu or Buddhist elements have altered the character of these incantations, turning them into *mantera* (Sanskrit mantra).

Puppets from a new form of Wayang Kuilt, recently developed in Kelantan.

One other Islamic or Middle Eastern feature that is prominent in traditional Malay theatre is the choice of stories. Such stories are found essentially in the repertoire of Bangsawan rather than in the older genres. Bangsawan borrowed much else from the Middle and Near Eastern traditions, including costumes, dance movements and language features. Eventually some of these Middle Eastern and Indo-Muslim features were to find their way into Malay films.

While Islamic, Middle Eastern and Indo-Muslim influences have been vital in shaping traditional Malay performing arts over the centuries, recent decades have seen a reversal of attitude towards these art forms due to strengthening of Islamic values. On the positive side, however, Islam has begun to reshape some of the traditional genres, evident in the revival of non-controversial art forms such as the Kelantanese Tarik Selampit and the development of new forms of shadow play, incorporating Islamic elements.

Middle East influences in traditional Malay theatre

Islam is believed to have entered the Malay Peninsula at various satges between the early 14th and 16th centuries. Middle Eastern influence predates the arrival of Islam. The impact of Islam was more spectacular than that of previous major religions that came into Southeast Asia. Together with Middle Eastern cultural aspects, Islam made inroads into all fields of life and cast its influence on Malaysia's performing arts.

The *gambus* is derived from the Middle Eastern *o'ud.*

Qur'anic influences

Records found in Java document the efforts of nine Muslim saints (*wali songo*) to imbue classical arts such as Wayang Kulit Purwa and gamelan music with Islamic elements. While similar documentation is non-existent in Malaysia, it is likely that Islam brought in its wake various forms of religious chanting (*zikir*) through missionary groups or members of Sufi orders. There is some evidence from Thailand to support such a view.

In Malaysia's northern states, particularly Kedah and Kelantan, there exist various forms of *zikir* (locally written as *dikir*) both within the context of religious ceremonies, and outside them. The best known of these is Dikir Barat, imported into Kelantan from Thailand.

Dikir Labah, active in Kelantan, and Kedah's Hadrah, are two forms of vocal and instrumental musical traditions connected with the praise of the Prophet Muhammad during his birthday (*maulud*). In the modern context, the religious character is diluted, and two strands of performances—the secular and the religious—have developed. In performance, Hadrah is combined with non-religious drama. It opens with singing and dancing to the accompaniment of frame drums (*rebana*). The performance is then continued with a play, in the style of Bangsawan, without any religious colouring.

However, gatherings of Muslims featuring genuine zikir still take place, and during maulud celebrations various famous forms of laudatory texts are utilized. Prayers, incantation texts and verses from the Qur'an continue to be used almost universally in the older traditions of Malay theatre, particularly in Wayang Kulit and Mak Yong theatre opening rituals. They are often a curious amalgam of elements derived from animism and other religions, such as Hinduism and Buddhism.

Connected with the use of invocation texts is the belief in invisible beings. Islam requires of its adherents a belief in supernatural beings such as angels (*malaikat*), demons (*syaitan*) and genies (*jinn*). Four principal arch-angels, Mikail, Jibrail, Izrail and Israfil feature in theatre opening invocations alongside the other various categories of beings. The demons appear mainly in their older Hindu form as evil spirits (*bhuta*) or ogres (*rakshaha*). The *jinn*, in particular Jinn Afrit, appear as characters in stories of Middle Eastern flavour. One of the most important of these stories in which Jinn Afrit appears as a character is *Gul-Bakawali*, the Islamic romance from India performed in Bangsawan.

Mystical ideas

The Islamic mystical tradition has provided traditional Malay theatre with a range of materials related to the Prophet Muhammad and other Muslim personalities. In theatre opening rites, greetings are addressed to the Prophet, to the first four caliphs (*khalifah*) of Islam, and to certain saints (*wali*). Sufism

Dabus

Dabus is a combination of vocal and instrumental music, martial art and dance from southern Perak and northern Selangor. It is semi-religious in content. The vocal music consists of religious songs (*nasyid*), while the orchestra is a combination of Middle Eastern and Javanese instruments. A performance begins with preliminary rituals and a musical prelude, followed by the entry of the Dabus dancers with metal skewers known as *anak dabus* (left). The dance begins and a state of trance is induced (pictured below). The dancers pierce themselves in the arm with their *anak dabus* until blood flows (right). According to the taboos of Dabus, only the leader of the troupe can stem its flow.

Dikir Barat
This form of *zikir*, imported into Kelantan from Thailand and secularized, is no longer performed in a strictly religious context. Where originally the lyrics of the performance praised Allah (God) or Prophet Muhammad, Dikir Barat (pictured, left) has been adapted to eulogize visiting dignitaries, newly married couples and even development projects. Its increasingly secular character led to problems in its home state. A ban on its performance was imposed by the state government in 1997, but it was lifted a year later.

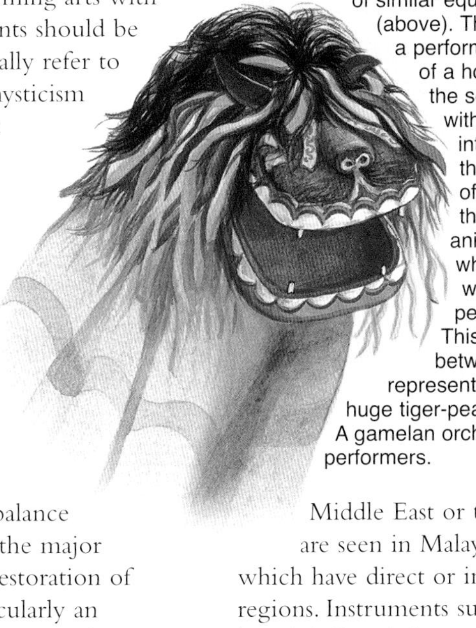

Kuda Kepang: From war dance to theatre form
Kuda Kepang, a hobbyhorse dance that is active in Johor, is sometimes staged as dance theatre with the incorporation of a story. The genre is reputed to have developed in Arabia during the time of Ali, the fourth caliph of Islam. Ali was a noted commander of the Muslim armies, and it is said that music was used to provide inspiration to soldiers during battle, with some of the soldiers going into a state of trance. In Java, the idea of a dance using horses was adapted, using artificial horses made of plaited bamboo or cut-out leather and other decorative trappings, to turn a war dance into theatre. Kuda Kepang performers in Johor make use of similar equipment (above). The first part of a performance consists of a hobbyhorse dance, the second commences with the dancers going into a trance, and the third section may consist of a Barongan—a dance theatre form using animal masks—in which performers wear huge peacock-lion masks (left). This represents the conflict between the *barong*, represented by an actor wearing a huge tiger-peacock mask, and evil forces. A gamelan orchestra accompanies the performers.

is manifested in theatre, with references to the Sufi stations (*maqam*), or states (*hal*), as well as to spiritual energy centres (*lataif*) within the human body which have to be energized for protection or power.

However, such elevated concepts and ideas are not to be found in the average theatre practitioner or Malay shaman (*bomoh*), but in a few who have interest and possible exposure to Islamic mysticism. There is the possibility that Javanese mysticism, which in some instances is tinged with Hinduism, may have been an influence.

In Malaysia, much controversy surrounds the issue of whether traditional performing arts with strong pre-Islamic religious elements should be permitted. Some practitioners usually refer to concepts associated with Islam's mysticism to justify their interest in these art forms. To them, no conflict exists between traditional theatre and Islamic teaching.

Alchemical ideas, especially those connected with healing processes, have an important place in traditional ritual theatre genres such as Main Puteri. The Islamic belief that the human body is made up of the four elements (*anasir arba'ah*) is persistent. The dislocation of the balance between these elements is one of the major causes of illness. Consequently, a restoration of balance in the elements, and particularly an adjustment in 'wind' (see 'Belief systems of traditional theatre') serves to bring about healing.

Cultural influences

Indirect Islamic cultural influences exist in many styles of Malaysian performing arts, including dances such as Zapin and musical styles such as Ghazal. At least two styles of theatre—Kuda Kepang and Dabus—claim inspiration from the earliest days of Islam.

Musical instruments and styles of music, both instrumental and vocal, emanating directly from the Middle East or through Indo-Muslim sources, are seen in Malay traditional theatre forms which have direct or indirect links with those regions. Instruments such as the *rebana*, the stringed lute (*rebab*) and the *gambus* are principal instruments used in Peninsular Malaysia. Vocal techniques derived from Islamic lands have been noted, a striking instance being the singing technique used in Mak Yong dance theatre (see 'Malay vocal music').

Stories with a Middle Eastern or Indian setting are taken from major cycles, including *One Thousand and One Nights*, stories of prominent heroes based on *hikayat* literature, and romances such as *Laila Majnun* and *Gul-Bakawali*. These stories appear mainly in Bangsawan.

Malay vocal music

Apart from existing as distinct art forms, Malay vocal music styles are manifested in some of the theatre genres found in Malaysia such as Mak Yong, Wayang Kulit and Main Puteri. These genres contain some of the most elaborate singing styles encountered in the country. Mak Yong in particular, with its melismatic songs, stands out as a unique form of Malay musical expression. The spread of Islam and its resurgence in the 20th century influenced performing art forms in Malaysia.

Nasyid, traditionally performed by a soloist and chorus, is sung in Arabic or Malay. Its melody and lyric pronunciation are Arabic-sounding.

Forms of Malay vocal music

The Islamic-influenced forms of Malay vocal music fall into two categories: that containing ordering of tones, or a recurring rhythmic pattern, such as Mak Yong songs; and tone melodies or non-rhymed music.

Rhymed vocal music

The musical repertoire of Mak Yong contains some 30 pieces in various categories, as well as vocal ululation (yodel). The songs are sung by male and female characters according to dramatic situations within the Mak Yong repertoire of 12 principal stories in a style described as polyphonic. The vocal as well as instrumental style of Mak Yong and some of its pieces are also used in the shamanistic Main Puteri dance. Middle Eastern influences are evident in instrumentation as well as performance techniques, even if the content is not religious in character.

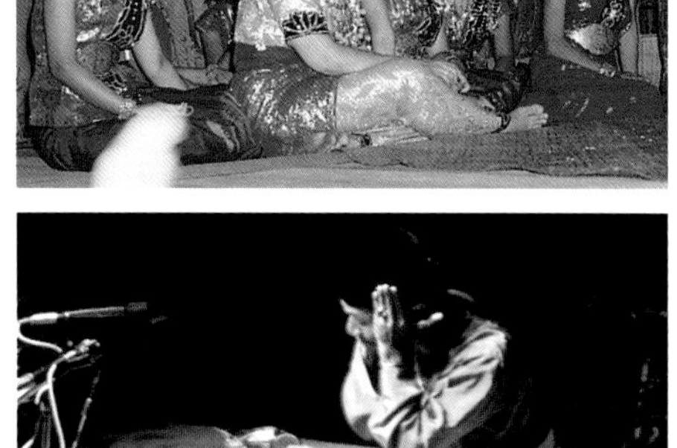

TOP: Mak Yong songs reflect Middle Eastern influences, and the vocal rendition is highly ornamented, typical of Islamic influence.

BOTTOM: Qur'an recitation is a characteristically monophonic, repetitive and highly improvised vocal genre.

Non-rhymed vocal music

The most important example of non-rhymed music is the art of Qur'an recitation (*tilawat al-Qur'an*), and the chanting or uttering of specific phrases in remembrance of Allah (*zikir*). Although the art of Qur'anic recitation is not generally regarded as music or even poetry, it has become the most important example of pitched sound-art in Malay culture, and specific methods of learning how to recite the Qur'an are learnt by the Malays from an early age. Local and international Qur'an assemblies held annually in Malaysia establish the significance of both the text of the Qur'an and the art of reciting it.

The call to prayer, *azan*, recited five times a day, is sometimes referred to as a form of poetry or music, although there is disagreement among scholars as to whether or not the *azan* should be termed poetry and music. This also applies to specifically religious ceremonies (*tahlil*) held to pray for those who have passed away, to bless those embarking on a journey or to offer thanks to Allah upon attaining success. Although one may see artistic or aesthetic merit in the manner in which some of the ceremonies are executed, in essence they would not be regarded as performances of 'art' as such.

Other examples of vocal music deriving from the Middle East, with social rather than religious functions and therefore non-controversial even if, occasionally, the content derives from the Holy Qur'an, include *qasidah, berzanji, marhaban* and *nasyid*.

Zikir

Several varieties of *zikir* or *berdikir*, which have been developed in more elaborate ways throughout the Islamic world, also exist in Malaysia. Some of the well-known 'Beautiful Names of Allah' (*al-asma-ul-husna*) or carefully selected phrases, particularly the attestation of the faith (*ashhadu Allah ilaha il Allah Muhammadur Rasul Allah*: There is no god but Allah and Muhammad is the messenger of Allah), are presented in diverse rhythmic patterns, often with accompanying body language. Several important styles of zikir are practised in Malaysia, the content and manner being dictated by the different Sufi movements found in the country. Zikir is also presented as the opening section of Dabus performances (above) in which religious chanting is done to the accompaniment of frame drums, gongs, and barrel drums. Other vocal musical forms connected with zikir include Rodat and Hadrah. Rodat is active in several states but is principally associated with Terengganu. Hadrah, active in Kedah and Perlis as a theatre form, started off as a form of zikir singing. One form of zikir, totally secularized, is Dikir Barat, performed in Kelantan (left).

Non-religious vocal music

The non-religious forms of vocal music include *syair* and *nazam*. The word syair itself and its structure comes from Arabic, Persian and Urdu literature, in which the form remains important to this day, as in Urdu lyric poetry and in particular in the romantic Ghazal, which developed from the 13th century. In form Ghazal consists of stanzas of four rhyming lines which principally deal with the theme of love—mundane or mystical—but with material that may come from fantasy, religion, or even history. Its most striking aspect is the manner in which it is presented, with or without musical accompaniment. Traditionally Ghazal was spontaneously improvised rather than fully written.

In addition to its essentially love themes the syair may be intended to teach a particular aspect of religion in a pleasant manner, to give advice or to serve as a vehicle of instruction. Ghazal also exists in Malay culture, and is active principally in the state of Johor (see 'Ghazal'). The Ghazal texts are originally believed to have come from the Middle East. But here the emphasis has shifted from the literary to the musical aspects of the genre. Nazam is a longer poem again containing some teaching, and presented without musical accompaniment.

Religious vocal music

Of the types of vocal music containing religious themes, the qasidah is the most important. This in fact is a long epic poem, the Poem of the Mantle by Sharafuddin Muhammad Al-Busiri (circa 1212–1295), the recital of which is sometimes to bring about miraculous cures.

Marhaban

Literally meaning 'welcome', the most important of the songs in this genre was composed to welcome Prophet Muhammad to Medina when he migrated with a small group of his earliest followers from Mecca to escape persecution. This event, the *hijrah*, marks the beginning of the Islamic Hijrah calendar.

The text of the *marhaban* contains praise of or salutations to the Prophet. Normal invocations praising the Prophet are incorporated into daily supplications (*doa*) following the prayers (*salaat*). Although these may at times be recited in a rhythmic manner, particularly by an assembly of worshippers, the recital does not take on any musical character. As a general rule, groups recite the marhaban while seated (pictured below), but stand at certain points of the recital to indicate respect for the Prophet.

Recitals begin with *salawat*, standard phrases invoking Allah to bless the prophet, his family and his companions, the earliest of the Muslims. These praises are done in keeping with the passages in the Holy Qur'an exhorting that such a thing be done, as for instance in the following verse:

Lo Allah and His angels shower blessings on the Prophet
O you who believe, ask for blessings on him
And salute him with a worthy salutation. (33: 56).

Many different texts are used for such purposes, and once again, gatherings of this sort are called *maulud*. Recitals are done by separate groups of men and women, usually without musical accompaniment, although most of the popular renditions of the original welcoming song are done to the accompaniment of hand-held, single-faced *rebana* drums. The most famous of the marhaban texts has been translated and sung in English by Yusuf Islam, the former Cat Stevens. The song opens with the following verse:

O the White Moon rose over us
From the Valley of Wada'
And we owe it to show gratefulness
Where the call is to Allah

Berzanji is a literary style or composition relating the life story of the Prophet Muhammad through an epic song. The Malay version of the texts recited possibly reached the Malays through Arabic and Urdu. This is usually presented during celebrations marking the birthday of the Prophet, and as such the name of the genre is sometimes changed to *mawlid* or *maulud*. The text comes from the Kitab Berzanji, composed originally by someone named Ja'afar who hailed from the village of Berzanj. The Kitab Berzanji is sometimes referred to as an epic. Its recitation in rhythmic form is done by groups of men and women, particularly during the month of Rabi-ul-awal commemorating the birth of the Prophet in 571 CE. Such recitals take place in mosques and prayer houses as well as in private residences.

The nasyid is an Arabic-Malay style of song again containing lyrics of a religious character. Traditionally monophonic in character, it is sung in a call-and-response manner to the accompaniment of a chorus and music, once again provided by the *rebana*. Nasyid groups tend to be bigger than those for other genres of vocal music, and the themes of nasyid are connected with the life of the Prophet as well as with general Islamic teachings. Recent years have seen a proliferation of nasyid groups producing imaginative nasyid in imitation of popular songs in styles that are more liberal and flexible, giving the artistes more freedom with harmony. The best-known of these groups in Malaysia is Raihan, which presents nasyid in English, Malay and Arabic, and which has earned an international reputation.

Berzanji **is one of the most common and traditionally practised religious vocal genres. It is a recitation of a composition relating Prophet Muhammad's life story through an epic song.**

LEFT: Towards the end of the 20th century, *nasyid* developed into newer styles, imitating popular commercial songs. Two of Malaysia's better known nasyid pop groups are Hijjaz (top) and Rabbani (bottom).

Zapin

Zapin is a dance form that combines both Middle Eastern and Malay elements. Introduced into Peninsular Malaysia by Arab communities who settled in the state of Johor before the 14th century, Zapin has since been transformed from a participatory and flexible village form of dance, performed only by men, to a more rigidly stylized form of expression in Malaysian popular culture.

Contemporary Zapin often incorporates fancy footwork and hand movements.

Origins of Zapin

Zapin developed from the dance traditions of the Hadhramis (the Arabs of Hadhramaut) who came to the region initially to trade and then to settle. The Arabic tradition of singing, prancing, hand clapping, jumping, yodelling and striking hand-held drums during wedding processions fascinated the Malays to whom it epitomized not only the Arabic way of life but also that of Islamic culture.

Experimental choreography has given Zapin a more stylized form.

The Malay communities in Peninsular Malaysia, as well as in other parts of the region (Singapore, the Riau Islands and Sumatra), selectively adapted and assimilated elements of the Arabic *zaffan* to create their own dance form, known in various dialects, as Dana, Zafin, Zapin, Japin and Jipin. They also toned down the more robust and energetic elements of the dance—big stepping motions, high skips and jumps, wide arm sways and exaggerated stooping and bending of the upper torso—and introduced more controlled movements. The singing of a monotonous refrain and the rhythmic clapping of the onlookers were replaced by a medley of Malay and Arabic verses sung to the accompaniment of the *gambus*, the local version of the Arabic *o'ud*, and small, hand-held drums. The music ensemble gradually expanded to include a single-headed long drum, violin and harmonium or accordion.

Musical and vocal accompaniment

The most distinctive musical instrument accompanying the Zapin dance is the pear-shaped, six-stringed lute (*gambus*), derived from the Middle Eastern *o'ud*. Other instruments include a number of cylindrical, double-headed hand drums (*marwas*), a long drum (*dok*), which sets the pace and acts as the time marker, a harmonium or accordion, and a violin. The solo vocal accompaniment is in the form of *pantun* sung either in Malay or in a mixture of Malay and Arabic verses. The Arabic verses are usually recited as exclamations at the end of a pantun stanza or interjected between complete quatrains.

1. Harmonium 2. *Gambus* 3. *Dok* 4. Violin 5. *Marwas*

Islamic influences

Zapin is not only associated with the Middle East, but also with Islam. Dance is not encouraged in Islam, but dance and music are part of secular Muslim celebrations such as weddings and festivals. Both the dance movements and the music of Zapin display Islamic ethics as well as elements from visual art. In accordance with the Islamic code of segregating men and women, Zapin was for a long time performed exclusively by males, while women were relegated to the passive role of spectators.

Islamic influences are also seen in the structure of the dance itself which is highly stylized. There are no overtly realistic dance gestures. Instead, the dance motifs are predominantly inspired by the movements of animals and plants. An exception is when the dancers trace letters from the Arabic alphabet with their feet as they form dance motifs and sequences. The symmetrical, repetitive dance motifs within a prescribed floor plan also invoke the idea of a continuous arabesque pattern.

The use of musical instruments consisting of the gambus, which is played by the vocal soloist, the hand drums and the long drum also give Zapin a Middle Eastern flavour.

Secular influences

The popularity of Bangsawan (a staged musical drama incorporating dialogue, songs, music and dances) in the 1930s and 1940s was partly responsible for introducing Zapin to the Malays in other parts of Peninsular Malaysia and for providing new venues for Zapin performances. In the interval between scenes in Bangsawan performances, the audience were treated to songs and dances ('extra-turns'), including Zapin, which was performed on stage by both men and women in pairs or in groups. Bangsawan choreographers also drew on Zapin for

Dance movements in contemporary Zapin

Zapin is a highly stylized four-beat dance form which emphasizes footwork. Hand and arm gestures act as a balance while reflecting movements from nature and the environment—the movements of birds, fish, bats, chickens—and humans doing daily chores. The arms may be swung freely or held, one in front, the other behind, with the palms loosely open or clenched with a protruding index finger elegantly curved. Although each dance motif can be performed separately, more commonly two rows of men (and, nowadays, women) in single file dance opposite each other. Performers enter the dance area in a single file or in double rows and present a salutation to the musical prelude or *taksim*, played by the *gambus* player. A set of predetermined dance steps is repeatedly performed throughout the length of the accompanying music and singing. Zapin is performed in numerous styles, but all feature basic steps, turns, and standing and squatting positions in sequences that are repeated. Depicted here are the steps of Zapin Melayu.

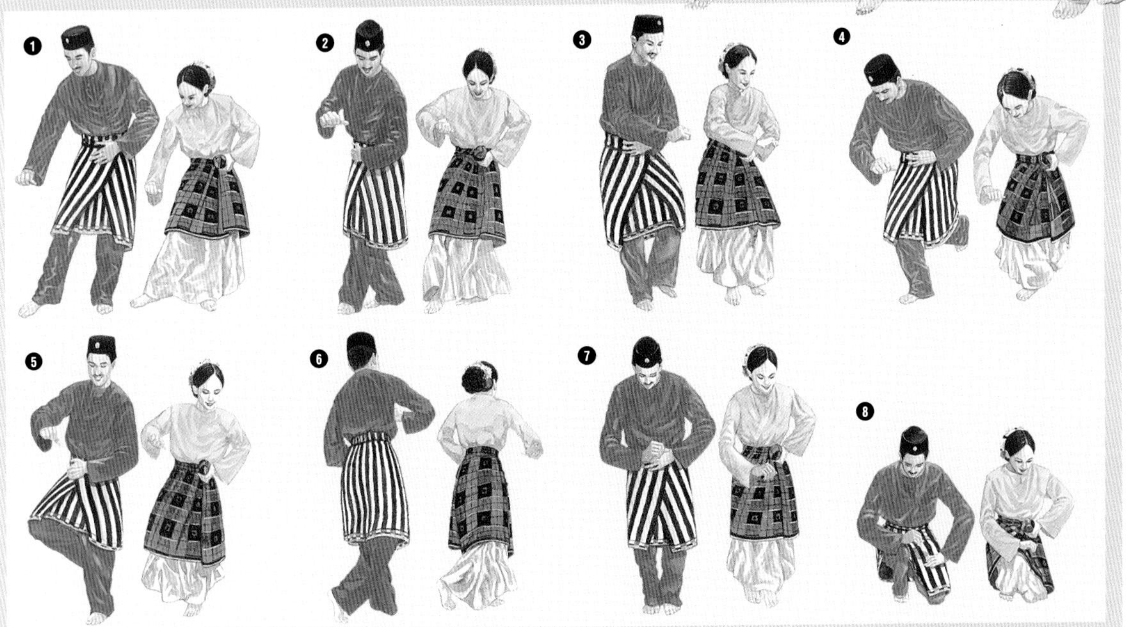

dance repertoire in the religious and Middle Eastern stories enacted by the troupe.

The establishment of dance stages, cabarets and dance halls in urban entertainment parks in the 1930s not only facilitated public dancing, but also established new trends in performing Malay folk dances, including Zapin. From the 1930s, movie directors in the fledgling Malay film industry drew on Zapin and other folk dances and music traditions when choreographing for the screen. Stories and plots introduced into the cinema from India were made palatable to Malay audiences by combining them with elements of dance and music from Malay folk traditions. Zapin, in particular, underwent a period of profoundly creative choreography. New dance motifs, performed by well-known film stars, and even chorus lines, were eagerly imitated, changing the course of Zapin from a folk tradition into a popular genre. Fancy footwork and hand movements, as well as improvised movements of the head and torso, became the norm. The genre came to be used extensively as a dance and musical idiom in a wide variety of contexts, from Malay classical stories to modern Malay tragedies.

Today, Zapin has become a dance to be viewed rather than one inviting popular participation. It may be seen as an accompanying dance routine in television entertainment programmes or as part of cultural performances and social festivities. Although traditional forms may still be seen, particularly in Johor, Pahang, Terengganu, Perak, Sabah and Sarawak, the new Zapin has shed much of its original dance style to include more experimental choreography, larger floor plans, new musical compositions and modern costuming. Both the old and new Zapin exist alongside one another, the former in villages and through rejuvenation as a state folk dance in Johor, the latter as one of Malaysia's national folk dances.

The Yayasan Warisan Johor (Johor Heritage Trust) actively promotes Zapin and produces video compact discs for the purpose.

Left: **Zapin is a popular dance especially in Johor, even among young children.**

Borea

Borea as a theatre style reached Penang in the mid-19th century. It is believed to derive from Shia Islamic passion plays performed during the Muslim month of Muharram to commemorate the martyrs of Kerbala. Originally incorporating chanting, processions and self-flagellations, these highly dramatic passion plays were adapted to create a form of secular theatre, choric in presentation with a lead singer.

Meanings of Borea

The term Borea refers to a mat or carpet on which grieved mourners or chanters would sit frenziedly wailing and crying during Muharram whilst commemorating the valour, heroic deeds and martyrdom of Caliph Ali, his sons and their families. Borea also means sack-cloth in Urdu and several other north Indian languages. As a linguistic term and as a theatre genre, the term is said to derive from Buhri or Bohri, the name of an Indian Muslim Shia community actively involved in early Borea in Penang.

TOP: Contemporary Borea performances are choric, with a lead singer, and include dances and modern bands.

BOTTOM: The lead singer's lyrics are made up of quatrains and poetic passages with social messages.

Background

Two possible dates for the arrival of Borea in Penang are generally given—1845 or 1874. The credit for its development goes to Muslims of Shia origin from North India belonging to the Indian Sepoy regiments based in Penang. Members of these regiments were in fact the earliest performers.

At the early stage, Borea activities consisted of costume parades with strolling minstrels singing songs connected with the martyrdom at Kerbala, drawing carts decorated with model tombs (*tabut*), and collecting donations. Although some elementary form of passion drama (*taziya*) seems to have been performed during the early days of Borea in Penang, this tradition did not last long. Religious drama eventually gave way entirely to secular plays. Similarly, secular songs in praise of wealthy patrons such as local merchants took the place of religious songs.

This reshaping of Borea's performance style was inevitable due to the small and diminishing number of Shia Muslims. The change also meant that non-Shia Muslims, especially those belonging to Tamil-speaking and mixed Indo-Malay (Jawi-Peranakan) communities, could now take part in Borea. These groups also became the principal presenters or organizers of Borea. In other states Borea is known but never performed. It remains a uniquely Penang art form.

Structure

Performances were divided into two sections—the day-time procession, called *kuli kalin*, and the night-time theatre performance. Participants in kuli kalin wore masks or painted their faces in various designs. Their costumes consisted of robes modelled upon sack-cloth garments characteristic of early Borea, and hats, often oddly shaped. With the secularization of this genre, Borea became a choric presentation with a lead singer (*tukang karang*) who also composes the quatrains and recites the poetic passages. He is accompanied by a chorus.

Full-length plays were generally not a feature of Borea, while comic sketches, with no well-defined functions, were presented. The costumes developed for this style of Borea were at times copies of military uniforms, while for comic sketches, normal costumes of Penang's many races were utilized.

In Malaysia, Borea remains characteristically and typically a choric performance. Dance movements or gestures are included and large modern bands accompany performances. Thus, from a religious activity, Borea has been moulded into a totally secular solo and chorus singing style. Performances grace special occasions such as birthdays of celebrities or public holidays. Borea competitions are occasionally held in Penang.

TOP: A modern Borea performance featuring participants in Western costume.

BOTTOM LEFT: Borea performances of the early 20th century included a day-time procession in which participants donned masks and wore sack-cloth robes.

A Borea procession making its way through George Town in Penang in the early 1900s.

Innovations

Innovations introduced into Borea over the decades include a platform or proscenium stage. Processional Borea has, as a result, died out, and even open-air staging has become rare. The original Indo-Persian music was replaced by Arab-Malay music played by such instruments as the frame drum (*rebana*), gongs, and *gambus* (*o'ud*). The use of Keroncong music later became fashionable, and following World War I came the involvement of women as singers and dancers. Western musical instruments, including the guitar, the ukulele, the flute and the bongo drums eventually came to replace traditional Malay instruments. Contemporary Borea groups make use of Indian, Western, as well as traditional Malay instruments in eclectic combination.

Unlike early Borea troupes which consisted of 40 or more performers, a contemporary one typically consists of one tukang karang, a dozen persons—male, female or mixed—constituting the chorus. Female impersonation, a necessity in the early days due to social restrictions prohibiting women on stage, has been retained as convention, its principal objective being that of heightening comedy.

Performers at one time wore a mixture of costume styles—Western, Middle-Eastern, Chinese, Indian and Malay. Such a mixture is seldom seen these days. The tukang karang is always clothed resplendently. The other members of the troupe, known as sailors, wear pants, with a clear preference for white ones, shirts and sashes. The women usually dress in the *sarung kebaya*, consisting of a long-sleeved blouse and a sarong, or other traditional costumes, although modern costumes are also sometimes worn.

The tukang karang's lyrics are sung to tunes borrowed from Western, Malay and Hindustani popular music, while the dance steps are based upon popular Western dances such as the cha-cha or tango. Preferred local dance styles include Zapin, Inang or Joget.

An absence of song texts meant the tukang karang had to improvise his lyrics extempore. In recent years the use of scripts has become the norm. They are vetted and sometimes censored by government licensing bodies.

At one time, the Borea repertoire consisted of a fairly large number of plots, based upon Malay folk tales, legends and history. Foreign literary sources were also used, these reaching Borea mainly through Bangsawan. Additionally, some of the skits dealt with social problems and issues affecting the Malay community. Over the years, Borea has abandoned the use of complete plays. Even the once highly popular comic sketches are rarely used. They had served the function of entertainment, channelling government propaganda, and advertising.

On the whole, however, Borea has not given up the function of providing humour or being an agent of social criticism. The bad effects of gambling or drinking or polygamy, for instance, continue to be a concern of contemporary Borea. What has changed is the manner of presentation. In current performances, everything is contained in the lyrics of the tukang karang. The traditional function of praising the rich, the famous and the powerful is still maintained with the difference that much of the praise is these days showered upon politicians or local dignitaries.

Left: While modern Borea performances no longer feature complete plays, humour remains a function of this theatre form.

Commemorating the martyrs of Kerbala

The vital events are the deaths of Ali Ibni Abu Talib, the fourth caliph of Islam, who was the Prophet's cousin as well as son-in-law, and Ali's two sons, al-Hassan and al-Hussein. Ali was murdered on his way to a mosque in Kufa in 661 and al-Hassan died in 669, possibly as a result of poisoning. The most tragic of the deaths was that of al-Hussein, who was beheaded at Kerbala close to Kufa, by followers of Yazid, son of Muawiyah, whose claims to the caliphate resulted in the killing of Ali in the first place. This took place on the 10th of Muharram, the first month of the Muslim calendar. Among Shia Muslim communities the singing of religious songs, and the performance of dramatic passion plays based on an extensive repertoire during Muharram perpetuate the memory of these events.

1
2
3
4
5

1. Rock and other forms of popular music in Malaysia have developed their own styles.

2. Scene from *The Miser*, a play produced by Penang Players, one of the oldest theatre groups in the country.

3. *Ronggeng Rokiah*, a Malay musical staged by Istana Budaya in Noir style in a 1950s cabaret club setting.

4. One of Malaysia's leading Chinese ensembles, Dama Orchestra, in performance.

5. A contemporary dance production by prominent artiste Ramli Ibrahim.

CONTEMPORARY PERFORMING ARTS

The contemporary scene in Malaysian performing arts is an exciting one, with vibrant activity in all the disciplines of the performing arts reaching a near feverish pace, particularly in Kuala Lumpur. The proliferation of professional, semi-professional and amateur organizations has meant that there is an increasing variety of performances available for the Malaysian audience, demonstrating a desire for variety and better quality productions, harking back to and utilizing the traditional in new ways, while also taking bold steps in new directions. One of the more exciting outcomes of such an approach has been the greater number of fusion productions amalgamating not only Western elements and the different genres, but also features from the rich heritage of cultures found in Peninsular Malaysia, Sabah and Sarawak.

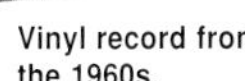

Vinyl record from the 1960s.

Indeed, with the new sense of discovery and the opportunities that have increasingly become available during the half century since Independence, and particularly since the 1970s, activities involving fusion and cross-cultural approaches have increased in pace. Individual talents—directors, actors, dancers and musicians—particularly from amongst the younger generation, have in many instances come into their own, some receiving international exposure as well as acclaim. Malaysian troupes have taken advantage of opportunities to travel abroad and to participate in international events. Much of this has been made possible through the generous grants and financial support that have become available for the arts from both the government and the private sector. The arts have also received stimulus from the establishment of the Akademi Seni Kebangsaan (National Arts Academy) and the Panggung Negara (National Theatre) in the 1990s. The academy has made significant contribution towards the development of traditional performing arts and contemporary dance. The overall spin-off effect of the academy has been considerable, with its graduates involved in various spheres of production. The national theatre has staged lavish productions of traditional performing genres, including the first major production of a Mak Yong play, and has also helped expose Malaysians to quality international productions.

The commercial scene in the performing arts has been equally active with the development of numerous local groups and companies, as well as local recording labels. Similarly, there has been considerable activity in the teaching and research of performing arts. Academic programmes in the performing arts are now available in several universities. Serious attention is thus being devoted to both teaching and research, resulting in an increasing consciousness for better and more professional productions, and more systematic documentation and research.

Contemporary dance in Malaysia is an evolving form, a fusion of classical traditions and indigenous elements.

Contemporary Malay drama

Modern Malay drama grew out of the struggle for independence in the 1950s. Early Malay writers created drama based on the history of their homeland and used it to inspire nationalism. Later events led Malay playwrights to reassess and reinterpret their role in society. Over the past 30 years dramatists have experimented with various forms and styles, incorporating elements from traditional arts, foreign cultures and other media to arrive at a distinct Malaysian identity in contemporary Malay theatre.

1. *Raja Lawak*, a 1992 comedy by Zakaria Ariffin. 2. Anwar Ridhwan's 1992 play *Yang Menjelma dan Menghilang*. 3. *Kerusi—Suatu Adaptasi*, adapted

Sandiwara

Malay drama began in the 1950s as Sandiwara. It replaced the Bangsawan theatre in terms of audience appeal and performances. Sandiwara dealt with historical themes, Malay legends and contemporary society. The aim was to remind the Malays of their history prior to colonization, and to instil and incite nationalistic feelings. Sandiwara playwrights used non-realism techniques of traditional theatre and Western classical drama, but the tendency was towards realism. Two of the foremost Sandiwara playwrights were Shahrom Hussein and Kalam Hamidy. Shahrom's most popular play, *Si Bongkok Tanjung Puteri* ('The Hunchback of Tanjung Puteri') (1956), was based on history and oral folklore, and looked at personal freedom and justice in a feudal society. Shahrom maintained the traditional elements of dance and use of *pantun* (quatrains), but the structure of his play was closer to modern drama than the loose episodic nature of Bangsawan.

Megat Terawis by Fatimah bte Abd Wahab was the first script to be printed in 1950. It had its sources in the oral tradition, depicting the heroism of a Malay warrior during the Aceh-Perak war of 1579.

Realism and social drama

Contemporary drama that developed in the early 1960s took after the realism plays that were popular in the West at the time. The works of Mustapha Kamal Yassin, Awang Had Salleh and Usman Awang portrayed contemporary life and revolved around issues faced by society after independence.

An important element of realism drama is its social message. In the early 1950s, a literary movement called Angkatan Sastera 50 was formed by young Malay writers such as Keris Mas, Usman Awang and A. Samad Said. The movement's motto was art for society, its purpose to eradicate social injustices. These writers chose ordinary people as their characters, used everyday speech and addressed problems that the audience could identify with. Most of the scenes took place in the living room, where debates over marriage and career were played out. The theme was almost always the conflict between urban and *kampung* (village) values and lifestyles.

Mustapha, who is credited with pioneering Malay realistic drama, wrote the memorable comedy satire *Atap Genting Atap Rembia* ('Tiled Roof, Thatched Roof') (1963). It revolved around class differences, portrayed in a love story between a rich city girl and a poor village boy. Mustapha imbued his characters with eccentricity and frivolity, showing that village folk had as much destructive pride as city dwellers.

Usman Awang's works such as *Serunai Malam* ('Flute of the Night') reflected his concern for the spirit of development and progress, while A. Samad Said wrote *Di Mana Bulan Selalu Retak* ('Where the Moon Always Cracks'), a play about human behaviour as being the result of a person's environment. He dramatized life in the slums of the 1960s, showing how unemployment turned a young former soldier who felt betrayed by society into an angry man.

In the post-war years, when Asian nations began to achieve independence, writers resolved to uproot Western colonialism. Later they sought to inspire society to respond to the challenge of change, and dedicated their work to the building of society.

Experimental drama of the 1970s

The 1970s marked a new era in the development of modern Malay drama with the staging of Noordin Hassan's *Bukan Lalang Di Tiup Angin* ('Tis Not the Grass That's Blown by the Wind). He abandoned the trend of realism, employing instead a more theatrical concept, filling the stage with symbols and abstract images. Noordin also used traditional theatrical elements such as music, song and dance, combining them with fantasy elements to dramatize his theme—the root cause of poverty among Malay

from Hatta Azad Khan's play *Kerusi* and staged by Universiti Sains Malaysia students in 2003. **4.** *Tok Perak*, staged by playwright Syed Alwi in 1972.

farmers and peasants. The play was his response to the political situation at the time, in particular the racial disturbances of 13 May 1969, which became a turning point in Malaysian history. Playwrights of this period, among them Noordin, Johan Jaafar and Syed Alwi directed their work at the Malay identity, reflecting the need for Malays to re-examine their aspirations and take pride in their national identity. They found realism too restrictive a style to address the complex problems of society, and experimented with new forms and presentation styles. Such experimental theatre was to engender the unique identity of Malay drama. Syed Alwi was the first playwright to use the multimedia theatre concept, blending theatre with film and photography. His play *Alang Rentak Seribu* ('Alang and his Myriad Ways'), which he wrote in 1973 as part of a trilogy with *Desaria* ('Country Joy') and *Z:OO – M 1984,* was produced by the Malaysian Arts Theatre Group under the direction of Krishen Jit. It was a thought-provoking play, addressing issues such as unity.

Anti-realism plays

A group of young, dynamic and educated dramatists emerged in the mid-1970s and excited the drama scene with their application of Noordin's theatrical concept in a more fervent way. Johan Jaafar, Hatta Azad Khan, Mana Sikana, Dinsman and Dr Anuar Nor Arai used experimentation to highlight the uneasiness of the post-1969 Malaysian society.

Their plays were anti-realistic in content and structure. Most of these playwrights adopted an anti-establishment stance, their plays emerging during a period of heightened student activities and street demonstrations in support of social and political causes. Johan, for instance, dealt with an unbalanced social system, exploitation and human suffering in *Angin Kering* ('Dry Wind') and *Kotaku O Kotaku* ('My City O My City'). Similarly, Hatta protested against social injustices in his allegorical plays *Kerusi* ('Chair') and *Patung-patung* ('Puppets'). Dinsman, on the other hand, did not address social concerns, exploring instead the existential level of human existence, as did Mana Sikana and Anuar.

New trends and modernism

The 1980s brought new trends in modern Malay drama. Playwrights turned to the traditional arts for inspiration. Noordin, for instance, assimilated Islamic elements in a theatre form called *teater fitrah* (religious theatre). His plays, *Tiang Seri Tegak Berlima* and *1400,* focused on religion as a solution to society's problems.

Zakaria Ariffin's *Pentas Opera* ('Opera Stage'), written in 1989, and *Perempuan Seorang Leftenan Inggeris* ('An English Lieutenant's Woman') were nostalgic plays about an era in Malaysian history: after the withdrawal of the British, the Japanese Occupation in Malaya prior to the bombing of Hiroshima. Depicting the influence of the Japanese Occupation on the social and political history of the country, both focused on the life and hardships of Bangsawan troupes, and how history marked the end of this theatre genre. Khalid Salleh's plays, meanwhile, were almost always criticisms of the local political-social situation. In *Bereng-bereng*, he urged his countrymen to be more critical and not to be blind followers. In 1990, Anwar Ridhwan brought a new style of realism, fantasy and symbolism to Malay theatre with *Orang-orang Kecil* and *Yang Menjelma dan Menghilang*. Both were allegories and criticized the social-political system, portraying man as power crazy, materialistic and opportunistic. About a decade later Faisal Tehrani emerged to show a new modernistic consciousness in *Angin Madinah* and *Misi*, the latter a multi-layered play about power, corruption and revenge.

Towards the end of the 20th century, Malay theatre groups began receiving assistance and support from organizations such as the Malaysian National Theatre Council. The establishment of the National Arts Academy (Akademi Seni Kebangsaan) in 1994 and the opening of the National Theatre (Istana Budaya) in 1999 have also augured well for Malay drama, the former nurturing budding playwrights and directors, and the latter staging a variety of theatrical productions, including musicals.

Syajar produced by Universiti Kebangsaan Malaysia students at a theatre festival organized by the Malaysian Universities Cultural Council in Kuala Lumpur in 2003.

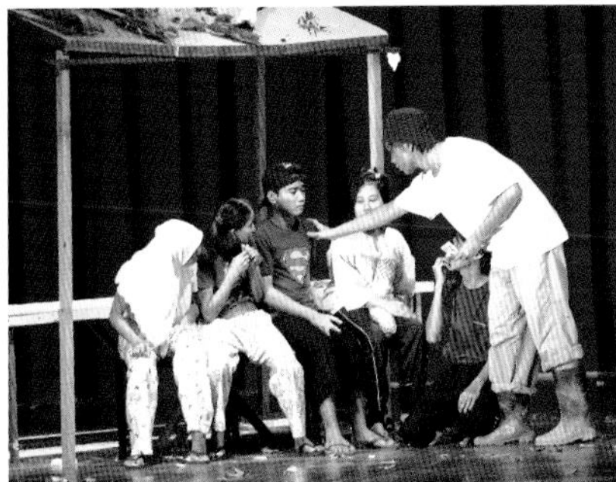

Fitrah dan Takdir was presented by students from the Multimedia Universiti at the festival.

Dalam Kehadiran Sofea, staged by the Budayasari Dance Theatre of Penang in 2003, was written and directed by Razali Ridzuan, who used prostitution as his theme to illustrate futility in a world of spiritual degradation and material entrapment.

English drama

English language theatre in Malaysia had its beginnings more than 50 years ago, and over the decades has been shaped and defined by the social and political events in the nation's development. An early drama scene largely influenced by historical experience as a British colony has engendered a lively theatre environment, reflecting 21st-century modernity and the multi-culturalism of a developing nation.

Pioneer playwrights

Edward Dorall

K. Das

Syed Alwi

Lee Joo For

ABOVE: A scene from *Henry V*, produced by the Malayan Arts Theatre Group in 1953, starring playwright Syed Alwi.

FAR RIGHT: Penang Amateur Dramatic Society, circa 1908.

1950–1960s

In the 1950s and 1960s, one theatre group in particular, the Malayan Arts Theatre Group, made up mostly of expatriates, had an impact on the local drama scene with its productions of Shakespeare, Shaw, Wilde and Ibsen. In the period from Independence in 1957 to the mid-1960s, early playwrights among English-educated Malaysians began yielding their pens and establishing for themselves an independent role in English theatre.

Most of these dramatists were inspired by a social conscience to portray the reality of the local people, sharing with their Malay-language compatriots the desire to depict the poverty that dogged society. Coupled with this was their search for a Malaysian identity as the newly independent nation attempted to build national unity. The first efforts to encourage writers to create quality, presentable scripts took place in 1965 with the launch of the Arts Council Playwriting Competition. Edward Dorall, a schoolteacher, won with his play *The Young Must Be Strong*. Dorall also wrote plays for his students to stage, such as *A Tiger is Loose in Our Community*, which looked at the restlessness and agitation of youth in an environment where children had no choice but to be bad and aggressive in order to survive. 'Tiger' was the nickname of protagonist Chan Choon Hoong, a leader of hard-core criminals.

While Dorall's plays had an underlying social theme, he attempted at the same time to create a Malaysian cultural landscape through his use of speech and language. His characters engaged in real-life conversations and argued in bad grammar, their sentences liberally punctuated with Malay and Chinese phrases. Patrick Yeoh, too, used everyday language in *The Need To Be*, his script interspersed with Malay and Cantonese phrases. These dramatists felt that a realistic portrayal of Malaysian life necessitated the use of authentic speech as spoken by the man on the street. Lee Joo For, however, left issues of social injustice to his peers, preferring instead to explore campus unrest in America and themes of non-violence, intrigue and the atomic explosion in *Nero Has Arisen in Malaya*, *Explosion and Four Left* and *Son of Zen*.

Late 1960s–early 1970s

In 1967, a group of Malaysians led by Syed Alwi and K. Das took over the Malaysian Arts Theatre Group. Their first production was *Lela Mayang*, an adaptation of a Bangsawan tale, in 1968. It was also the first joint effort by Malay-language and English-language playwrights. The group later produced *All The Perfumes* by K. Das and Syed Alwi's *The More We Get Together* that he wrote as a student in the United States. Syed Alwi also scripted *Going North* in 1965, set in the time of the Emergency (1948–1960).

In his 1994 play *We Could **** You, Mr Birch* Kee Thuan Chye used the Brechtian technique of letting his actors step out of their historical characters to address the audience directly and in so doing, drove home his point that history is subject to interpretation by those with vested interests.

RIGHT: A scene from *The Trees* written by Malik Imtiaz Sarwar in 1997, and produced by the Actors Studio the same year.

The proliferation of English-language plays in the late 1960s was stymied in the following decade, when contemporary Malay theatre gained popularity with Malaysian urbanites. This was due in part to the fostering of Malay culture by the government in the aftermath of the racial riots of 13 May 1969. There was increased emphasis on the use of the national language and the promotion of Malay culture, which affected all aspects of Malaysian life, including theatre. In 1971 the National Educational Policy was introduced and with it, Malay replaced English as the medium of instruction in schools.

In such a scenario, theatre groups pursued their art in the spirit of nationalism and the quest for identity. Syed Alwi turned to writing Malay plays, and theatre groups staged Western plays in Malay,

English Theatre Groups

Group/Company	Founders	Year
Malayan Arts Theatre Group	Expatriates	1952
Penang Players	Expatriates	Early 1950s
Lidra, Universiti Malaya	UM students	1959
Angkatan Sasaran, Universiti Sains Malaysia	USM students	Early 1970s
KL Theatre Club	Shuhaimi Baba, Norma Nordin & Mustapha Nor	Early 1970s
Phoenix 61	Chin San Sooi	1980s
Kami	Kee Thuan Chye, Thor Kah Hong, Faridah Ibrahim & Sabera Shaik	1981
Five Arts Centre	Krishen Jit, Chin San Sooi, Marion D'Cruz & Anne James	1984
Actors Studio	Faridah Merican & Joe Hasham	1989
Instant Café Theatre	Jo Kukathas, Jit Murad, Andrew Leci & Zahim Albakri	1989
Kuali Works	Ann Lee & Karen Quah	1994
Drama Lab	Zahim Albakri, Jit Murad & Uria Oliveiro-Kirchuebel	1994
East 100 Theatre	Kannan Menon & Girija Nair	1990s

giving them a Malaysian treatment in terms of plot, set, characters and cultural traits. Chin San Sooi, one of the few dramatists who was producing English plays during this period, looked to the traditional arts for inspiration and subject matter. In 1977, he wrote and directed *Lady White*, a retelling of the popular myth about Lady White Snake. While the story has Chinese origins, Chin used Wayang Kulit music in his production. Drawing on the heritage of Malaysia's multi-ethnic population, he created a unique modern Malaysian theatre, writing and directing *Yap Ah Loy* and musicals such as *Morning Into Night*, *Reunion* and *O Brickfields/KL Sentral.*

Stella Kon wrote futuristic plays such as *To Hatch A Swan* and *Z is for Zygote*. She also wrote a musical drama, *The Bridge*, in which she used the traditional *Ramayana* protagonists, Rama and Sita, in a modern story about drug addicts struggling to find themselves and a way out of their addiction. *The Bridge*, which was presented by the inmates of a drug rehabilitation centre, fused elements of Western drama and Asian theatre, and was experimental in nature, mixing masks, mime, dance and music.

It was during the lull in English drama that Ghulam-Sarwar Yousof, a literature lecturer at Universiti Sains Malaysia, wrote and staged *Halfway Road, Penang* in 1971, in which characters from the lower income group grappled with social problems. He went on to write *Golden Lotus* in 1974 and *The Trial of Hang Tuah the Great* in 1980.

1980s onwards

The dearth of English drama continued into the 1980s before enjoying a resurgence towards the end of the decade. In 1983, K. S. Maniam scripted *The Cord*, one of the few plays written by a Malaysian Indian about Indians. Maniam's characters were rural Indians in the plantation sector. Kee Thuan Chye wrote and staged politically charged plays *1984 Here and Now* in 1985 and *The Big Purge* in 1988, both dealing with the detentions of dissenters, and *We Could **** You, Mr Birch* in 1994, that was inspired by the 1875 murder of British Resident J. W. Birch and which Kee turned into a comment on issues of the day. Syed Alwi, who resumed writing English plays in the 1990s, scripted *I Remember the Rest House*.

Theatre companies set up in the 1980s have kept English drama alive since. They produce plays, and train and nurture actors, designers and directors. The new breed of playwrights deal with a range of issues in various forms of artistic expression and have created a truly Malaysian theatre. Among them are writer-actor-director Huzir Sulaiman, who produced *Atomic Jaya* in 1998, a political satire of a nation caught up in the mania of mega projects, and first staged as a monodrama. Other leading playwrights include Jit Murad, Malik Imtiaz Sarwar, Bernice Chauly, Amir Muhammad, Mira Mustaffa, Dina Zaman and Mahani Gunnel.

A scene from *Yap Ah Loy*, written by Chin San Sooi in 1985 and produced by Five Arts Centre.

Penang Players productions

1

2

4

Penang Players, one of the oldest theatre groups in the country, has produced a variety of plays, including:
1. *Antigone*, 1977.
2 & 3. *The Battle of Coxinga*, 1977.
4. *Six Characters in Search of an Author*, 2001.

Chinese and Tamil drama

Chinese and Tamil drama were brought to Malaysia in the early 20th century by immigrants—traders, merchants and indentured labourers. Both theatre forms initially adhered closely to, and were influenced by, cultural developments in their country of origin. They underwent almost similar phases of development in the years leading up to World War II, and in the post-Independence years paralleled the development of Malay and English drama in Malaysia, sharing themes influenced by historical and social circumstances, and incorporating elements from local as well foreign cultures.

A joint production by Dan Dan Theatre Productions and Sisyphus Theatre entitled *Shall We Off....?* that was invited to a theatre festival in Tokyo in 2001.

Scenes from Chinese drama of the 1970s: (Top) *Qiao Qian Zhi Xi* ('The Happiness of Moving') and (bottom) *Yuan Ye* ('Wild Field') produced by the Dramatic Arts Society.

Brochure of *Hang Li Po*, produced by the Dramatic Arts Society in 1971.

Chinese drama

Chinese drama activities in Malaysia began in 1919, and in the 1920s–30s reflected domestic issues and developments in China, often responding to movements and campaigns launched on the mainland. Plays were staged mostly for charitable purposes, such as raising funds for storm and flood victims in China. Dramatists wrote against feudalism, aggression and appealed to overseas Chinese to save China. The most active drama group at the time was the Ren Jing Ci Shan Bai Hua Ju She (Ren Jing Drama Society), led by dramatists such as Leong Chi Seng, Deng Ruqin and Xie Linyao. Leong, considered the most prominent playwright at the time, staged *Can Zhong Can* ('The Tragic Within Tragic') in 1920, *She Hui Guai Xiang* ('The Sickness of Society') in 1923, and *Fu Gui* ('The Return of Father') in 1929.

A scene from *Hui Niang Goes to School*, produced by Do Do Children's Theatre.

When the Pacific War broke out in 1941, dramatists used nationalism as their theme, appealing to people to join forces to protect Malaya, although their works lacked aesthetic appeal, and were generally crude productions. Post-World War II drama was increasingly less China-centric. Playwrights such as Guan Xinyi and Song Ren focused on the local situation, addressing socio-economic problems facing the people, including inflation, unemployment and poverty. In the 1950s, their attention was directed at similar social circumstances and contained elements of anti-communism and patriotism. Their plays often depicted the friendship between the Chinese and the other races, and theatre became a platform to convey messages of inter-ethnic cooperation, goodwill and unity.

In 1963, Leong and other playwrights formed the Dramatic Arts Society. The society staged a number of plays based on legendary Chinese scripts such as *Lei Yu* ('Thunderstorm') in 1963, *Qu Yuan* ('Resting Garden') in 1968, *Yuan Ye* ('Wild Field') in 1979 and a Chinese operetta *Hang Li Po* in 1971. The society, credited with laying the foundations of modern Chinese drama in Malaysia, began conducting drama training courses in 1975. It remains an influential force in Chinese drama circles.

In 1988, the Malaysian Institute of Art established a Diploma of Drama course (conducted in Mandarin), which had a significant impact on the development of contemporary Chinese drama in Malaysia, especially with the introduction of Western literature and experimental theatre as part of the course. The institute's drama department was set up by Leong, who still serves as adviser to the Dramatic Arts Society. Graduates and teachers of the institute set up a number of theatre groups in the 1990s that have been at the forefront of Chinese drama since, producing plays and offering training in acting, directing, production and scriptwriting. In 1993, a group of the institute's graduates formed the Theatre Education Foundation with the aim of generating interest in drama activities among Chinese secondary school students.

In 2001, the country's first Chinese children's theatre—Do Do Children's Theatre—was set up by Happy Kee, an MIA graduate who had worked with the Song Song Song Children's Theatre in Taiwan from 1998–2000. Do Do's first production was *Hui Niang Goes to School*, written and directed by Kee.

Modern Chinese drama groups

Company/Group	Directors/Producers	Productions
Dan Dan Theatre Productions (1992)	• Soon Choon Mee • Loh Kok Man • Charles Jung • Woo Guo Xiong	*Three Genarations; Aku; Love Stories* and *Cabo-Cabo.*
Sisyphus Theatre (1992)	• Leong Sook Fung • Koh Choon Eiow	*Si Shen Ku Qi De Shi Hou* (When The Dead Cried); *Zai Ri Chu Shi Zhong Jie*, (Ended When The Sun Rises).
Ping Stage Consultants & Services (1994)	• Goh You Pin • Ho Shih Phin • Sunny Ng	*Chuan Shuo Nie Zi; Tauke.*
Need Entertainment (2001)	• Ling Tang • Andrew Low	*Chup! Take a Break!*
Do Do Children's Theatre (2001)	• Happy Kee	*Hui Niang Goes to School*
O-Hi Team (2002)	• Ryon Lee • Osver Tan • Rorn Lew	*The Angles; The Sleeping Heart.*

Tamil drama

Tamil drama was first staged in Malaysia in 1910 by visiting Indian playwright-director Kalia Perumal Devar Vathiyar. These dramas were based on the Indian mythology taken from the *Ramayana* and *Mahabharata* epics, were poetic in structure and performed by actors from India. In 1929, Kalia joined his compatriots Shestari Vathiyar and Mangala Vathiyar to set up the Hindu Vinayaga Sabha, which, together with the Sangeetha Abhivirdhi Sabha formed by a group of art lovers in 1923, were the prime movers of Indian cultural activities in the country. In the ensuing years, drama troupes from India staged performances in various parts of the country, especially in estates where the Indians were mainly settled.

The popularity of Tamil drama grew in the 1930s–40s as it provided the main source of entertainment for Indian settlers. Drama productions continued to draw stories from Indian literature and mythology, and the plays were staged by societies that were formed in various parts of the country. After World War II and the Japanese Occupation, Tamil drama began experiencing significant changes. Drama was no longer based on Indian literature and local playwrights focused on nationalistic and social themes as a result of political developments in the country, and plays often contained messages of freedom and justice. Women began taking to the stage in the mid-1950s, and Tamil theatre shed its simplicity for sophisticated sets, costumes, props and make-up. Other themes popular with playwrights and audiences alike ranged from romance and friendship to comedy and murder mysteries. Titles of plays often reflected the subject matter, such as *Natpu* ('Friendship') written by K. P. Samy; *CID Segar,* a detective story co-written and directed by K. Raman and Palaniappan; *Drohi* ('Betrayer'), *Marma-kolai* ('Mysterious Murder'), *Oviyam* ('Art'), *Ithaya Thabam* ('Affairs of the Heart'), *Maranam* ('Death') and *Mottaiyan Magane* ('Bald Man's Son', a comedy).

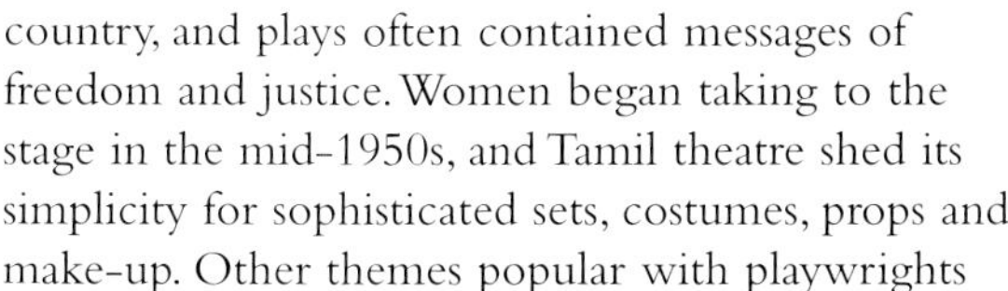

Poster of a 1970s historical drama *Kulothunga Cholan.*

In the 1960s dramatists turned their attention to the social and economic conditions of Indians, highlighting the poverty and other problems facing the community. It was also during this period that Tamil playwright-directors staged translations of popular Malay classics such as *Mahsuri* and *Hang Tuah.* At the same time, Radio Television Malaysia (RTM) began producing and airing radio dramas, which were immensely popular with listeners. In the decades that followed Tamil drama further assimilated elements from other local cultures as playwrights endeavoured to promote unity among the various ethnic groups through their work. In 1972 Azhi Aruldasan staged *Kadharam* ('Kedah'), a groundbreaking drama with dialogue in both Tamil and Malay. Meanwhile, there were also efforts to bring in foreign drama productions, notably by Rajalingam, a teacher, who arranged for India's Manohar's Drama Troupe—comprising more than 70 artistes and 200 tonnes of props—to stage 10 major theatre productions in Malaysia.

The late 1980s marked the debut of Tamil television dramas, produced by a new generation of writers and directors. Some of these playwright-directors, such as Kumar Thangaiah, were trained in India, and upon their return wrote and directed dramas for television. In 1987 Suhan Panchatcharam became the first Tamil/Malay drama director to produce a local Tamil movie, *Naan Oru Malaysian* ('I Am A Malaysian'). Since the 1990s the burgeoning television drama and film industry as well as a growing market for home videos and digital discs have been at the expense of Tamil theatre. Playwrights too, generally prefer writing for the screen rather than stage productions.

Scene from *Vivekanandar*, a drama based on Indian literature.

Scene from *Manivasagar*, also based on Indian literature.

Heroes, heroines and buffoons

Early Tamil drama featured an all-male cast, and actors often played dual-gender roles, taking the role of the male protagonist known as *Rajapart* as well as that of the female lead called *Sripart.* An actor's script comprised poetry and singing. An ensemble comprising a harmonium, tabla and mirdangam drums provided the musical accompaniment. A play almost always included comic relief between acts, and the clown's role was called *Buffoon-part.* In the 1930s–40s stage settings, props and facilities were minimal, and drama groups used simple flyers and pamphlets to advertise their shows. Actors had to depend on the power of their voices to be heard. Gasoline lights were used where electricity was not available. Tickets were priced at between 50 cents and two ringgit.

Scene from *Drohi* ('Betrayer'), produced in 1954, in which the lead male and female roles were played by men.

Prominent Tamil playwright-directors

1950s
- Guru Santhanam
- K. Raman
- Palaniappan
- K. P. Samy.

1960s

- Azhi Aruldasan
- Reh Shanmugam (top left)
- Vijayasinggam (top right)
- M. S. Maniam
- Arivananthan

These playwright-directors often acted in their own productions.

1970s
- Manu Ramalinggam
- Bairoji Narayanan

1980s

- Suhan Panchatcharam (top right)
- Reh Sha. Ananthan (top left)
- Kumar Thangaiah
- Francis Silvan
- Devarani
- Raj Kamal

1990s
- S. T. Bala
- Raj Morgan Amala Rooban

Contemporary dance

Contemporary dance in Malaysia is a fusion of classical traditions and ethnic elements. Three generations have influenced this dance movement to its present state, best described as an evolving form with a vocabulary that strives to be uniquely Malaysian. Since the 1990s, choreographers have been integrating elements from various dance traditions while exploring creative movements and improvisation. The works are often stimulated by intercultural interaction and reflect the choreographers' interpretation of the Malaysian psyche.

AWAS! **choreographed by Joseph Gonzales, merges Mak Yong dance movements with modern dance techniques.**

Pioneers of contemporary dance

Lee Lee Lan

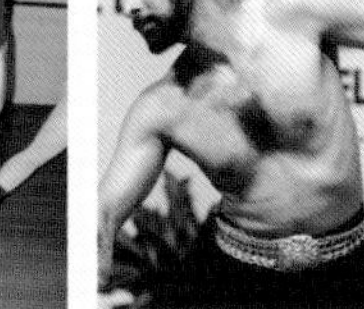

Ghouse Nasuruddin

Oh Eng Sim

Frances Teoh

BOTTOM LEFT: *Re: Lady White Snake*, choreographed by Mew Chang Tsing and Lee Swee Keong, is recognized as one of best contemporary dance performances by Malaysians.

BOTTOM RIGHT: *A Cherry Bludgeoned A Spirit Crushed* is a arrangement by Lee Swee Keong in which he experiments with multi-media and Butoh techniques.

The Pioneers

The pioneers of modern dance in Malaysia were trained in classical ballet and performed regularly in the early 1970s, appearing in television variety shows and productions organized by the Universiti Malaya and the Selangor Philharmonic Society. Among these pioneers were Lee Lee Lan, Wong Suet Lin, Frances Teoh, Peggy Lum, Oh Eng Sim, Suzan Manen and Mohammad Ghouse Nasuruddin.

Their works were mainly the reconstruction and staging of Western musicals such as *Hello Dolly, West Side Story* and *Show Boat*. There was also an effort to incorporate local cultural elements into their choreography. Oh Eng Sim, for instance, fused ballet and local styles using indigenous themes in her productions *Sang Kancil Suite* and *Manorah*. Ghouse Nasuruddin also experimented along the same lines, producing such work as *Dimanakah Pusakaku?* ('Where is my heritage?'), which marked the beginning of synthesis of Eastern and Western forms in contemporary dance.

In 1967, Lee Lee Lan established the Federal Academy of Ballet, one of the biggest dance schools in Southeast Asia. She had graduated from the Royal Academy of Dance and also studied modern dance, jazz and tap. She later founded the Kuala Lumpur Dance Theatre, which nurtured much talent, the most outstanding students being Andrew Pan and Catherine Yong who went on to pursue successful careers in ballet and contemporary dance in Europe.

The Kuala Lumpur Dance Theatre invited international choreographers to create works for the local dance scene. These choreographers—including Sean Greene from Bela Lewinsky Company, Claudio Assante from the June Lewis Company of New York and the late Anthony Then, co-founder and artistic director of the Singapore Dance Theatre—inspired the young dancers who worked with them, such as Viknendren Sivalingam, Ungku Majid, David Lee and Joseph Gonzales, all of whom pursued dance education in the United Kingdom and subsequently worked in London's West End and Europe.

A government-initiated effort in the late 1970s to develop a Malaysian cultural identity captured the imagination of dance choreographers. In 1982, Lee Lan choreographed a full-length Malay ballet *Soraya* to music by Julia Chong. It marked one of the earliest attempts to incorporate Malaysian traditions into a ballet performance. In the libretto of *Soraya*, a shaman character (similar to Rothbart in *Swan Lake*) abducts Princess Soraya and her knight rescues her. While the movements of that production were classical ballet, the finale was a medley of dances from traditional repertoire, using steps of the Tarian Lilin and Joget, Chinese and Indian dances.

The 1980s

The search for creativity, identity and original development in modern dance took off with the arrival on stage of Wong Fook Choon, the late Lari Leong, Ramli Ibrahim and Marion D'Cruz in the early 1980s. These dancers had trained abroad and returned to begin the transcultural process in Malaysian contemporary dance.

Leong, who had worked extensively in Paris, incorporated Tai Chi and Eastern philosophy into his choreography. In 1981 his dance work won first prize at the International Choreographic competition in Switzerland. His choreography for the Kuala Lumpur Dance Theatre, *Lurah*, was influenced by his love for village life and the Malaysian countryside, and incorporated gestures of typical village activities such as farming, harvesting, children's games and simple ritual ceremonies. In *A river… the sea*, set to Jean Michel Jarre's music, he created fluidity of movement and quiet energy. He was ahead of his time, working an intriguing blend of theatre and drama into his experimental productions.

Ramli Ibrahim trained in classical ballet and performed with the Sydney Dance Company before turning his focus to Indian classical dance. The fact that he is a Malay immersed in another tradition and culture created waves and he has his critics among the Malay community. Ramli began creating contemporary work in the early 1980s. In *Gerhana*, he worked with local talent and material, such as the songs of legendary actor-director-singer-songwriter P. Ramlee. He has since established himself as a leading artiste.

Wong Fook Choon was a taxi driver and noodle maker who began dancing at a late age. Nevertheless, he excelled in ballet and was a professional dancer in Switzerland prior to his return to Malaysia. His works reflect an in-depth knowledge of Chinese tradition and culture, and a strong sense of drama. He uses music, voice and thematic material from various cultures in groundbreaking productions such as *Orphan's Tears*, *Prince Charming* and *Hang Li Po*, the last based on a local historical tale. These represent Wong's successful explorations into ballet and contemporary dance using Eastern themes.

Marion D'Cruz spent some time in New York and Indonesia, subsequently exploring the Graham technique with Balinese movements as seen in her choreography *4 x 4*. She explores construction and deconstruction extensively in her choreography, the more notable of her efforts being *Urn Piece*, *Immigrants* and *Malaysia Boleh!*

The new generation

A new generation of Malaysian dancers and choreographers is continuing the work of the pioneers, drawing on Malaysia's cultural heritage and traditions for inspiration and charting their own course. The more prominent among them are Vincent Tan, Suhaimi Magi, Mew Chang Tsing, Aida Redza, Loke Soh Kim, Choo Tee Kuang, Lena Ang, Lee Swee Keong, Loh Pit Fong and Anthony Meh. All received their early training in traditional Malay, Chinese and Indian dance, and even other Southeast Asian forms such as Balinese and Javanese dance. They were also trained in ballet and modern dance abroad.

These dancers often explore issues of identity, history, heritage and roots in their work. Some of them are motivated by human rights and social justice issues and use the stage as their forum. Others seek to rebel against convention, presenting dance in avant garde ways, incorporating elements of Japanese Butoh forms, experimenting with space and video technology, and giving new interpretation to the meaning of dance.

Malaysian contemporary dance became more experimental in the 1990s, continuing into the new century. Recent works demonstrate the dancers' eclectic training, their innovativeness and creativity, as well as their ability to merge traditional dance vocabulary with the modern. Many new works depict traditional dance vocabulary set to vibrant fusion music. *Re: Lady White Snake*, choreographed by Mew Chang Tsing and Lee Swee Keong, is a dance-drama retelling the famous Chinese legend, its characters fusing Javanese, Balinese, Malay, Indian, Chinese and Western dance movements that evolved through improvisation. The work stands out as one of the best dance performances and productions in Malaysia in recent times, and toured Southeast Asia. It was commended by the Ford Foundation and earned the choreographers the International Artist Programme grant.

AWAS! is a full length dance drama that merges Mak Yong dance movements with modern techniques, set to Asian music. Choreographed by Joseph Gonzales, it looks at the effect of the dominance of one man over another, and explores the issues of status, power and justice; while in *AKAR: A Pilgrimage*, Aida Redza deals with issues of culture and identity within the context of migration.

The influence yielded by the new generation of choreographers on contemporary dance since the 1990s is due in part to the opening of more private dance schools and the establishment of Akademi Seni Kebangsaan (National Arts Academy) in 1994, which gives younger dancers the opportunity to express a more multi-cultural, multi-faceted approach to dance.

Marion D'Cruz in *I Dreamed*, which she choreographed in 1988 to a poem of the same title by Chin San Sooi, about visions of the past, present and future.

Indian classical dance guru Ramli Ibrahim began creating contemporary dance work in the 1980s.

TOP: *Urn Piece* (2002 version) choreographed by Marion D'Cruz and produced by the Akademi Seni Kebangsaan in a show featuring teachers' choreography.

ABOVE: *Watermelon Juice*, choreographed by Loke Soh Kim and produced by the Akademi Seni Kebangsaan.

BELOW: The late Lari Leong's works were often experimental and reflected Eastern philosophy incorporated in modern dance.

Early recording industry

The 78-rpm gramophone era began in Malaya in the early 20th century with the emergence of the recording industry and recording artists. Since then, recorded popular music in Malaysia has expanded to encompass a string of local record companies, a vibrant consumer market and recording artists of international standing.

Labels of the first companies to record in Malaya in the early 1900s.

Early industry

By the 1920s and 1930s, recording companies such as The Gramophone Co. (also known as His Master's Voice or HMV) and Columbia of England; Pathe of France; Beka, Hindenburg and Odeon of Germany were recording music in Malaya. In the first two decades of the century, recording engineers of the respective companies made trips to Asia and, with the assistance of local agents, identified artistes and songs, the repertoire to be recorded and used hotel rooms to set up their recording equipment.

Recording process

Recording was done on hard wax. Performers had to sing into the recording horn, and were only given two to three minutes to sing each song. This limitation restricted improvisation; if mistakes were made, the wax had to be thrown away. The wax matrices were then sent to factories of the respective recording companies to be processed and duplicated.

Prior to 1907, recordings made by The Gramophone Co. were pressed in Hanover. From 1908, wax matrices were sent to Calcutta where a factory had been set up. The factory processed records from India and Southeast Asia till the 1920s. It also assembled gramophone machines with parts imported from Europe. Due to the rapid increase in record production, The Gramophone Co. built a bigger factory at Dum Dum, India in 1928.

The finished products had coloured paper labels and were placed in simple brown paper sleeves. It was only later in the 1920s and 1930s that pictures of artistes, the trademark and other illustrations were printed on the brown paper sleeves. These products were then sent back to local agents appointed by the respective companies in Malaya to be sold. The introduction of electrical recording in the mid-1920s provided a stimulus for increased sales. The microphone that came with electrical recording eliminated overcrowding of performers around the recording horn. Soft instruments could now be heard.

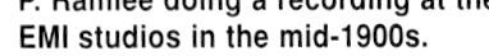

P. Ramlee doing a recording at the EMI studios in the mid-1900s.

Major labels in Malaya

The Gramophone Co. of London was the first company to record in Malaya. Records were made under the label of HMV (Chap Anjing or Dog Label), which featured a fox terrier listening to the gramophone as its trademark. The Gramophone Co. dominated the recording industry in Malaya. In 1931, following the Depression, The Gramophone Co. and Columbia merged to form the Electric and Musical Industries Ltd (EMI). EMI brought under its umbrella other companies such as Beka, Odeon, Pathe and Parlophone.

Most of the Malay records of the 1930s were products of EMI and were manufactured at Dum Dum, India even though their labels had the trademarks of the various companies. Pathe or Chap Ayam displayed the rooster, Odeon or Chap Gajah the elephant or domed theatre, Parlophone the sign of the pound and Columbia two music notes on either side of the head of a tiger as their respective trademarks. As the companies were all part of EMI, there was little competition between them.

Early 20th century 78 rpm gramophone.

The Gramophone Company was also able to dominate in Malaya as it did in other parts of the world by encouraging local dealers to set up their own recording companies bearing their own names and labels. In this way, The Gramophone Co. cut its own costs yet made it difficult for competing companies to break into the market. Chap Kuching (Cat label) was started by S. Moutrie and Co. and Chap Singa (Lion Label) by M. E & T. Hemsley & Co. of Singapore. Both were distributors and local agents of The Gramophone Co. To cater for the increased number of recordings, a proper recording studio was set up by The Gramophone Co. in

Labels and jackets of vinyl gramophone records.

Singapore in 1934. This studio was used by all companies under EMI as well as local companies. Recording engineers of The Gramophone Co. made the recordings in the studio.

Artists and repertoire

Most of the songs recorded in the first two decades of the 20th century were vocal pieces from Bangsawan plays and extra turns (see 'Bangsawan and Jikey operatic theatre' and 'People in Bangsawan'). The repertoire consisted of Asli, Joget, Dondang Sayang and Keroncong pieces as well as social dance music such as waltzes, polkas, marches and mazurkas. The recording artists were either famous Bangsawan stars such as Miss Norlia, Miss Julia, Miss Tijah and Mr K. Dean, or they were the winners of competitions organized by the recording companies.

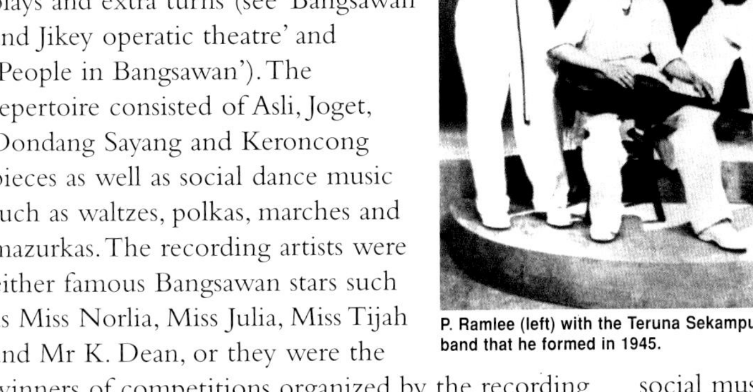
P. Ramlee (left) with the Teruna Sekampung band that he formed in 1945.

In the 1920s and 1930s, in addition to the Bangsawan repertoire, recording artists began to sing songs with lyrics that were meaningful and that advised audiences to be kind 'Stamboel Junjongan Hati' (Stamboel Respects the Heart) by Miss Nancy, to help the poor 'Kesian' (Pity) by Che Aminah and not to be greedy for money 'Ingat-Ingat' (Remember) by Che Wantora. They employed modern dance rhythms such as the rumba and keroncong rumba. Comic songs (*lawak/jenaka/sinderan*) were also recorded. These were topical songs in the 1930s and 1940s.

In the late 1940s and 1950s, film stars such as P. Ramlee, Nona Asiah (who was dubbed the nightingale of Malaya), Lena, Momo Latif and Normadiah were also recorded. P. Ramlee was the most famous of these singers and had a few hundred songs to his credit. His voice was also dubbed over that of other film stars. The most highly skilled musicians formed the orchestras of the recording companies. The HMV and Columbia orchestras were led by A. Rahman, Ahmad Jaafar and Osman Ahmed.

In the 1950s, songs from P. Ramlee movies were popular. 'Engkau Laksana Bulan' (You are like the Moon) from the film *Penarek Becha* (Trishaw Puller) describes the difficult life of a trishaw puller while 'Menceceh Bujang Lapuk' (Old Bachelor's Nonsense) from the film *Bujang Lapuk* (Old Bachelor) illustrates the poverty faced by unemployed youths.

The film songs were eclectic. Singers used crooning voices and were accompanied by orchestras that included violins, flute, trumpet, piano, double bass and conga drums. They sang newly arranged Malay social music such as 'Joget Baru' (new joget) and 'Masri Moden' (modern masri) as well as new songs to the beat of Latin American dances such as the cha cha.

P. Ramlee composed and recorded 249 songs in the 1950s–70s.

Cover of *Irama*, a music magazine from the 1950s.

Recording artists of the 1920s–50s

1. Momo Latif
2. Rubiah
3. Lena
4. Nona Asiah
5. Normadiah

Popular music

Popular music is the genre that is most pervasive in Malaysia. Performers, composers and audience cut across ethnic, class and age distinctions, and the music is disseminated through radio, television, film, cassettes, videos and digital discs. Singers perform in all the Malaysian languages. From the wealth of influences in the country, Malaysian musicians have initiated their own styles and projected their own identities by combining Western, Malay, Chinese and other elements in the melodies and lyrics.

Pop diva Sheila Majid sings in a variety of styles.

Mainstream popular music

Most popular music in Malaysia comprises music influenced by chart-oriented and easy-listening pop from America and Europe. Styles include commercial folk-rock, folk-blues, soul, ballad, rap and country and Western music. Like their Western counterparts, the songs are 'strophic' in form. Electric guitars, synthesizers, drum sets and other Western instruments are used. Most pop lyrics are about romantic love.

Prominent exponents of mainstream Malaysian pop include the late Sudirman Arshad, Sharifah Aini, Francissca Peters, Andre Goh, Dato S. M. Salim, Rafeah Buang, Tres Amigos, Orkid Abdullah, The Alleycats, Sweet Charity, The Blues Gang, KRU, Noor Kumalasari, Siti Nurhaliza, Astura, Ning Baizura, Aishah, Era Fazira, Too Phat, Poetic Ammo and many others. They combine internationally distributed styles with local musical elements, themes and sometimes regional dialects.

Sudirman, once acclaimed as Asia's top entertainer, was known for his songs 'Chow Kit Road', *Balik Kampung* ('Return to the Village') and patriotic songs such as *Tanggal 31* ('Dated 31'). The Blues Gang's *Apo Nak diKato* ('What is There to Say') fuses the rambling rocking rhythm of American folk-blues with Malay antiphonal singing style. Sung in the dialect of Negeri Sembilan, the lyrics comment on the difficulties of working on the rubber estates and paddy fields. In her album *Legenda* ('Legend'), Sheila Majid sings new arrangements of P. Ramlee's songs such as *Getaran Jiwa* ('Quivering Soul'), *Jeritan Batinku* ('Cry of my Inner Self'), combining new instruments such as synthesizers, guitars, drums, shakuhachi (Japanese bamboo flute) and saxophone. The Alleycats incorporate Malay dance rhythms into their songs. In *Mari Berdendang* ('Let Us Dance'), they invite the audience to sing and dance to the Joget rhythm which is characterized by the alternation of three notes against two.

Since the 1990s new pop melodies, known as *Irama Malaysia*, have been composed using rhythms and musical elements of Malay traditional social music such as Inang, Joget, Asli, Ghazal, Zapin, Dikir Barat and Dondang Sayang. Noraniza Idris' 'Puteri Dikir' uses the antiphonal style of singing and handclaps of the Dikir Barat, Siti Nurhaliza's 'Cindai' employs the Zapin rhythm, Jamal Abdillah's 'Ghazal untuk Rabiah' is accompanied by the Ghazal ensemble while Amir's 'Zikir Kasih' is a modern version of *zikir*.

Popular mainstream singers and groups include: 1. Too Phat; **2.** Andre Goh; **3.** Siti Nurhaliza; **4.** Sharifah Aini; **5.** Francissca Peters; **6.** The Blues Gang; **7.** S. M. Salim; **8.** Sudirman.

Jazz fusion

The pioneers of jazz fusion in Malaysia are Asiabeat (below), who, since 1976, have been fusing Asian instruments like the Malay gamelan and *kompang*, the Indian *tabla*, *nagaswaram* and sitar, Chinese drums, Japanese *shakuhachi* (bamboo flute) and Western electric guitar and drums. Asiabeat combines Asian performance styles with jazz. 'Bamboo Groove' begins with a solo shakuhachi introduction played in a style reminiscent of Japanese shakuhachi music for meditation. In the next section, the shakuhachi plays the melody while the electric guitars and drums provide the harmony and beat respectively. This is followed by a section which features the *saron* (metallophones) of the Malay gamelan playing interlocking melodies together with the shakuhachi and electric guitars.

Rock

A Malaysian brand of rock music has flourished. Rock bands and singers such as Ella, Search, Lefthanded (right), Bumiputera Rockers, XPDC, Bloodshed and Wings are extremely popular. These singers promote two main styles. The first—known as slow rock—resembles the core of mainstream popular songs except that it is amplified and the beat is hardened. Lyrics are usually about love. The second style refers to heavy metal songs with heavily amplified drums and electric bass and guitar riffs. Themes include rockers' rights, peace, injustice, power and money.

Lucu (comical) songs

Lucu songs refer to songs which incorporate topical issues including comment on problems in Malaysian society such as excessive gambling, motorbike racing, womanizing and the plight of taxi drivers. These songs are invigorated by humour in the tone of voice and in the lyrics. The relevant and amusing lyrics become the focal point for listeners. Melodies combine Chinese, Indian, Malay and Western elements. Album titles reflecting the topical nature of the songs include *Dunia Materialistik* ('Materialistic World') by Rampa and *Tak Faham! Tak Faham!* ('Cannot Understand! Cannot Understand!') by Hang Mokhtar (pictured above, left).

Rampa's song *Senasib* ('Of the Same Fate') shows how working people of all ethnic groups in Malaysia (such as Malay shoemakers and Chinese and Indian street hawkers) share the same fate and aspirations. They are poor and hope to become rich one day. Indian *nagaswaram*, bells and drums, Chinese gongs and drums, and Western electric guitars and synthesizers are used to provide the accompaniment. Chinese and Indian words are mixed with Malay.

Hang Mokhtar's *Tampal Korek* ('Patch and Dig') employs a popular tune from a Chinese television serial and Chinese sentence construction and speech manner to highlight lyrics about the perpetual digging of roads, to the frustration of commuters.

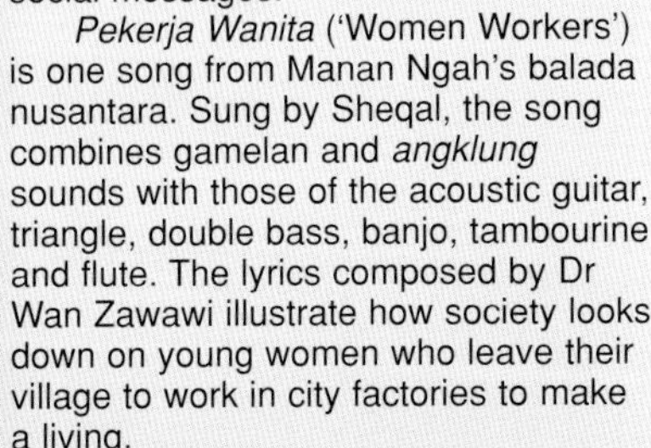

Balada nusantara

In 1989, two composers Manan Ngah and M. Nasir initiated a different type of popular music they called *balada nusantara* and *muzik nusantara* respectively. This music combines Arabic, Hispanic, European and Asian music. Traditional instruments such as *caklempung*, gamelan, *gendang, seruling, tabla, gambus*, sitar and *kompang* are combined with guitars and synthesizers. The lyrics are not just outpourings of love, but also portray social messages.

Pekerja Wanita ('Women Workers') is one song from Manan Ngah's balada nusantara. Sung by Sheqal, the song combines gamelan and *angklung* sounds with those of the acoustic guitar, triangle, double bass, banjo, tambourine and flute. The lyrics composed by Dr Wan Zawawi illustrate how society looks down on young women who leave their village to work in city factories to make a living.

Singer and composer, M. Nasir defines his muzik nusantara as a blend of traditional music and sounds with foreign influences. In his hit song 'Mustika', literally meaning 'magic stone' and often used as a woman's name, M. Nasir combines angklung and gamelan with electric guitar sounds and uses the asli rhythmic pattern played on the kompang.

***Left top*: M. Nasir. *Left bottom*: Manan Ngah**

World music

As the name of Zainal Abidin's new recording company Afrozapin implies, Zainal (right) fuses African rhythms and singing style with Malay rhythms such as Joget, Keroncong, Asli and Zapin. In his song *Hijau* ('Green'), Zainal combines Malay drums, Indian *tabla* and the Negeri Sembilan dialect to remind audiences to take care of the environment. In the song 'Gamal Bongkar', he includes a live recording of the music of the Kenyah and Kayan of Sarawak and mixes it with his own song played with guitars and drums.

Nasyid pop

Nasyid style singing with percussion backdrop and Western harmony has become a commercial force to reckon with in the 1990s. The album of nasyid group Raihan (below), *Puji Pujian* ('Praises'), contains 10 songs which praise Allah and advocate morality and devotion to Islam. They are sung in contemporary manner with the backing of a full percussion ensemble playing Latin American and Nusantara rhythms. In their debut album *Cahaya Ilahi* ('Light of Allah'), the nasyid group Hijjaz sing praises to Allah, religious recitations and other songs which carry advice on ways to curb social ills. The album features sounds of the *kompang, marimba*, gamelan and guitar. The nasyid group Rabbani presents P. Ramlee's songs *Assalamualaikum* ('Peace Be With You') and *Berkorban Apa Saja* ('Sacrifice Everything') in nasyid style with percussion accompaniment.

Chinese orchestral music

The modern Chinese orchestra (huayue tuan) *combines Chinese and Western elements. While the ensemble comprises mainly traditional Chinese instruments, Western instruments such as the cello and double bass are often added. The rendering of new arrangements of Chinese and local Malay music using Western harmony reflects contemporary efforts to create a Malaysian identity.*

The Penang State *huayue tuan* brings together the best musicians from orchestras belonging to various schools and associations.

Top: Dama Orchestra, one of the country's leading Chinese orchestras, is reputed for its classical and experimental music.

Bottom: The Professional Cultural Centre Orchestra. Chinese orchestral music consists of compositions for small ensembles or full orchestras, and Western instruments are often used.

Development in Malaysia

Chinese immigrants of the 19th century used to get together on an ad hoc basis to improvise regional Chinese opera and folk tunes in the various clan and regional associations. There was no conductor, but the bowed fiddle would take the lead. No scores were used. In the 1960s, the new sounds of the modern Chinese orchestra (formed in China in the 1930s) attracted the interest of Chinese associations. They began to add new instruments, played the repertoire of the modern orchestra and called the ensemble *huayue tuan*.

Prevalence

The huayue tuan enjoys much popularity, especially among Chinese youths. It plays an important function within the Chinese community, providing the opportunity for youths to socialize and interact, make music, and at the same time, learn new skills. Musical societies also provide leadership and musical training. Members help in the running of the organization by taking charge of printing scores, organizing concerts and maintaining the instruments. Membership fees of such societies or associations are relatively low, affording Chinese youths of lower socio-economic background the opportunity to join the orchestra. The huayue tuan also contributes to the development of Chinese culture and the betterment of society through annual concerts organized to raise funds for Chinese cultural bodies and activities.

The modern Chinese orchestra is organized as part of voluntary associations such as clan associations, Chinese school musical clubs and alumni clubs, and political and religious groups.

Chinese-medium schools play an increasingly important role in promoting the huayue tuan. In the state of Penang alone there are about 15 Chinese orchestras belonging to these schools and associations. The Penang state orchestra, formed in 1998, comprises the best musicians from these orchestras. It was formed to raise the level of the huayue tuan and nurture local talent in collaboration with internationally renowned conductors and composers, and receives sponsorship from the state government. Youths are inspired to master Chinese instruments by the performances of local professional musicians who have graduated from the Shanghai Conservatory and the Beijing Music Academy of China.

Musical styles and repertoires

Chinese orchestral music combines Chinese melodies and scale with Western musical forms, harmony and intonation, and sometimes Malay melodies and rhythms. Most of the new compositions of the huayue tuan are programmatic.

The *liuqin* (willow leaf-shaped lute) is used in solo and in ensemble as the soprano part of plucked string instruments.

With titles such as 'Moonlight over the Spring River' or 'Dance of the Yao People', the music describes a specific scenery or human activity. The repertoire consists of pieces performed by the whole orchestra, compositions for small ensembles or chamber music (sometimes accompanying singing, dance or chorus) and solo pieces for the *guzheng*, *erhu*, *dizi* and *suona* (the last three usually accompanied by piano or *yang qin*).

Compositions played by the entire ensemble comprise new arrangements of folk songs played in heterophony as in regional music 'Crazy Dance of the Golden Snake', new compositions played in triadic harmony as in 'Dance of the Yao People', and mini-concertos where a soloist plays with the orchestra such as 'A New Song of the Herdsmen' for the dizi and orchestra.

Malaysian folk and patriotic songs such as 'Tanah Air Ku', 'Ayam Didik', 'Inang Cina', 'Burung Kakaktua' and 'Chan Mali Chan' have also been arranged for the modern Chinese orchestra. New compositions incorporating Masri dance rhythms and those using the Malay *kompang* drum such as 'Potong Padi' have been created. Groups such as Dama Orchestra (Malaysian Chinese Ensemble), the Professional Chinese Cultural Organization of Kuala Lumpur and the Penang state *Huayue Tuan* have expanded the boundaries of Chinese music by experimenting with Western chamber musicians, classical Indian instrumentalists and jazz fusion musicians. By so doing, they have been able to attract non-Chinese audiences to their performances.

Instruments of the *huayue tuan*

The modern Chinese orchestra consists of four sections:

- Bowed strings—treble section: *erhu, banhu* and *gaohu*; tenor section: *zhonghu*; bass section: *gehu, beida gehu*. The cello and double bass are often added.
- Plucked strings—*pipa* (pear-shaped lute), *yueqin* (moon guitar), *liuqin* (willow leaf-shaped lute), *sanxian* (three-stringed guitar), *guzheng* (zither); and strings struck by hammers, *yang qin* (dulcimer).
- Wind—*dizi* (transverse flute); *xiao* (vertical flute); *sheng* (mouth organ); *suona* (double-reed oboe).
- Percussion—*gu* (drum); *bo* (cymbal); *luo* (gong); *yunluo* (small gongs); *ling* (bell); *maling* (horse bell); *bangzi* (wood block).

Western influence is evident in the division of the orchestra into four sections with the bowed string section dominating, the presence of a conductor and in the seating of the players. As in the Western orchestra, the bowed strings are seated to the left, the bass instruments to the right, the wind instruments in front of the conductor and the percussion at the back of the stage. The design of the instruments has been modified to increase the range, to temper the scale and to increase the volume.

The *dizi* (traverse flute) is traditionally made of bamboo and produces an expressive sound.

The *erhu* is a versatile bowed string instrument.

The *ruan* comes in three sizes.

Instruments of the modern Chinese orchestra

1. *Ganggu*
2. *Paigu* (five drums)
3. *Banhu*
4. *Muyu*
5. *Jingdaluo*
6. *Dizi*
7. *Suona*
8. *Sheng*
9. *Yunluo*
10. *Timpani*
11. *Gaohu*
12. *Zhonghu*
13. *Liuqin*
14. *Zhongruan*
15. *Daruan*
16. *Pipa*
17. *Yang qin*
18. Cello
19. *Erhu*
20. Double basses

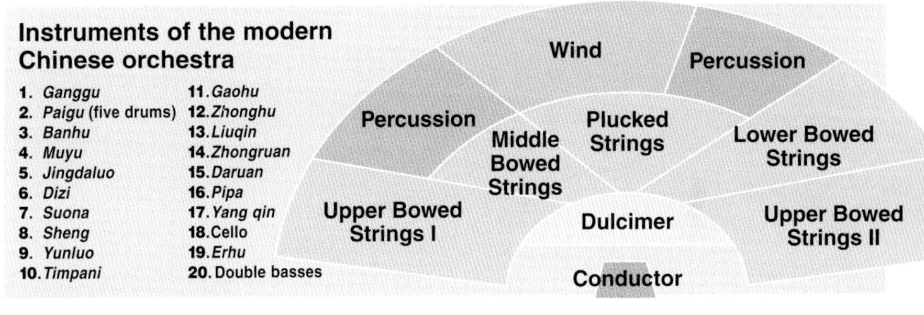

Penang State Huayue Tuan

Contemporary art music

By the mid-20th century many Malaysian musicians were well trained in the performance of Western and local instruments, and in the basic theory and elements of Western classical music. Composers of that era, such as Johari Salleh, Alfonso Soliano and Gus Steyn, played in the Radio Television Malaysia Orchestra, writing arrangements of pieces as well as original compositions. These early composers planted the seeds for a contemporary art music movement in Malaysia.

A performance featuring the Malaysian Philharmonic Orchestra with the BBC Symphony Orchestra, Petronas Performing Arts Group and Rhythm in Bronze.

Datuk Ooi Chean See conducting the Malaysian Philharmonic Orchestra.

Art Music

Art music refers to a musical tradition in which pieces are composed with serious intent and written using music notation and in the format of a score by a trained composer. There is usually a high degree of refinement, sophistication and individual expression in the creative process and in the resulting composition. Art music is disseminated through published scores, recordings in the form of long-playing discs, cassette tapes, compact and digital discs, live concerts, and by broadcasting via radio and television. Although appreciated by only a small audience, contemporary art music in Malaysia is cast in a Western-based musical idiom, which often incorporates elements from folk music that exists in an oral tradition.

The mid-20th century and *muzik seriosa*

The composers of art music in the mid-20th century (*muzik seriosa* or serious music) looked to Western forms such as the lyric song, the symphonic poem, theme and variations and other forms. Their compositions of the 1950s–60s featured Western solo instruments, the full orchestra and the use of harmony. These elements symbolized the emergence of Malaysia as a modern nation in Southeast Asia. They also attempted to write music that would have some appeal to all ethnic groups in the country. Even though these early composers relied heavily on Western musical elements, they also attempted to incorporate Malay, Chinese and Indian musical features to give a Malaysian flavour to their music.

Late 20th-century developments

Throughout the second half of the 20th century many young Malaysians went abroad to study performance and music composition. They attended conservatories and schools of music at universities in Australia, Europe and the United States. In the 1980s and 1990s many of these talented musicians returned home to apply their skills and exercise their creative ability in composing new music. They used the resources of the 20th–21st-century music world, including serial technique, atonality, polyrhythm, new

State-of-the-art acoustics

The hall of the Dewan Filharmonik Petronas takes its inspiration from the traditional shoe-box shape of the great 19th-century European concert halls, and seats an audience of 885. Unique acoustic devices have been incorporated into the design of the auditorium to maximize its natural acoustic qualities. A perforated metal ceiling vault allows sound to travel to an upper ceiling, comprising seven panels which can be moved to alter the volume of the hall and simulate a wide range of acoustic environments. The resonance of the auditorium can also be adjusted by opening or closing absorptive panels in the side walls. Walls, ceilings and balconies have been shaped to reflect sound both to the audience and the musicians while avoiding echoes.

1. Highest point of moveable ceiling.
2. Moveable acoustically reflective ceiling adjusts volume of concert hall.
3. Lowest point of moveable ceiling.
4. Moveable acoustically absorptive panels.

The RTM Orchestra, formed in 1957, combines local ensembles such as the gamelan and *gendang* drums with the Western orchestra.

tone colours, electronic media and computers. In addition, they looked to the musical and philosophical elements from traditional Asian cultures, seeking to establish their own stylistic traits and, at the same time, an Asian, if not a Malaysian, identity. As an integral part of the music itself, many compositions from the 1980s–90s are rooted in Asian sensibilities.

Influences in art music

While contemporary Malaysian art music can be documented from only the second half of the 20th century, many factors have shaped its development. The fact that countless talented musicians went overseas to study Western instruments brought a high degree of skill, discipline and excellence to the performance arena in Malaysia, albeit with a focus on Western musical instruments. In addition, young musicians went abroad to study composition, to learn the techniques of composing music that emerged in the larger post-World War II music world.

Other talented musicians studied music education (at first abroad and now locally) in the training of schoolchildren. With the emergence of local music educators, music programmes are taught in government schools and in teachers' training colleges. These programmes focus not only on general music concepts and principles, but also on local, traditional music, giving young schoolchildren a foundation in the music of their own country.

Malaysian universities have also contributed to the growth of art music by teaching courses in music. In the early 1990s, Universiti Sains Malaysia was the first institution of higher learning to offer the Bachelor and the Master of Arts in music (and later a Bachelor of Music), and in the late 1990s and early 2000s many other institutions followed suit. The building of the Dewan Filharmonik Petronas (Petronas Concert Hall) in 1998, and the establishment of a philharmonic orchestra in Kuala Lumpur the same year, as well as the proliferation of smaller orchestras, have given stimuli to the further growth and nurturing of a Malaysian art music tradition. The continued dedication of music teachers as well as the creative efforts of Malaysian composers and performers attest to a rich, vibrant and continually developing art music tradition in the country.

Malaysian art music

Muzik seriosa (1950-1970)

Alfonso Soliano, who conducted the Radio–Television Malaysia (RTM) Orchestra in the 1950–60s, wrote many arrangements of popular tunes of the time for voice and piano, songs like 'Dondang Sayang', 'Jingli Nona' and 'Bunga Tanjung'. He also used Asli rhythms in his original compositions for orchestra and borrowed musical elements from other ethnic groups. Composer Tan Chong Yew also wrote arrangements of local melodies for voice and piano, and throughout his career composed new music for the RTM Orchestra. Other composers such as Johari Salleh (above right) combined local ensembles such as the gamelan with the Western orchestra, as in the piece entitled 'Gurindam Gamelan', and Gus Steyn (above left) wrote programmatic music in a Western idiom, but with a story line or a scenic description taken from local legends (his 'Si-Tanggung').

Art music (1980 onwards)

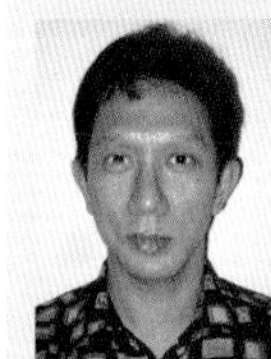

Abdul Razak Aziz

The work '10 Nyanyian Settings' (10 Song Settings) for Soprano, choir and 2 Pianos (1981–90) by Abdul Razak Aziz (left) uses lyrics entirely from Malay children's nursery rhymes, while another work, an opera in progress, finds its inspiration from a novel by the Malay author Fatimah Busu. A set of 'Five Piano Etudes' that he completed in 2002, exploring various elements of harmony, rhythm and texture, will be published in 2004 by The Asian Centre in Penang, where Razak is based.

Valerie Ross

The works of Valerie Ross (right), a highly versatile composer, also show strong Asian influences. In her piece 'Karma', Ross combines instruments from various ethnic groups along with melodies cast in the slendro scale from the gamelan tradition, rhythms and time organization based on the Indian *tala* and certain musical textures commonly found in traditional Malay music. In many of her works traditional musical instruments are played in both old and new ways, but she also looks for new sound resources, especially those from the natural environment, sounds such as the chirping of crickets and birds (as in her 'Web 2'). She has also composed multi-media works ('Nadis-Chakra', a sound sculpture), and music with dance composition for theatre ('Fatamorgana').

John Yong, Julia Chong, Tan Su Lian and Raymond Kong

Other contemporary Malaysian composers from the 1980s–90s maintained close ties with Western forms like their predecessors in the 1950s–60s. These composers included John Yong Lah Boh and the late Julia Chong from Sarawak, and Tan Su Lian (left) and Raymond Kong from Peninsular Malaysia. Both Yong and Chong tended to compose long works, many of them programmatic. Yong's symphonic poem in three movements, 'The Mystery of The South China Sea', uses a Western chamber orchestra. Much of the music is based on atonality but Yong also employs the Chinese pentatonic scale.

Local motifs are often found in the musical works by the late Chong. Her ballet suites, 'Sang Kancil', 'Soraya' and 'Manorah', are based on local legends and theatre forms, and the music is permeated with local motifs and scale structures. She also used Sarawak instruments, as in the work 'Rushing Waters', a programmatic piece depicting the swift flowing waters of the Rajang River. In this musical piece she uses the *suling* (flute), *engkerurai* (mouth organ), *sapeh* (plucked lute), *jatung utang* (xylophone), and *engkerumong* (gong-chime).

Old music, new treatment

The main traditional music genres in Malaysia to experience development in the context of an art music tradition are the Joget Gamelan and the Keroncong repertoires. The number of instruments in the Malay gamelan increased in the 1980s–90s and composers such as Ariff Ahmad and Sunetra Fernando have attempted to bring a new Malaysian identity to gamelan music. Large and new formal structures, vocal parts, and adaptations of other Southeast Asian gamelan styles have become part of the music vocabulary in this genre. The contemporary Keroncong Malaysia is coloured with popular and pre-existing Malay melodies as well as newly composed melodies by Malaysian composers, pieces such as 'Baba dan Nyonya' by Baba Ong Cheng Ho, 'Keroncong Bakti' by A. Rahman Ghani, and 'Indahnya Malaysia' by Sudar Majid Aliyas.

LEFT: The Rhythm in Bronze ensemble integrates and modernizes elements from traditional music.

RIGHT: Composer Sunetra Fernando.

Arts organizations and their contributions

Apart from universities, several institutions and organizations, both government and private, are actively involved in promoting the performing arts. While the National Theatre and the National Arts Academy, in particular, have played major roles and served as catalysts for the promotion of the traditional arts forms, the contribution of private organizations is no less significant as they have nourished and nurtured a thriving performing arts environment in Malaysia.

Built at a cost of RM210 million, the National Theatre's auditorium has a seating capacity of 1,445. The stage comprises four proscenium stages that can be modified to suit any performance.

The National Theatre

In 1999, the National Theatre was opened, 35 years after the idea was first mooted. The decades in between witnessed the setting up of the National Cultural Troupe in 1972; the formation of the Youth Symphony Orchestra in 1982, which became the National Symphony Orchestra in 1993; and the establishment of the National Choir in 1992.

The objectives of the National Theatre, popularly known as Istana Budaya, are to cultivate excellence and professionalism in the arts and to promote arts and culture sponsorship by the corporate sector as well as individuals.

Technically impressive, the National Theatre is often compared to the Sydney Opera House and the Royal Albert Hall. Its architecture is striking, based on a moon kite in flight. The shape of the building takes the form of the *sirih junjung*, a multi-layer arrangement of betel leaves used in Malay weddings and welcoming ceremonies. Its interior design contains elements of traditional Malay architecture, with the royal boxes being patterned after the large windows of a Malay house, and the design of the theatre lobby on the third floor taking its shape from the large Malay *rebana ubi* drum.

A world ethnic music fusion production staged by Istana Budaya entitled *Mohram*.

Initially Istana Budaya's policy was to stage only Malay language productions, a move that alienated non-Malay theatre artists, enthusiasts and audiences. In recent years, however, there have been efforts to stage foreign productions, such as *Fame* and *Cats*.

Istana Budaya productions

1. *Alang Rentak Seribu*, written by playwright Syed Alwi and set in a *kampung* (village).
2. *Raja Tangkai Hati*, a spectacular performance of Mak Yong theatre.
3. *Geeta Gangsa*, a concert of music, dance, theatre and lyrical poetry in a fusion of East and West.

The National Arts Academy (Akademi Seni Kebangsaan)

Unlike the universities and institutions of higher learning in the country, the National Arts Academy emphasizes the practical aspects of the various disciplines it offers. The academy, which opened its doors in July 1994 to the first batch of 80 students, offers five disciplines: theatre, music, dance, creative writing and cinematography.

Graduates of the academy are taught to be arts practitioners and experts in their chosen field, at the same time gaining some theoretical knowledge. The rationale behind this approach is that well-trained performers and creative artistes leaving the academy after a three-year programme will, through their involvement, be in a position to raise the standard of the arts in the country. The intention is that they will be agents of change towards better quality theatre, music or dance productions, as well as original literary works.

The academy foresees that graduates will, for instance, work as members of an orchestra, music composers, actors or directors, scriptwriters or choreographers, as well as teachers of these arts. It is the hope of the academy that its students will find a niche in the expanding arts industry in the country, and that some will make an impact

internationally. Whether or not these objectives will be achieved it is too early to tell. There are other concerns as well: recognition and acceptance of the diplomas offered by the academy, the quality of its curriculum and graduates; the cost of educating its students and the direction of the academy.

Undoubtedly its students have an obvious advantage in that, with the financial resources available for the academy, they are taught by the best academicians in the country. The academy does not stint on appointing part-time staff from universities in the country as well from the private sector, in addition to recruiting teaching staff from Singapore. Staff members have also come from Indonesia and other countries. Almost the entire teaching staff of the academy works on a part-time basis. Some of the academy's students have already made a name for themselves on stage and in television. Others have entered local universities to pursue degree programmes, with a handful at post-graduate level. This augurs well for the academy. Equally impressive is the attention a few of its graduates have attained in performances. On the other hand, the academy has produced many 'generalists' rather than dedicated specialists, unlike similar institutions in other countries, particularly Indonesia.

The academy has also done especially well in its own productions of traditional Malay genres, particularly Wayang Kulit, Mak Yong and Bangsawan. In these areas it has become a leader, with regular productions resulting from the courses taught by professional practitioners and highly qualified academicians. Through these efforts the academy has introduced these traditional performing arts forms to Kuala Lumpur audiences, and has generated considerable enthusiasm for them. Students at the academy have had the benefit of learning from the country's foremost Wayang Kulit puppeteer, the late Hamzah Awang Amat, its best-known Mak Yong performer, the late Khatijah Awang; and famed Bangsawan artiste, Rahman B. But these instructors and practitioners are a threatened breed, and the future of courses in traditional theatre remains unclear. Some quarters feel the academy has not taken an active enough role in preserving and conserving traditional genres of the performing arts (See 'Teaching and research in the performing arts').

Students at the Akademi Seni Kebangsaan have the benefit of learning from professional practitioners, such as Dr Zamin Haroon, better known as Chandrabanu, who teaches traditional Terinai dance.

The academy also organizes productions in traditional Malay performing arts, such as Bangsawan.

An adaptation of Shakespeare's *A Midsummer Night's Dream* staged by the students.

Other Arts Organizations

Temple of Fine Arts

Founded in 1981 by Swami Shantanand Saraswathi, a Hindu monk, with the late V. K. Sivadas and the late Gopal Shetty as dance directors. Its underlying concept is to make dance and music affordable to all, and teaches various dance forms ranging from Indian classical and folk dance to Malay, Chinese and modern dance, as well as north and south Indian music. It has centres in Kuala Lumpur, Penang, Johor Bahru and Melaka. It conducts an annual festival of dance, drama and music that is choreographed and produced entirely by its teachers and students.

Butterfly Lovers, a Temple of Fine Arts production, is a contemporary dance drama based on the Chinese legend, with music composed by local musicians.

Five Arts Centre

A performing and visual arts collective of artists and producers. Its activities include drama, music, young people's theatre, visual arts and multimedia performances. Founded by Krishen Jit, Chin San Sooi, Marion D'Cruz and Anne James in 1984, it also houses resident companies Marion D'Cruz and Dancers, and Teater Muda (Young Theatre).

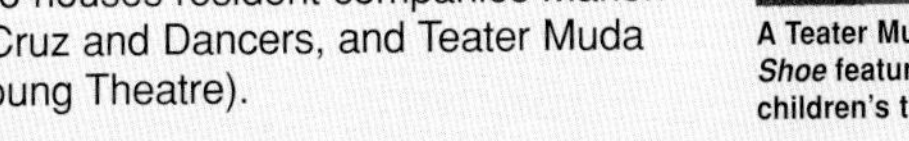

A Teater Muda production *Red and Gold Shoe* featuring teenagers directed by children's theatre specialist Janet Pillai.

Sutra Dance Theatre

Established by Indian classical dance guru Ramli Ibrahim to promote theatre and the arts. It offers training in traditional, classical and contemporary dance as well as in lighting, stage management and theatre production.

Suasana Cultural Centre

A leading company and teaching institution in traditional dance established by Azanin Ahmad, one of Malaysia's top traditional Malay dancers and choreographers. Her first dance drama *Dayang Sari*, produced in 1978, included elements of Mak Yong, Gamelan, Terinai and Asyik, as well as traditional musical accompaniment.

The Actors Studio

Malaysia's first privately owned theatre to present professional theatre. Owned and managed by Joe Hasham and Faridah Merican, who also set up an academy to train actors, directors, writers, designers and production personnel.

The Actors Studio and Five Arts Centre production of Lloyd Fernando's play *Scorpion Orchid* in 1995.

Teaching and research in the performing arts

Although traditional performing arts in Malaysia have a history centuries old, formal education in this field is a relatively new development, having started in the 1970s, and in only one institution of higher learning at the time. Since then, however, many universities have set up performing arts programmes, generating interest and research in both indigenous and modern theatre, dance and music.

In 1980 Universiti Sains Malaysia produced a Malay language version of *Hamlet*, in an attempt to expose students to foreign plays.

Top: Performing Arts students at Universiti Sains Malaysia are taught puppet making as part of practical courses offered by the university.

Above: New Wayang Kulit forms produced by the university draw on characters and stories from local legends, instead of the traditional *Ramayana*.

Universiti Sains Malaysia: The pioneers

Teaching of the performing arts in Malaysia began in 1970 with the establishment of the first full-fledged degree programme in performing arts at Universiti Sains Malaysia (USM) in Penang. The focus of the programme, set up by Ghulam-Sarwar Yousof, was on theatre and drama, while some courses in music and dance were offered as well. Prior to that, courses in theatre production were available to students in the English Department of Universiti Malaya.

The programme at USM soon developed into a unique one, and one of the most exciting in Southeast Asia, mainly due to the fact that it provided for the teaching of dance, music and theatre in one place, while recognizing the need to balance Western elements with Asian traditions. For the first time in the country, cognizance was given to the importance of indigenous performance traditions. Outstanding practitioners of the arts were recruited to teach these traditional theatre genres. The country's leading shadow play puppeteer, the late Hamzah bin Awang Amat, taught in the programme from 1977 to 1994. Penang's last Bangsawan artistes, the late Pak Alias bin Abdul Manan and his wife, the late Puan Aminah binti Nani, were also involved in the programme.

The music curriculum at the university also attempted from the mid-1970s to achieve an East-West balance. Of particular importance was the work done by ethnomusicologist Patricia Matusky, who was later joined by Tan Sooi Beng. Tan went on to head a separate music programme at the university that was established in the early 1990s.

Narukami, an adaptation of a Kabuki play, was produced and directed by playwright Kee Thuan Chye in 1976 under the auspices of the Penang Players. It was staged at Universiti Sains Malaysia's Panggung Sasaran (experimental theatre).

Although some attempt was made in the early years of the programme to introduce the work of non-Malaysian writers, such as that of Indonesian playwright Ariffin Noer's *Kapai-kapai*, most of the drama productions in the following years were based on the work of local writers, offering students little opportunity to work on major plays by foreign playwrights, or to witness foreign productions, as such productions rarely found their way to Penang. The opportunities to view international plays came through the efforts of the most active local drama troupe at the time, Penang Players. USM's exception to the palette of local plays was the significant production of *Hamlet* in the Malay language in 1980, a production which became the subject of much controversy, given the growing polarization that was taking place within and outside campuses due to nationalistic policies. To date that production of *Hamlet* remains the high point of USM's performing arts programme.

Most of the outstanding research in the various genres of traditional theatre and music undertaken in the country has come from people attached at one time or other to USM. The research output from the academic staff members of the programme has been groundbreaking and quite phenomenal, and not only significant by virtue of its quantity. For the first time serious research work from a local academic institution became available to the rest of the world. The research done was timely, for many of the traditional performing arts were, in fact, dying out. Since the early pioneering research in the traditional performing arts, many of the genres have become extinct. This research contribution remains the most important aspect of USM's performing arts programme.

Universiti Malaya

The next institution to develop a performing arts programme was Universiti Malaya (UM) at its Cultural Centre, which was established in 1997. The programme's main focus is on history and theory as well as productions, with some work on radio and television drama, and theatre management. The programme also includes courses in dance and music, with an emphasis on production. Recent changes in the curriculum have seen the introduction of courses in Asian genres and a postgraduate programme.

In terms of research, the most important work done on Malay dance has come from UM. With the consolidation of its curriculum and the development of its postgraduate courses, the programme will undoubtedly make valuable contributions to Malaysia's performing arts. Non-academic activities in the performing arts involving the university's various residential colleges are noteworthy.

Growing emphasis on performing arts

Other public universities have pockets of strength, particularly in music; however, these newer departments of performing arts have yet to develop solid academic programmes. The situation, in many cases, is underscored by certain constraints, mainly a lack of qualified academic staff as well as the small numbers of students who enter the programmes.

Universiti Malaya's programme in theatre includes Mak Yong.

UM regularly stages dance and drama performances by its students and those from other institutions and theatre groups.

These problems are related to that of limited opportunities for serious work in the performing arts, particularly for university graduates.

Universiti Malaysia Sarawak developed the country's third performing arts programme, offering theatre and cinematography courses. Universiti Putra Malaysia has developed a reasonably strong programme in music, although its offerings in other areas of the performing arts are less than substantial. In theatre, for instance, the emphasis is on the use of technology and the development of drama, particularly for television. Music has also received some emphasis at Universiti Pendidikan Sultan Idris in Tanjung Malim, while Universiti Technologi MARA (UiTM) is in the process of stabilizing a very basic programme in theatre studies.

The existence of such programmes at local universities has meant a larger pool of talent being made available, resulting in the upgrading of productions, particularly those of the many amateur and professional performing arts companies in Kuala Lumpur.

Preservation, conservation and documentation

Preservation of traditional performing arts has become increasingly urgent in recent years with rapid modernization and changing values that have caused many of the genres to die out. Even such important genres as Wayang Kulit, highly active in recent decades, have suffered a decline for various reasons, including economic, social and religious ones.

Efforts at documentation have largely been initiated by individuals rather than organizations, although some older archival material does exist in the collections of the National Archives and Radio Television Malaysia (RTM), including RTM's regional offices. One of the earliest private efforts was made by William Malm of the University of Michigan in the late 1960s. A collection of about 100 hours of video recordings made by him is stored in the Music Department of that university, with some copies being brought back to Malaysia.

The largest single collection, consisting of videotaped material and photo documentation of genres such as Mak Yong, Wayang Kulit Siam, Dikir Barat, Main Puteri and Menora, was put together by Ghulam-Sarwar Yousof in the 1970s and 1980s. Some of this collection was destroyed by fire, and additions were later made to the existing collection. The material collected by Malm (with the assistance of Mubin Sheppard) and Ghulam-Sarwar Yousof has been made use of by several scholars, both local and foreign. Some of this material also has been distributed in the form of recordings. In recent years Pesaka, a local company, has been documenting the traditional performing arts and attempting to make them available to Malaysian and international audiences.

Masters of Tradition

Semangat Insan is a series of six documentaries that profile some of Malaysia's cultural legends. The first four, written and narrated in English by Bernice Chauly and produced by Perin Petrus of Planet Films Malaysia, premiered in May 2000. The others were produced in 2002.

Wayang Kulit—*Feast of the Shadow Spirits* features Pak Dollah Baju Merah, the popular Wayang Kulit Siam puppeteer.

Chinese Opera—*Daughter of Heaven* (right) features the career of Choy Yin Heong, a charismatic performer in Cantonese Opera.

Mak Yong—*Pageant of the Ancients* focuses on Cik Ning's melodramatic saga as a Mak Yong performer.

Main Puteri—*Dance of the Inner Winds* features the shaman Pak Yusuf.

Menora—*Flights of Grace* is a feature on Eh Chom, one of the last masters of Menora.

Bangsawan—*Star of the East* tells of the career of Pak Rahman B., the last Bangsawan star.

Rehearsal in theatre production at Universiti Malaya.

Professional dancer and teacher Umesh Shetty (pictured) trained in Indian dance at the Temple of Fine Arts before furthering his studies and contemporary dance training abroad.

Producing practitioners

A certain amount of training in the performing arts comes through private institutions and organizations, such as the Academy TV3, Temple of Fine Arts and Actors Studio Academy, as well as the government-run Akademi Seni Kebangsaan. These organizations have been producing practitioners in theatre, drama and dance. At the same time, the numerous private music and dance schools are the principal source of dancers and musicians. Students from these institutions are specifically trained to be practitioners and have the opportunity to contribute to Malaysian performing arts.

1. *Cili Padi*, a children's drama series aired by TV3 in the mid-1990s.

2. P. Ramlee, artist extraordinaire of the 1950s–70s.

3. Saloma, well-known actress and singer of the 1950s and 1960s.

4. TV3's sitcom *Senario* has enjoyed top ratings since its 1996 debut.

5. *Layar Lara*, an award-winning film by Shuhaimi Baba in 1997.

6. P. Ramlee with Saloma and Mak Minah in his film *Ahmad Albab*.

MALAY FILMS AND TELEVISION DRAMAS

At the beginning of the 20th century traditional Malay performing arts went through various phases of development brought about by urbanization and an increasingly significant middle class audience. Classical traditions, with the exception of Nobat music, almost totally lost their support, and folk forms adjusted to the new circumstances. The new urban audiences began to look for new forms of performing arts to fulfil their wish for escapism or fantasy. Ironically, it was Bangsawan that the most powerful of all performing arts—the cinema—exploited, making its debut in 1933 with *Laila Majnun*.

This was to usher in, first the film industry, and later on, television dramas. Some of the influences that shaped Bangsawan and the succeeding drama forms remain important today. These came from the Middle East, India, the Southeast Asian region as well as the West. Nevertheless, culturally the early films manifested an Asian ethos and local values.

Realism entered Malay drama in the 1950s–60s, eventually finding its way into films. However, only in recent decades has the attraction for fantasy and legendary material given way to greater realism in Malay films. Experiments there were, with horror films, detective films, and in recent years science fiction, but the essential ingredients that made the films attractive to Malay audiences were to remain in place for a long time. However, recent productions have begun to demonstrate a degree of originality, inter alia, through the abandoning of formula films and nurturing of new themes. Experimental films have begun to find their own footing.

Television was introduced into the country in 1963, with colour television coming in 1978. The pioneering effort in Malay language television drama came with *Tetamu Malam* ('Night Guest') by Aziz Wok in 1964. There were to be many successors, and with the initiation of the 'Drama Minggu Ini' ('This Week's Drama') slot in the early 1970s, Malay TV drama for the first time began to be taken seriously. The range of offerings expanded, as did the themes, centred around social events, nation building, integration, and upon moral instruction. The greatest impact, however, was to come in 1984 with the development of privatized television, marked by technical sophistication, contemporary themes, and concepts that developed from imitation of the best Western productions.

Despite impressive technical and artistic developments in cinema and television drama, however, the problem of censorship continues to inhibit serious film making. Television dramas and films remain highly constrained, and compared with its counterpart in neighbouring countries, the Malaysian film industry has a long way to go before it can be taken seriously.

Posters of two of the 30-odd films directed by P. Ramlee in the 1960s and 1970s.

The development of Malay films

Hollywood and Hindustani films had been popular in Malaya for several decades before the emergence of the Malay film industry in 1933 with the production of Laila Majnun, *a Middle Eastern romance. Like its forerunner, Bangsawan, from which many of its best-known actors and actresses, designers and musicians migrated to the cinema, this new medium was multiracial in character, with contributions from Malays, Chinese, Indians, Filipinos and Indonesians. This situation changed in the 1960s with the Malay domination of the artistic aspects of film-making. Films of the 1990s, particularly those directed by younger directors, have once again developed to be multiracial in content, theme, and casting.*

Selubung ('Veil of Life'), directed by Shuhaimi Baba, was selected for exhibition at the Brussels Film Festival in 1997.

Ringgit Kasorga, another of Shuhaimi's films that was shown at the Brussels Film Festival in 1997.

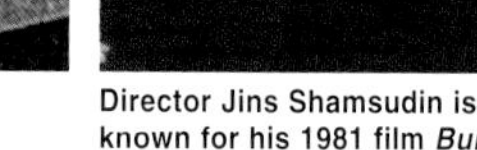

Director Jins Shamsudin is best known for his 1981 film *Bukit Kepong* ('Kepong Hill').

P. Ramlee was among the pioneer Malay directors, his first effort being *Penarek Becha* (1955), in which he also acted with co-star Saadiah.

Bangsawan influences

Laila Majnun, directed by B. S. Rajhans, was one of several important Middle Eastern stories that found their way into Malay films through Bangsawan. Others originated from Indian, Javanese, as well as from Malay literary sources (see 'Bangsawan and Jikey operatic theatre').

The success of *Laila Majnun* set the stage for the rapid development of the Malay film industry. In 1939, brothers Runme Shaw and Run Run Shaw started the production of Malay films in Singapore. The Japanese Occupation interrupted production of Malay films, and following World War II, Malay Art Productions, in an attempt to counter Japanese cultural influence, came up with *Seruan Merdeka* ('Call for Freedom'), the first Malay realistic film with a nationalistic theme as well as Sino-Malay characters. Shaw Brothers resumed production with *Singapura di Waktu Malam* ('Singapore at Night'), a musical comedy directed by B. S. Rajhans, in 1947. During the 'golden years' of Malay films (1950s–early 1960s), many films became box office hits. The range of subject matter expanded considerably, and included history, politics, religion and contemporary social issues.

Pioneer Malay directors

The success of films directed by Indians prompted several Malay directors to venture into the field beginning with Haji Mahdi, whose film *Permata Diperlimbahan* (1952), however, was a failure. Shaw Brothers attempted to remedy the situation by inviting several directors from the Philippines, among them B. Avellana who directed *Sergeant Hassan* (1958), the first Malay war film. In a sense, P. Ramlee's successful directorial debut in 1955 with *Penarek Becha* ('Trishaw Puller') was to become a landmark. P. Ramlee was followed by S. Roomai Noor who directed *Adam* in 1956 and *Bawang Puteh Bawang Merah* in 1959, financially the most successful film of the 1950s.

The golden era of Malay films was also the decade of the Malay director, with the emergence of P. Ramlee, S. Roomai Noor, Jamil Sulong and others. Jamil Sulong directed *Batu Belah Batu Bertangkup* (1959) and *Lanchang Kuning* (1961). From that time on, Malay directors were to dominate the industry, their films increasingly demonstrating a return to roots through the use of local folklore and history.

Indian Influences

Apart from the repertoire which came through Indian sources, many of the early Malay films were characterized by a great deal of singing and dancing, a trend seen in Indian films. These elements were introduced into Malay films at their formative stage by Indian directors between 1947 and 1962. The Indian pioneering directors who followed in the footsteps of B. S. Rajhans, most of whom were brought in by Shaw Brothers, included S. Ramanathan, K. M. Bhasker, B. N. Rao, V. Grimaji, K. R. S. Shastri, Phani Majumdar, Dhiresh Ghosh and Kidar Sharma. Several local Indian directors, including L. Krishnan and K. M. Bhasker, also found a place in the industry.

LEFT: Indian director Phani Majumdar. RIGHT: L. Krishnan, who directed *Bakti* in 1950.

The rise of film companies

Motilal Chemical Company of Bombay, which produced *Laila Majnun*, was the first known company to get into the business of film production. Malay Film Productions remained active until 1967. The short-lived Nusantara Films produced about a dozen films. In 1952, Ho Ah Loke, a film distributor, established Rimau Film Productions in Singapore, with the company changing its name to Keris Film Productions the following year.

Loke Wan Tho's Cathay Organization came into being with the opening of Pavilion Cinema in Kuala

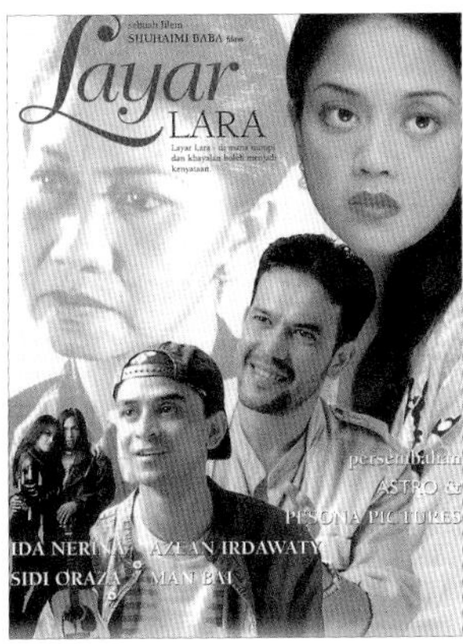

Lumpur in 1935, as well as Singapore's first cinema at the Cathay Building in 1939. By the 1970s Cathay had grown to become an established name in cinema operations with many classics and award-winning films to its credit. Its productions included the *Pontianak* series and *Orang Minyak* series, thus introducing into the Malay film world the genre of horror films. Important names attached to its studios included Wahid Satay and Rose Yatimah. In 1956 Keris Film Productions merged with Cathay Organization to set up Cathay-Keris Film Productions with its studio in Singapore.

Merdeka Film Productions of Kuala Lumpur, set up by H. M. Shah, attracted top stars from Singapore's two studios in the 1960s. This company grew dramatically but closed down in 1977, ironically with *Loceng Maut* ('Death Knell'). Today, its buildings serve as the headquarters of Perbadanan Kemajuan Filem Nasional (National Film Development Corporation, also known as FINAS), which was established in 1981 to develop the Malay film industry and provide support such as investment incentives and credit facilities for budding film-makers.

The huge profits made by Sabah Films, set up in 1975, from its maiden offering, *Keluarga Comat*, prompted the mushrooming of other companies, revitalizing the industry and initiating a renaissance. The new companies included Perfima, Syed Kechik Productions, Indra Film Productions, and Jins Shamsudin Productions.

Second-generation directors

Shaw Brothers sent several of their directors including L. Krishnan, P. Ramlee, Salleh Ghani, Jamil Sulong, Omar Rojik, S. Kadarisman, Sudarmadji, and Jins Shamsudin, to make films at Merdeka Studios in Hulu Kelang in the 1960s. These in fact comprise the second generation of directors, some of them, including Jamil Sulong and Jins Shamsudin, connecting the 1960s with the 1970s and 1980s.

Film content

The 1970s marked the increasing influence of Hollywood, with Malay films searching for new types of content. Jins Shamsudin imitated James Bond films, but his fame rests upon *Bukit Kepong* ('Kepong Hill') (1981). Jamil Sulong, on the other hand, directed a range of films following *Batu Belah Batu Bertangkup*, including *Raja Bersiong* ('Fanged King') (1968) and *Sumpahan Mahsuri* (1989), both based on local legends. Jamil is perhaps best known for *Ranjau Sepanjang Jalan* ('Suffering All the Way') (1983), based on a novel of the same title by literary laureate Shahnon Ahmad.

Recent decades have seen Malay films making use of increasingly sophisticated techniques of film making on the one hand and low budget productions on the other. The shift away from the formula of the 'golden era' is evident, too, in the choice of scripts. Films depicting family situations have given way to lightweight melodramas or comedies such as *Sikit Punya Gila* (1982), *Mekanik* (1983), *Azura* (1984), *Kaki Bakar* (1995), *Ali Setan* (1986), *Scenario The Movie* (1999), *Spinning Gasing* (2001) and *KL Menjerit* (2002). Increasingly too, there is less emphasis on promoting traditional family values and good citizenry. Instead, more serious themes and social issues have begun to emerge. Entertainment is not necessarily the only objective of these new films, some of which are experimental in character. Several directors, including U-Wei Saari, Adman Salleh, Teck Tan, Shuhaimi Baba, Aziz M. Osman, Erma Fatimah and Yusuf Haslam, have had a strong impact on audiences at home and internationally. At the same time, a crop of new actors and actresses has begun to make waves in the industry, among them Amy Mastura, Deanna Yusof, Ramona Rahman, Jalaluddin Hassan, M. Nasir and Rosyam Nor.

Tun Tijah was directed by L. Krishnan and produced by Merdeka Studios in 1960.

LEFT: Posters of *Ranjau Sepanjang Jalan*, which was directed by Jamil Sulong in 1983 and critically acclaimed; and *Layar Lara*, Shuhaimi Baba's 1997 directorial effort that was awarded Best Foreign Film at the Brussels Film Festival.

Malay films in international festivals

Over the years selected Malay films have been exhibited overseas, particularly at international festivals, and a number have been successful in garnering awards at the Asia-Pacific, Cannes and Brussels film festivals.

Year	Award	Film	Film festival
1956	Best music	*Hang Tuah*	Asia-Pacific Film Festival
1957	Best actor	*Anak-ku Sazali* (P. Ramlee)	Asia-Pacific Film Festival
1958	Best cinematography	*Sumpah Orang Minyak*	Asia-Pacific Film Festival
1959	Best comedy	*Pendekar Bujang Lapok*	Asia-Pacific Film Festival
1960	Best comedy	*Nujum Pa' Belalang*	Asia-Pacific Film Festival
1963	Most versatile talent	*Ibu Mertua-ku*	Asia-Pacific Film Festival
1964	Best comedy	*Madu Tiga*	Asia-Pacific Film Festival
1983	Best screenplay	*Ranjau Sepanjang Jalan*	Asia-Pacific Film Festival
1992	Best sound production	*Kanta Serigala*	Asia-Pacific Film Festival
1995	Best foreign film	*Kaki Bakar*	Brussels Film Festival
1997	Best foreign film	*Layar Lara* (Shuhaimi Baba)	Brussels Film Festival
1998	Best actor	*Jogho* (Khalid Salleh)	Asia-Pacific Film Festival
2000	Best sound production	*Leftenan Adnan*	Asia-Pacific Film Festival
2001	Best actress	*Spinning Gasing* (Ellie Suriaty)	Cinemaya Film Festival

Malaysia's first premier, the late Tunku Abdul Rahman (left) with film producer Runme Shaw in 1967.

Scripts

Many of the early productions were based on folk tales, Bangsawan scenarios, local legends, events taken from history or upon the lives of historical figures. Malay Film Productions' *Hang Tuah*, done in Eastman Colour, was directed by Indian director Phani Majumdar. By the time they ceased operations, Malay Film Productions and Cathay-Keris had produced three colour films each. Shaw Brothers produced *Ribut* ('Storm'), *Hang Tuah* ('Hang Tuah') and *Raja Bersiong* ('The Fanged King'). The script for *Raja Bersiong*, a Kedah legend, was written by Malaysia's first Prime Minister, Tunku Abdul Rahman. Cathay-Keris produced *Buluh Perindu* ('The Magic Flute'), *Cinta Gadis Rimba* ('The Virgin of Borneo') and *Mahsuri* ('Mahsuri'), another Kedah legend, also scripted by Tunku Abdul Rahman.

The P. Ramlee era

The Malay film industry began in 1933, and in the decades since there have been several periods marked by outstanding contributions by one or more personalities. During one such peak period—1950s–60s—one name stood out: P. Ramlee. This artiste extraordinaire was multi-talented; wearing alternately the hats of singer, composer, lyricist, actor, playwright, director and producer, and is, in fact, regarded as the Malaysian film industry's most outstanding personality.

Ibrahim Din, A. R. Tompel and P. Ramlee in the 1972 film *Laksamana Do Re Mi.*

Top: A 1952 picture of P. Ramlee.

Bottom: Sarimah, one of P. Ramlee's leading ladies in the 1950s–60s.

A star is born

Born in Penang on 22 March 1929, and given the name Teuku Zakaria Teuku Nyak Puteh, P. Ramlee began his career in the arts playing on the ukulele. He later took formal lessons in music from Tuan Kamaruddin, studying the piano and the guitar. In his films P. Ramlee was often shown playing musical instruments. Indeed, apart from his considerable talent as an actor, his reputation is based upon his songs, which have enjoyed a resurgence in interest in recent years. Around the figure of P. Ramlee has developed an image of what someone unschooled in the performing arts can attain.

Film career

Discovered while singing at a fair in Penang in 1948, P. Ramlee was introduced to the art of the film by B. S. Rajhans, one of several Indian film directors active in the Malay cinema in its early phase. P. Ramlee joined Malay Film Productions in August 1948, initially as a background singer, making his debut as an actor the same year in the film *Chinta*, playing a villain. The film had S. Roomai Noor and Siput Sarawak in the leading roles. During the two-year period of the initial contract, P. Ramlee appeared in eight films, manifesting his remarkable versatility—playing a musician in *Noor Asmara* (1949), a comedian in *Nasib* and *Nilam* (both in 1949), and a villain once again in *Rachun Dunia* (1950). *Bakti* (1950) made P. Ramlee a star whilst *Takdir Illahi* (1950) sealed his reputation and set him on the road to fame.

With Shaw Brothers' backing, P. Ramlee's first effort as a director materialized in 1955 with *Penarek Becha* (see 'Development of Malay films'). P. Ramlee also wrote the original story for the film, as well as the dialogue and music. On top of that he played the lead role of Amran, a trishaw operator. The score included one of his most famous songs, the enigmatic 'Azizah'. The role of the heroine was played by a Singaporean actress, Saadiah, who began her career at the age of 13. She appeared in P. Ramlee's two earlier films *Rachun Dunia* and *Bakti*. P. Ramlee also cast Saadiah in *Semerah Padi*, his next film, and in several others.

Almost all P. Ramlee films became box-office hits. Malay audiences, and increasingly over the decades non-Malay audiences as well, adored his looks, his charismatic smile and personality, his skill as an actor and his 'golden' singing voice. His strength as an actor lay in his portrayal of the romantic hero.

Contribution of other talented artistes

P. Ramlee's films owed their success as much to the actresses and supporting stars as they did to him. The talented actresses with whom P. Ramlee was paired were Saadiah, Kasma Booty, Siput Sarawak, Siti Tanjong Perak, Rokiah, Neng Yatimah, Rosnani, Aini Hayati, Normadiah, Sarimah, Saloma, Zaiton and Latifah Omar. Kasma Booty was regarded as the first 'star' in the Malay film world with her appearance in *Chempaka* in 1947.

The supporting actors in the P. Ramlee's films, mainly recruited from the Bangsawan theatre, were Haron Omar, Yusof Banjar, Ahmad Nesfu, A. R. Tompel, S. Kadarisman, Jaafar Wiryo, Daeng Idris, Mustarjo, Malek Sutan Muda, D. Harris, Sharif Medan, Nordin Ahmad, M. Amin and M. Zain. Apart from Salleh Kamil and S. Kadarisman, two other supporting actors who played the role of villains with great effect in films directed by P. Ramlee were A. Rahim and Omar Suwita. All these stars embellished the films that P. Ramlee acted in and directed.

In *Pancha Delima* (1958), which he directed, P. Ramlee introduced a new talent, Jins Shamsudin, who soon became a celebrated figure. He starred in and directed over 50 films, garnering many awards and distinctions and building a reputation as a creative leader in the Malay film business. In 1969 Jins Shamsudin directed two films—*Di Belakang Tabir* and *Bukan Salah Ibu Mengandung*—in which P. Ramlee acted.

Left: P. Ramlee with Zaiton in the 1956 film *Anak-ku Sazali.*
Top right: P. Ramlee holding Kasma Booty and looking at Rokiah in *Sejoli.*
Right: *(Left to right)* D. Harris, Siput Sarawak and P. Ramlee.

Asian Film Festival awards won by P. Ramlee

Award	Film	Year
Best music	*Hang Tuah*	1956
Best actor	*Anak-ku Sazali*	1957
Best cinematography	*Sumpah Orang Minyak*	1958
Best comedy	*Pendekar Bujang Lapok*	1959
Best comedy	*Nujum Pa' Belalang*	1960
Most versatile talent	*Ibu Mertua-ku*	1963
Best comedy	*Madu Tiga*	1964

Recognition

P. Ramlee's work as an outstanding film artiste was acknowledged not only by cinema audiences throughout Malaya, Singapore and Indonesia, but also by international organizations. Many of his films became perennial classics, with *Antara Dua Darjat, Sumpah Orang Minyak, Sergeant Hassan, Musang Berjanggut, Bujang Lapok, Labu Labi* and *Do Re Mi* the series and many more continuing to be screened over and over again.

Child actors

One of the most successful child actors of early Malay films was Bat Latiff. His portrayal as the son of Pa' Belalang in *Nujum Pa' Belalang* (1959) was an enchanting blend of guile, resourcefulness and sheer youthful high spirits. It was no surprise that Bat Latiff won the 'Best Performance for a Child Actor' award at the Asian Film Festival in 1960 for his role in the film and again in 1963 and 1964 for his roles in *Lela Manja* and *Gerhana*, both directed by Jamil Sulong. Another child actor awarded 'Best Performance by a Child Actor' at the Asian Film Festival was Tony Castello (*Anak-Ku Sazali*, 1957).

From Singapore to Kuala Lumpur

Merdeka Film Productions was established in 1961 by H. M. Shah and Ho Ah Loke, one of the founders of Cathay-Keris Productions. In 1964, the capital of Malay films moved from Singapore to Merdeka Studios in Hulu Kelang, near Kuala Lumpur. Most of the actors, directors and studio workers in Singapore migrated to the new base. Among them were P. Ramlee, L. Krishnan, Jamil Sulong, Omar Rojik and S. Sudarmadji. P. Ramlee's first film at Merdeka Studios was *Si Tora Harimau Jadian* (1964), featuring the legend of the 'wolf-man'. P. Ramlee also took on the leading double role as the Jekyll and Hyde character. After two years at Merdeka Studios, P. Ramlee became the most productive figure, directing and/or acting in at least one film each year.

In 1972, P. Ramlee directed and acted in the comedy, *Laksamana Do Re Mi*. It was to be his last film. Aided and abetted by his old friends A. R. Tompel and Ibrahim Din, he brought back the three zany characters whose antics had delighted audiences in the old days.

P. Ramlee died of a heart attack on 29 May 1974, after having acted in no less than 62 films between 1948 and 1972, directed 34 films and composed 249 songs.

P. Ramlee's contribution

P. Ramlee was an immensely original and creative artiste. It is almost impossible to assess his contribution to the Malay film and music industries. He affected them in various ways, becoming a model to emulate and a source of inspiration for future generations of artistes. Through his films, he reflected the ethos of the Malays, their traditions and values, and their relations with Allah. While serving as a medium for social criticism, his films also served the cause of national unity. Over the years, his films have become popular not only among Malays, but with non-Malay audiences as well. In 1990, P. Ramlee was posthumously honoured and conferred an award by the Yang di Pertuan Agong (King) in recognition of his lifetime of contributions to the film industry.

P. Ramlee in the 1958 film *Sumpah Orang Minyak*.

P. Ramlee (second from left) with co-star Ahmad Nesfu (right) in the 1959 film *Nujum Pak Belalang*.

LEFT: Left to right: Saloma, Normadiah, P. Ramlee, Neng Yatimah, Mariani and S. Sudarmadji at the Asian Film Festival in 1958.

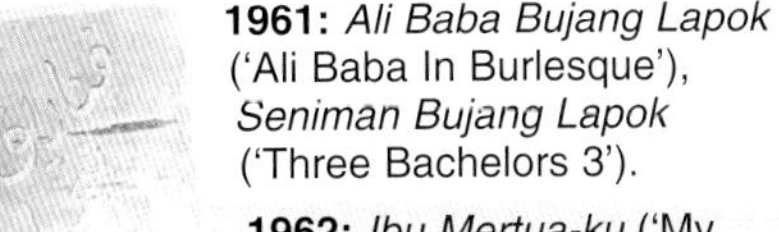

P. Ramlee films

1948: *Chinta* ('Love')

1949: *Nilam, Nasib* ('Fate'), *Noor Asmara*

1950: *Aloha, Bakti, Rachun Dunia, Takdir Illahi.*

1951: *Juwita, Penghidupan, Sejoli.*

1952: *Anjoran Nasib, Antara Senyum dan Tangis* ('Between Smile and Tears'), *Patah Hati* ('Broken Heart'), *Miskin* ('Poor'), *Sedarah.*

1953: *Hujan Panas, Ibu* ('Mother'), *Putus Harapan* ('Lost Hope'), *Siapa Salah* ('Who's Guilty?').

1954: *Perjodohan, Panggilan Pulau, Merana.*

1955: *Abu Hassan Penchuri* ('Abu Hassan The Thief').

1956: *Hang Tuah* ('Legend of Hang Tuah'), *Anak-ku Sazali* ('My Son Sazali'), *Semerah Padi.*

1957: *Bujang Lapok* ('Three Bachelors').

1958: *Pancha Delima Sumpah Orang Minyak* ('Curse of the Oily Man'), *Sergeant Hassan.*

1959: *Musang Berjanggut, Nujum Pa' Belalang* ('Fortune Teller'), *Pendekar Bujang Lapok* ('Three Bachelors 2').

1960: *Antara Dua Darjat*

1961: *Ali Baba Bujang Lapok* ('Ali Baba In Burlesque'), *Seniman Bujang Lapok* ('Three Bachelors 3').

1962: *Ibu Mertua-ku* ('My Mother-in-Law'), *Labu dan Labi* ('Labu and Labi').

1963: *Love Parade, Nasib Si Labu Labi* ('Labu and Labi 2').

1964: *Madu Tiga* ('Three Wives'), *Melanchong Ke Tokyo, Si Tora Harimau Jadian* ('Tiger Man'), *Tiga Abdul* ('Three Abduls').

1965: *Masam Masam Manis* ('Sweet Sour'), *Dajal Suchi, Ragam P Ramlee & Damaq.*

1966: *Sabarudin Tukang Kasut* ('Sabaruddin the Cobbler'), *Do Re Mi, Nasib Do Re Mi* ('Do Re Mi 2').

1967: *Keluarga 69* ('Family 69'), *Sesudah Suboh* ('After Dawn').

1968: *Anak Bapak* ('Like Father Like Son'), *Ahmad Albab, Gerimis.*

1969: *Bukan Salah Ibu Mengandung, Di Belakang Tabir, Kanchan Tirana.*

1970: *Enam Jahanam* ('Six Plunderers'), *Doktor Rushdi, Gelora.*

1971: *Jangan Tinggal Daku, Putus Sudah Kasih Sayang* ('Lost Love').

1972: *Laksamana Do Re Mi* ('Do Re Mi 3').

Malay television dramas

With the introduction of television services into Malaysia in November 1963, it was to be expected that eventually television drama would come into being. Malaysian audiences, in fact, did not have to wait long, for a year later almost to the day the first television drama was aired. Thus in addition to the cinema and live drama, television was to provide even greater entertainment choices. Since 1964 television drama, particularly in the Malay language, has provided a mixed fare, catering for both urban and rural audiences.

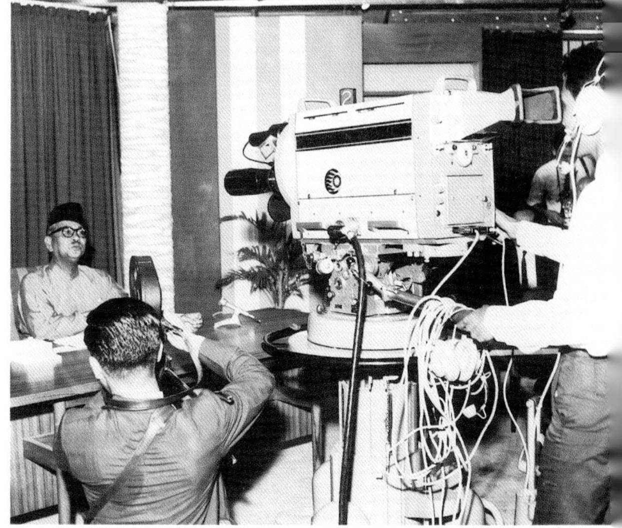

The first Prime Minister Tunku Abdul Rahman at the inauguration of Television Malaysia, Kuala Lumpur on 28 December 1963.

Development of TV

1963
Radio Television Malaysia

First terrestrial TV station. Government owned under purview of Information Ministry.

1984

First private free-to-air TV station. Owned and operated by Sistem Television Malaysia Berhad.

1994

First subscription cable TV network. Owned by Cableview Services Sdn Bhd, which stopped broadcasting in 2000 due to financial problems.

1995

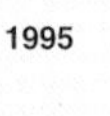

Second private TV station. Owned by Metropolitan TV Sdn Bhd. Transmisson supended in 1999 due to financial difficulties.

1997

Second pay cable TV network. Owned by MEASAT Broadcast Network Services Sdn Bhd. Offers over 40 TV channels and 16 radio channels.

1998

Private terrestrial TV station. Owned by Natseven TV Sdn Bhd.

2003

Private TV station. Owned by Medanmas Sdn Bhd.

2004

Private TV station. Owned by Metrovision.

Malay drama on television

On 13 November 1964, the first Malay television drama, 'Tetamu Malam', was broadcast by the state-owned Radio Television Malaysia (RTM) station. Produced by Abdul Aziz Wok, it was followed by fortnightly series such as 'Keluarga Tompel', and 'Telatah Mak Mah', both written by prominent pioneer scriptwriter A. R. Tompel. In 1972 RTM introduced a weekly drama slot called 'Potret Pekerti', which was aired for three years, followed by the series 'Jiran' and 'Drama Minggu Ini'. 'Jiran' featured characters from three races—Sahar, a Malay; Ayapan, an Indian; and Wong Peng, a Chinese—and was a portrayal of the lives of these people as neighbours, dealing with everyday social, economic and political issues. 'Drama Minggu Ini', on the other hand, featured individual dramas with different stories and characters.

The weekly drama was a complete story with a different cast and location that ran for about 45 minutes, while the weekly series featured the same cast and set, with half-hour episodes. RTM also aired a full-length drama of about 75 minutes duration on special occasions in the slot called 'Panggung RTM'. Other series produced later were 'Opah' and 'Bangsawan'.

Television drama was initially produced in black and white. RTM began broadcasting in colour on 28 December 1978. The earliest weekly series shot in colour were 'PJ' and the station's first sitcom, 'Santan Berlada'.

Popular serial dramas and sitcoms

Since the launch of TV3, the first private television channel in Malaysia on 1 June 1984, followed by other networks, including cable television stations, many slots have been introduced to offer a wide selection of locally produced dramas, serials and sitcoms. TV3's 'Cerekarama' slot airs a 90-minute drama every week and is a favourite with viewers while its longest running sitcom 'Pi Mai Tang Tu' has completed 33 seasons. The station's other dramas include 'Samarinda Badai Metropolis'. Its sitcoms include 'Senario', which has enjoyed top rating since its first run in 1996, '2+1' and 'Jangan Ketawa'. NTV7, which commenced operations on 7 April 1998, broadcasts Malay drama series and sitcoms in its 'Bintang Prima' slot. This slot runs on prime time from Monday to Thursday. The station's popular sitcom is 'Spanar Jaya', which revolves around the daily life of a group of car mechanics. ASTRO, too, airs many Malay dramas and series on its Ria Channel.

A slot introduced by NTV7 in the early 2000s, 'Odissi', showcases the work of budding directors and independent filmmakers, with the objective of encouraging local drama production. Some of the dramas aired in this slot are commendable productions, for instance, 'Piala untuk Mama', written and directed by Bernard Chauly; 'Rambutan

Popular TV dramas and sitcoms

1

3

Personalities in early television drama

The first television drama producers and actors came from the film industry, among them A. R. Tompel, Mak Minah and P. Ramlee. They were succeeded by Ahmad Tarmini, Omar Abdullah, Tawfik Kang, Zain Ismail and Khalid Salleh in the mid-1970s. Actresses of the 1970s–80s included Azean Irdawatty, Rubiah Suparman, Asmah Hani Hussein, Nancy Foo and Lai Joo Lian.

Early RTM producers were Zainuddin Nordin, Aziz Abass, Hasiah Ariffin, Zohara Gani Batusha, Othman Hafsham and Abdullah Zainol. Most of them were trained by the British Broadcasting Corporation as well as the London School of Film and Television Technique.

The late Zain Mahmud, Zainuddin Hamzah, Mohd Noor Ghani and Zain Haji Hamzah were among prominent scriptwriters. Abdullah Zainol's memorable 'Panggung RTM' slot featured scripts written by Johan Jaafar, Mana Sikana and Othman Haji Zainuddin.

Abdullah Zainol

Johan Jaafar

Direct Selling', written and directed by Mohamad Napi Dollah; and 'Tomi Cinta Delia', written by Julian Jayaseela and directed by Shanmugam.

Both RTM and TV3 give annual awards to dramas aired over television based on creativity, artistry and content. Since 1972, RTM has honoured several directors, producers, actors and actresses with its Anugerah Seri Angkasa (Seri Angkasa Awards). Similarly, TV3 honours outstanding dramas aired by the station at its annual Anugerah Skrin TV3 (TV3 Screen Awards), which it started in 1998.

Drama content

The initial television dramas of the 1960s placed little emphasis on themes and issues, and were mainly imitations of Western productions. In the 1970s, however, a consistency developed in terms of story ideas, and drama, both print and audio-visual, took a more active role in nation building. Drama themes often had moral, social and political messages, and exhorted the pursuit of development and harmony in a multi-ethnic society. For instance, 'Harapan dalam Lumpur' (1974), written by Azizi Haji Abdullah, was the story of a young Malay man returning to his *kampung* upon completing his tertiary education and channelling his energy and knowledge into developing his rural environment. Dramas of the period also sought to foster nationalism and patriotism, as in 'Wira' (1979) written by Zakaria M. Z. and produced by Abdullah Zainol, which was based upon history, in particular the struggle of Maharaja Lela against the colonialists.

In the 1980s and 1990s, television drama appeared to follow trends seen in films and staged dramas in terms of content. Popular themes of contemporary television drama range from crime, love and family stories to corporate conflicts.

Top: Sitcom '2+1.kom.my' was favourably received by viewers when TV3 aired it in the late 1990s.

Above: 'Jangan Ketawa', a sitcom broadcast by TV3 in the 1980s.

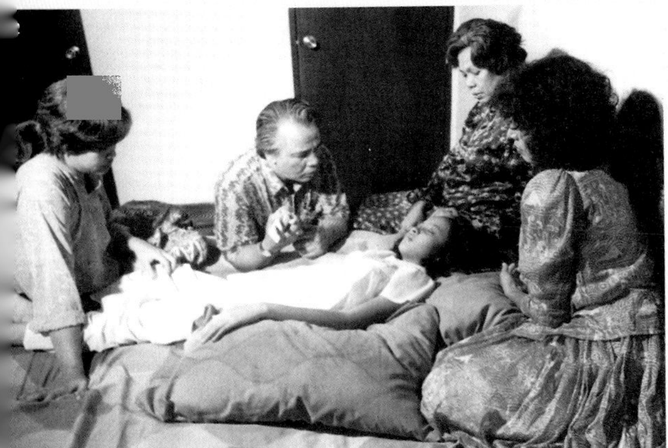

1. 'Hilang' 2. 'PJ' 3. 'Rumah Kedai' 4. 'Antik' 5. 'Panggung RTM'

The production process

Initially all dramas were shot indoors. A studio was used which could accommodate large sets comprising a living room, dining area, kitchen and a bedroom complete with furniture and fixtures. The action of the drama in the studio was recorded on videotape using studio cameras which were electronically linked to recorders in a control room where the director or producer, assistant director, technical director, audio technician and video technician worked. This production team also operated from the control room during camera rehearsals. Usually three studio cameras on tripods and pedestals would be used simultaneously to frame the actors and their actions in different shots and angles. During a location shoot (electronic field production), the control room may be located away from the shooting scene in a remote production control truck or outside broadcast unit.

During the mid-1980s, the scenario for Malay television drama began to take a new course. Private production houses were given the opportunity to submit proposals for drama productions of their own choice. Malay television dramas were then shot entirely on location on a single video camera using film techniques. Production houses engaged in film production began to work on shorter drama scripts meant for television. Among the companies active at the time were Sabah Films, Indra Films and Syed Kechik Film Productions.

Now there are more than 300 film companies and production houses registered with the Perbadanan Kemajuan Filem Nasional (National Film Development Corporation) producing Malay television dramas for both the government and private television and cable stations. Among them are HVD Film Productions which produced the action series 'Pendekar' starring Raja Azura in 1995; Kuasatek Pictures Sdn Bhd which produces many series and dramas for TV3 such as 'Cinta Antara Benua' starring Azah Aziz, Ahmad Idham and Rusdi Ramli, which was shot in London in 1997, and 'Salam Taj Mahal', which was shot in India and starred Sidi Oraza, Umie Aida and Vaneeda Imran.

The shooting of TV3 sitcom 'Senario'.

Glossary

A

Aerophone: A wind instrument such as *serunai* and other flutes.
***Angin*:** Literally wind, but indicating repressed emotions or desires.
Asli: One of the three most important categories of Malay dances, as well as the accompanying music.
Asyik: Infatuation; genres of dance and music that evolved from a palace tradition in Kelantan in the 18th century.
Awang Batil: A form of solo theatre involving storytelling in which a performer uses a brass bowl as an accompanying instrument.

B

Bagih: Traditional Malay healing ritual involving trance.
***Bakaba*:** Storytelling, verse recitation.
Bangsawan: Malay opera.
Bantogen: Hero of *Darangen*, an epic poem popular in the Philippines and Sabah.
Barongan: Javanese theatre form using animal masks.
Batil: Brass bowl used by traditional Malay storytellers to provide musical accompaniment.
Belian: A shaman dance of the Orang Asli and Malays.
Benzoin: White crystalline solid in natural resins used in incense.
***Berjamu*:** Ritual in which spirits are fed by a *dalang* in trance.
***Bertabik*:** To salute or pay respects.
***Berzanji*:** A literary style of composition relating to the life of Prophet Muhammad.
Bhangra: Traditional Punjabi dance accompanied by a small ensemble.
Bharata Natyam: South Indian classical dance.
Bhota: Ogre character in Wayang Kulit.
***Bintang*:** Star performer.
***Bobohizan*:** A female shaman.
***Bomoh*:** Healer or shaman.
Borea: Theatre form said to derive from Shia Islamic passion plays.
***Buah pinang*:** Betel nut; areca nut.
***Buka panggung*:** Ritual involving the 'opening' of the theatre before a performance.

C

Caliph: Islamic ruler, successors of Muhammad.
Canggung: A popular dance performed in Perlis.
Carnatic: 'South Indian' (derived from Karnataka, South India); also Karnatic or Karnatak.

D

Dabus: A performance that combines dance, music and martial art, and contains a display of self-mutilation.
***Dalang*:** Puppeteer, originally from the Javanese for storyteller.
***Dalang muda*:** In Wayang Kulit Siam, the apprentice puppeteer; also the opening section of a performance.
***Dangdut*:** Romantic, melancholic music with Indian and Islamic flavour.
***Darangen*:** An epic poem popular in the Philippines and Sabah.
Dikir Barat: A secularized form of Islamic religious chanting.
***Doa selamat*:** Islamic invocations.
Dondang Sayang: Love songs; an elaborate form of pantun singing.

E

***Engkerumong*:** An Iban musical ensemble, including hanging gongs and drums.

G

***Gambus*:** A lute fashioned after the Arabic *o'ud*.
Gamelan: Traditional Indonesian percussion orchestra, comprising mainly bronze or brass instruments.
Gawai: Sarawak harvest festival.
Gebiah: Animistic healing ritual involving trance.
***Gendang tarinai*:** Percussion and wind ensemble accompanying dances at a wedding during the staining of the bride's hands and feet with henna.
Ghazal: The singing of religious and romantic verses.

H

Hadrah: Musical performance with Middle Eastern influences.
Hamdolok: A theatre form derived from the Middle East.
Hanuman: Monkey character in the *Ramayana* epic.
***Hikayat*:** Legendary or historical story.
***Hikayat Maharaja Wana*:** An oral Malay version of the *Ramayana*.

I

Idiophone: A percussion instrument such as cymbal, xylophone or gong, made of sonorous material.
***Inang*:** Female court attendant; also a Malay dance genre.

J

Jataka Tales: A collection of 547 stories and tales about the Buddha in his previous lives.
Jikey: A form of operatic theatre active in Kedah and Perlis.
Joget: One of the three most important categories of Malay dance.
Joget Gamelan: A court dance and music form that evolved in Pahang and Terengganu in the 19th century.

K

Karagattam: A impromptu dance seen during the Thaipusam festival; also the pot placed on the head during such a dance.
Kathakali: South Indian classical dance drama based on the *Ramayana* and *Mahabharata* epics.
Kavadi Attam: An impromptu dance sometimes performed by *kavadi* carriers.
***Kelir*:** White cloth screen in shadow play onto which shadows of puppets are projected.
***Kemenyan*:** Benzoin; incense.
***Kenduri*:** Feast; also items used in rituals connected with theatre consecration.
Keroncong: The singing of love songs with origins in the 16th century music of the Portuguese in the Moluccas and Batavia.
Kuda Kepang: Hobbyhorse made from plaited bamboo slats; form of dance originating from Java.
***Kulintangan*:** A row of six to nine kettle gongs.

L

***Lagu*:** Song, melody.
***Lakhon*:** Thai word meaning performance or story.
Lakhon Chatri: The proper name for the dance theatre form popularly known as Menora or Nora.
Laksamana: Rama's brother in the *Ramayana* epic.
Likay: Thai opera, said to have developed from Bangsawan.

M

***Mahabharata*:** Important Hindu epic, dealing with the conflict between the Pandawa and Korawa clans.
Maharisi: A sage in the *Ramayana* epic.
Main Puteri: A shamanistic healing ritual active in Kelantan.
Mak Hiang: Rice spirit.
Mak Yong: Ancient Malay dance theatre of Kelantan and Patani in

present-day Thailand.

Mantera: Incantation or ritual formula.

Marhaban: Literally, welcome; songs of this genre, with particular reference to songs played to honour the Prophet Muhammad.

Maulud: Celebrations marking the birthday of the Prophet Muhammad; also another term for *Berzanji*.

Mek Mulung: A dance theatre form active in Kedah.

Membranophone: A membrane-covered percussion instrument.

Menghadap rebab: The opening dance and song sequence in a Mak Yong performance; salutation to the *rebab*.

Menora: A Thai-influenced dance theatre form.

Muzik seriosa: 'Serious' music.

N

Nang Sbek Thom: Cambodian shadow play using large puppets.

Nang Talung: Southern Thai shadow play style.

Nang Yai: Thai version of the Cambodian Nang Sbek Thom.

Nasyid: Form of Islamic religious music.

Natyasastra: The most important classical work on Indian performing arts, by Bharata.

Ngajat: A dance of the Iban, Bidayuh and Melanau associated with bravery.

Nobat: Royal orchestra.

O

Odissi: A form of Indian classical dance.

Orang Asli: Indigenous, or aboriginal, peoples of Malaysia.

P

Panggung: Stage, operating box used for presenting shadow play; also theatre or venue for performances.

Panjak: Musicians in Wayang Kulit Siam ensemble.

Panji tales: A series of stories developed around the character of the mediaeval Javanese culture hero Raden Inu Kartapati, popularly known as Panji.

Pantun: A poem of four (or sometimes more) lines with alternate rhyming lines.

Parsi theatre: A genre of Indian operatic theatre which evolved into Bangsawan.

Pencak Silat: Indonesian form of the art of self-defence.

Pentas joget: Dance hall.

Pi: Thai reed wind instrument.

Pohon beringin: Banyan tree; leaf-shaped puppet that opens and ends Wayang Kulit performances.

Proscenium: The arch separating the stage from the auditorium together with the area immediately in front of the arch.

Proto-theatre: Elementary or early theatre.

Q

Qasidah: Arabic poetry sung to the accompaniment of frame drums.

Quatrain: A stanza or poem of four lines, especially one having alternate rhyming lines.

R

Raja Bali: One of two monkey kings in the *Ramayana* epic.

Rama: Hero of the *Ramayana* epic.

Ramakien: Thai version of the *Ramayana*, used in Wayang Kulit Gedek.

Ramayana: Literally 'Rama's wanderings', an Indian epic.

Randai: Dance theatre involving acting, singing and *silat* martial art movements.

Ravana: Demon king, and villain in the *Ramayana* epic.

Rebab: Two or three-stringed lute.

Rodat: A dance of Arab origin.

Ronggeng: A type of music to accompany dance; also the dance.

S

Salawat: Phrases invoking Allah to bless the Prophet Muhammad, usually incorporated in genres of Islamic vocal music.

Sandiwara: The first form of Malay theatre using scripts.

Sang Thong: The story of the Prince of the Conch Shell, performed in Mak Yong as *Anak Raja Gondang*.

Sapeh: A lute of the Kenyah, Kayan and Kelabit communities of Sarawak.

Selampit: A simple form of theatre involving a single storyteller.

Semah: To cleanse. In traditional theatre it implies cleansing from some psychological malady.

Semangat: Soul, spirit, or universal vital energy.

Semar: Ancient deity; principal comic figure in Javanese traditional theatre forms.

Sembah: To pay homage to invisible beings or superior persons in the Hindu-Buddhist manner.

Sembah guru: Ceremony involving paying homage to teachers or officially graduating in a traditional art form.

Sewang: Dance ritual of the Temiar.

Silat: Form of martial art.

Sita Dewi: The heroine and Rama's wife in the *Ramayana* epic.

Sudawil: A *pantun*-like genre performed by the Kadazandusun.

Sugriva: The other monkey king in the *Ramayana* epic, and brother of Raja Bali.

Sumazau: An important dance of Sabah associated with the spirit world.

T

Taklempong: Knobbed gongs.

Tandak: Social dance form that includes call and response singing.

Tarian lilin: Candle dance.

Tarik Selampit: A form of solo theatre involving storytelling to the accompaniment of a rebab.

Tarsila: Genealogies.

Terinai: Court dance genre in Perlis, Kedah and Kelantan.

Tok Minduk: The shaman's assistant and interrogator in a Main Puteri performance.

Tok Puteri: The shaman in a Main Puteri performance.

Tutup panggung: Rite to close a theatre after a performance.

U

Ulik Mayang: Trance dance in Terengganu involving young girls.

W

Wayang Cina: The name locally given to the Chinese opera.

Wayang Kulit: Shadow play; puppet theatre form using skin figures.

Wayang Kulit Gedek: Shadow play form derived from Thai Nang Talung, performed in Kedah and Perlis.

Wayang Kulit Melayu: Javanese-derived shadow play form performed in Kelantan.

Wayang Kulit Purwa: Classical Javanese shadow play based on *Ramayana* and *Mahabharata* epics performed in Johor.

Wayang Kulit Siam: Principal form of Malay shadow play performed in Kelantan (also referred to as Wayang Kulit Kelantan).

Z

Zapin: Dance genre adapted from the Arabic version.

Zikir: Remembrance; repeated uttering of specific names of Allah usually in a rhythmic manner; locally Dikir.

Randai performance.

Bibliography

Abbreviations

JMBRAS *Journal of the Malaysian Branch of the Royal Asiatic Society*

MIH *Malaya in History*

Abdullah bin Mohamed (1971), 'The Ghazal in Arabic Literature and in Malay Music', *MIH*, 14(1): 24–31.

Affan, Seljuq (1976), 'Some Notes on the Origin and Development of the Naubat', *JMBRAS*, 49(1): 141–142.

Ahmad Omar (1984), 'Joget Gamelan: the Art of Orchestral Dance', *Performing Arts* (Singapore), 1: 38–41.

Ainon Abu Bakar and Zulkeply Mohamed (eds.) (1993), *Modern ASEAN Plays: Malaysia*, Kuala Lumpur: The ASEAN Committee on Culture and Information.

Ang Bee Saik (1997), 'Perkembangan dan Struktur Persembahan Menora di Utara Semenanjung Malaysia'. M.A. Thesis, Universiti Sains Malaysia.

Baden, Cass (1966), 'Malayan Musical Instruments', *JMBRAS*, 45: 285–286.

Bamroongraks, W. (1986), 'Manohra': The Cultural Traditional Media of Asean. Manila: Asean Committee on Culture and Information.

Banks, David J. (1976), *Trance and Dance in Malaya: The Hindu-Buddhist Complex in Northwest Malay Folk Religion*, Special Series No. 74, Council on International Special Studies, Buffalo: State University of New York.

Brandon, J. R. (1967), *Theatre in Southeast Asia*, Cambridge, Mass: Harvard University Press.

—— (1993), *Brandon's Guide to Asian Theatre*, Cambridge, Mass: Cambridge University Press.

Brunet, Jacques (1971), *Wayang Kulit de Kelantan: Theatre d'Ombre de Malaysia*, Berlin: Institut International d'Etudes Comparative de la Musique.

Burridge, K. O. L. (1961), *Kuda Kepang in Batu Pahat, Johore, Man*, 61: 33–36.

Camoens, Cantius Leo (1981), 'History and Development of Malay Theatre', M.A. Thesis, Universiti Malaya.

Chia, Felix (1980), *The Babas*, Singapore: Times Books International.

Chin, Lucas (1980), *Cultural Heritage of Sarawak*, Kuching: The Sarawak Museum.

Chopyak, James D. (1986), *Music in Modern Malaysia: A Survey of the Music Affecting the Development of Malaysian Popular Music, Asian Music*, 18 (1): 111–138.

Coedes, George (1969), *The Making of Southeast Asia*, Trans. H. M. Wright. Berkeley: University of California Press.

Cuisinier, Jeanne (1936), *Danses Magiques de Kelantan*, Travaux et Memoires de l' Institut D'Ethnologie de l'Universite de Paris.

—— (1957), *Le Theatre de Ombres a Kelantan*, Paris: Gallimard.

D'Cruz, Marion F. (1979), 'Joget Gamelan: A Study of its Performance Practice', M.A. Thesis, Universiti Sains Malaysia.

Endicott, Kirk Michael (1970), *An Analysis of Malay Magic*, London: Oxford University Press.

Fatimi, S. Q. (1963), *Islam Comes to Malaysia*, Singapore: Malaysian Sociological Research Institute.

Fernando, J. Sunetra (1996), 'Lagu Menghadap Rebab in the Mak Yong Theatre of Kelantan and South Thailand: An Interpretative Musical Analysis', M.A. Thesis, Universiti Malaya.

Fernando, Lloyd (comp.) (1972), *New Drama One*, Kuala Lumpur: Oxford University Press.

—— *New Drama Two* (1973), Kuala Lumpur: Oxford University Press.

Firth, Raymond (1967), 'Ritual and Drama in Malay Spirit Mediumship', *Comparative Studies in Society and History*, 9.

Frame, Edward (1975), 'A Preliminary Survey of Several Major Musical Instruments and Form-Types of Sabah, Malaysia', *Borneo Research Bulletin*, 7(1): 16–24.

Ghulam-Sarwar Yousof (1976), 'The Kelantan Mak Yong Dance Theatre: A Study of Performance Structure', Ph.D. Dissertation, University of Hawaii, Honolulu.

—— (1982), *Halfway Road, Penang*. Penang: Teks Publishing Co. Reprinted by the Asian Centre, Penang, 2002.

—— (1982), *Mak Yong: The Ancient Malay Dance Theatre*, Asian Studies, University of the Philippines.

—— (1983), 'Feasting of the Spirits: The Berjamu Ritual Performance in the Kelantanese Wayang Siam Shadow Play', *Kajian Malaysia*, 1(1): 95–115.

—— (1986) *Ceremonial and Decorative Crafts of Penang*. Penang: The State Museum.

—— (1992), *Panggung Semar: Aspects of Traditional Malay Theatre*, Kuala Lumpur: Tempo Publishing.

—— (1994), *Dictionary of Traditional South-East Asian Theatre*, Kuala Lumpur: Oxford University Press.

—— (1997), *Angin Wayang: A Biography of a Master Puppeteer*, Kuala Lumpur: Ministry of Culture, Arts and Tourism, Malaysia.

—— (1997), *The Malay Shadow Play: An Introduction*, Penang: The Asian Centre.

Ginsburg, Henry (1972), 'Sudhana-Manora Tale in Thai: A Comparative Study Based on Two Texts', Ph.D. Dissertation, University of London.

Goldsworthy, David (1979), 'Malayu Music of North Sumatra', Ph.D. Dissertation, Monash University, Melbourne.

Guntavid, Joseph, John-Baptist, Judeth, Lasimbang, Rita and Pugh-Kitingan, Jacqueline (1992), *Introduction to Sabah's Traditional Musical Instruments*, Kota Kinabalu: Department of Sabah Museum and State Archives.

Hamilton, A. W. (1982), *Malay Pantuns*. Singapore: Eastern Universities Press.

Hamzah Awang Amat and Matusky, Patricia (1998), *Muzik Wayang Kulit Kelantan*. Penang: The Asian Centre.

Hill, A. H. (1949), 'Wayang Kulit Stories from Trengganu', *JMBRAS*, 22(3): 85–105.

Ho Mei-Lu (1991), *The Royal Nobat of Kedah, Malaysia*, M.A. Thesis, University of California, Los Angeles.

Iyengar, Sreenivasa (ed.) (1983), *Asian Variations in Ramayana*, New Delhi: Sahitya Akademi.

Kee Thuan Chye (1987), *1984 Here and Now*, Kuala Lumpur: Vintex Trading Company.

—— (1994), *We Could **** You Mr. Birch*, Kuala Lumpur.

Khoo, S. N. (1990), 'Thai Menora: The Initiation Ceremony'. *Pulau Pinang*, 2(3): Penang: Georgetown Printers.

Ku Zam Zam Ku Idris (1975), *Traditional Malay Musical Ensembles in Northern Kedah*, Quezon City: University of the Philippines.

—— 'Nobat: Music in the Service of the King—the Symbol of Power and Status in Traditional Malay Society', Tinta Kenangan. Kuala Lumpur: Universiti Malaya.

Laderman, Carol (1991), 'Main Puteri: Malay Shamanism', *Federation Museums Journal*, 31 (New Series).

—— (1991), *Taming the Wind of Desire: Psychology, Medicine and Aesthtics in Malay Shamanistic Performance*, Berkeley: University of California Press.

Langub, Jayl (2001), Suk_t: Penan Folk Stories. Dayak Studies Oral Literature Series, No. 2. Kota Samarahan: Universiti Malaysia Sarawak.

Le May, Reginald E. (1954), *Culture of Southeast Asia: The Heritage of India*, London: Allen and Unwin.

Lee Joo For (1970), *'Son of Zen' in Three Southeast Asian Plays*, Kuala Lumpur: Universiti Malaya.

Linehan, W. (1951), 'The Nobat and the Orang Kalau of Perak', *JMBRAS*, 24(3): 60–68.

Low Kim Chuan (1976), 'Dondang Sayang in Melaka', B.A. Thesis, Monash University, Melbourne.

Malm, William P. (1971), 'Malaysian Ma'Yong Theatre', *The Drama Review*, 15(3): 108–121.

Maniam, K. S. (1983), *The Cord*, Kuala Lumpur:Aspatra Quest Publishers. Republished (1994) in *Sensuous Horizons*. London: Skoob Books Publishing Ltd.

Manisegaran, A. (1987), *Malaysiavil Medai Nadagangal (Tamil Dramas in Malaysia)*, Kuala Lumpur: Anban Press.

Manusama, A. (1992), *Th. Komedie Stamboul of De Oost-Idische Opera*, Batavia.

Matusky, Patricia (1986), *'Aspects of Musical Style Among the Kajang, Kayan and Kenyah-Badong of the Upper Rejang River: A Preliminary Survey', The Sarawak Museum Journal*. XXXVI(57): New Series, 185–229.

—— (1997), *Malaysian Shadow Play and Music: Continuity of an Oral Tradition*, Penang: The Asian Centre (Reprint).

Matusky, Patricia and Tan Sooi Beng (1997), *Muzik Malaysia: Tradisi Klasik, Rakyat dan Sinkretik*, Penang: The Asian Centre.

Miettinen, Jukka O. (1992), *Classical Dance and Theatre in South-East Asia*, Singapore: Oxford University Press.

Mohamad Kassim Bin Haji Ali (1974), 'Kuda Kepang', *Federation Museums Journal*, 19: 1–20.

Mohd Anis Md Nor (1986), *Randai Dance of Minang Kabau with Labonatation Scores*, Kuala Lumpur: Universiti Malaya Press.

—— (1993), *Zapin: Folk Dance of the Malay World*, Singapore: Oxford University Press.

Mohd Taib Osman (ed.) (1974), *Traditional Drama and Music of Southeast Asia*. Kuala Lumpur: Dewan Bahasa dan Pustaka.

Munan, Heidi (1990), *Iban Stories*, Petaling Jaya: Penerbit Fajar Bakti.

Nanney, Nancy (1983), 'An Analysis of Modern Malaysian Drama', Ph.D. Dissertation, University of Hawaii.

Ongkili, James P. (1970), 'The Traditional Musical Instruments of Sabah', *Universiti Malaya Historical Society Journal*, 8: 35–41.

Osnes, Mary Beth (1992), 'A Survey of Shadow Play in the Malaysian Traditional Shadow Puppet Theatre', Ph.D. Dissertation, University of Colorado.

Pugh-Kitingan, Jacqueline (1988) 'Instruments and Instrumental Music of the Tambunan Kadazan/Dusun', *Sabah Museum and Archives Journal*, 1(2): 24–61.

—— (1990), *Cultural Dances of Sabah*, Kota Kinabalu: Sabah Tourism Promotion Corporation.

Raghavan V. (ed.) (1980), *The Ramayana Tradition in Asia*, New Delhi: Sahitya Akademi.

Rahmah Bujang (1987), *Boria: A Form of Malay Theatre*, Singapore: Institute of Southeast Asian Studies.

Raja Badri Shah, Sheppard, Mubin, and Tunku Nong Jiwa (1962), 'The Kedah and Perak Nobat', *MIH*, 7(2).

Ramli Ibrahim (1994), *In the Name of Love*, London: Skoob Books Publishing Ltd.

Roselina Khir Johari (1977), 'The Role of the Playwright in Contemporary Malaysian Theatre', Masters Thesis, Indiana University.

Roseman, Marina (1991), *Healing Sounds from the Malaysian Rainforest: Temiar Music and Medicine*, Berkeley: University of California Press.

Rubenstein, Carol (1985), *The Honey Tree Song, Poems and Chants of Sarawak Dayaks*, Athens, Ohio: Ohio University Press.

Sandin, Benedict (1980), *The Living Legends: Borneans telling their Tales*, Kuala Lumpur: Dewan Bahasa dan Pustaka Malaysia.

Saong, Charles (1974), 'Sabah's Traditional Dances', *Sarawak Gazette*, 264–270.

Sather, Clifford 'Apai Alui Becomes a Shaman and Other Iban Comic Tales', Dayak Studies Oral Literature Series, No. 3. Kota Samarahan: Universiti Malaysia Sarawak.

Seeler, Joan DeWitt (1975), 'Kenyah Dance, Sarawak, Malaysia: A Description and Analysis', M.A. Thesis, University of Hawaii.

Shaw, William (1975), *Aspects of Malaysian Magic*, Kuala Lumpur: Museum Negara.

Sheppard, Mubin (1960), *The Magic Kite and Other Ma'Yong Stories*, Kuala Lumpur: Federal Publications.

—— (1973), 'Manora in Kelantan', *JMBRAS*, 46(1): 161–170.

—— (1974), *Taman Indera: Malay Decorative Arts and Pastimes*, Kuala Lumpur: Oxford University Press.

—— (1983), *Taman Saujana*, Petaling Jaya: International Book Service.

Skeat, Walter William (1967), *Malay Magic—Being an Introduction to the Folklore and Popular Religion of the Malay Peninsula*, New York: Dover Publications Inc.

Solehah Ishak (1987), *Histrionics of Development: A Study of Three Contemporary Malay Playwrights*, Kuala Lumpur: Dewan Bahasa dan Pustaka.

Sweeney, P. L. Amin (1971), 'Peran Hutan, a Malay Wayang Drama', *JMBRAS*, 44(2): 71–107.

—— (1972), *Malay Shadow Puppets: The Wayang Siam of Kelantan*. London: Trustees of the British Museum.

—— (1972), *The Ramayana and the Malay Shadow Play*, Kuala Lumpur: Universiti Kebangsaan Malaysia Press.

Tan Sooi Beng (1997), *Bangsawan: A Social and Stylistic History of Popular Malay Opera*, Penang: The Asian Centre (Reprint).

—— (1980), 'Chinese Opera in Malaysia: Changes and Survival', *Review of Southeast Asian Studies*, 10: 29–45.

—— (1984), *Ko-Tai Chinese Street Theatre in Malaysia*, Singapore: Institute of Southeast Asian Studies.

—— (1984), 'An Introduction to the Chinese Glove Puppet Theatre', *JMBRAS*, LVII(1): 40–45.

Taylor, Eric (1989), *Musical Instruments of South-East Asia*, Singapore: Oxford University Press.

Teeuw, A. and Wyatt, D. K. (1970), *Hikayat Patani*, 2 vols. The Hague: Martinus Nijhoff.

Thomas, Phillip (1986), *Like Tigers Around a Piece of Meat*, Singapore: Institute of Southeast Asian Studies.

Tilakasiri, Jayadeva (1970), *The Puppet Theatre of Asia*, Colombo: Department of Cultural Affairs.

—— (1999), *Asian Shadow Play*, Sri Lanka:Vishva Lekha.

Tunku Muda Mohamad (1968), 'The Silver Nobat of Trengganu', *MIH*, 12(1).

Usman Awang (1995), *Selected Plays* (trans by Solehah Ishak), Kuala Lumpur: Dewan Bahasa dan Pustaka.

Vente, Ines (1984), *Wayang: Chinese Street Opera in Singapore*, Singapore: MPH Booksellers (S) Pte Ltd.

Winstedt, R. O. (1961), *The Malays: A Cultural History*, London: Routledge and Kegan Paul.

—— (1961), *The Malay Magician: Being Shaman, Saiva and Sufi*, London: Routledge & Kegan Paul.

Wright, Barbara S. (1980), 'Wayang Siam: An Ethnographic Study of the Malay Shadow Play of Kelantan', Ph.D dissertation, Yale University.

—— (1981), 'Islam and the Malay Shadow Play', *Asian Folklore Studies*, 40: 51–63.

Zakaria Ali (1994), *Islamic Art in Southeast Asia 830 AD–1570 AD*, Kuala Lumpur: Dewan Bahasa dan Pustaka.

Zieseniss, A. (1963), *The Rama Saga in Malaysia*, Singapore: Malaysian Sociological Research Institute.

Index

Q

R

S

T

U

V

W

Y

Z

Picture Credits

A. Kasim Abas, p. 78, Rama and Sita. **Abdul Razak Aziz**, p. 123, Abdul Razak Aziz. **Actors Studio**, pp. 110–1, The Trees. **Adam Ariel**, p. 6, Indian classical dance; p. 86, *nagasvaram* player, *mridanga* drums player; pp. 106–7, contemporary dance; p. 115, Ramli Ibrahim. **Ahmad Sarji**, p. 56, Siput Sarawak; p. 117, Rubiah, Normadiah, Nona Asiah, Lena, P. Ramlee; pp. 128–129, scene from Ahmad Albab; p. 129, Saloma; p. 130, P. Ramlee in Penarek Becha, Phani Majumdar; p. 131, the late Tunku Abdul Rahman with Runme Shaw; pp. 132–3, P. Ramlee (all pictures). **Akademi Seni Kebangsaan**, p. 4, Bangsawan; p. 11, Tari Asyik; p. 54, Bangsawan scene; p. 88, Terinai dancers; p. 91, Terinai dance and ensemble; p. 94, modern Mak Yong performance; p. 110, Syed Alwi; p. 115, Urn Piece and Watermelon Juice dances; p. 125, Terinai dance class, Bangsawan, adaptation of A Midsummer's Night Dream; p. 126, puppet making; p. 143, characters from A Midsummer's Night Dream. **Anban Press**, p. 113, scene from Drohi, Kulothunga Cholan poster. **Anderson, Peter**, p. 45, Melanau dancers **Anuar bin Abdul Rahim**, pp. 26–7, the Wayang Kulit Siam theatre; p. 102, Zapin musical instruments. **Ariff Ahmad**, p. 85, Ghazal performance, Ghazal singer. **Arkib Negara Malaysia**, p. 88, Joget Gamelan; p. 104, early 20th century Borea performance; p. 116, P. Ramlee at EMI recording studio; p. 117, Momo Latiff, Irama cover; p. 134, inauguration of Television Malaysia; p. 141, early Bangsawan theatre. **Benjamin, Geoffrey**, p. 37, Temiar ritual séance; p. 62, healing ceremony; p. 71, man playing jaw's harp, woman playing flute. **Budayasari Dance Theatre**, p. 109, scene from *Dalam Kehadiran Sofea*. **Cadman, M. C.**, p. 44, Murut dancers. **Chai Kah Yune**, p. 1, Malay man playing musical instrument; p. 5, Menora dancer; p. 12, Malay *keris*; p. 16, Awang Batil masks; p. 32, Chinese puppet's facial features; pp. 38–9, Mak Yong costumes; pp. 42–3, Menora Dance of the Master, costume and tail-piece; p. 53, Chinese opera mask; p. 55, Bangsawan costumes, stage backdrops; p. 58, Chinese opera actors' painted faces; p. 92, Nobat instruments; p. 94, Long Abdul Ghaffar; pp. 94–5, Mak Yong dance movements; p. 95, Kampung Temenggung gateway; p. 99, Kuda Kepang dancers, peacock-lion mask; p. 138, Chinese opera painted face. **Chauly, Bernice**, p. 10, shadow puppet; p. 22, Wayang Kulit Siam shadow play; p. 28, Dalang Dollah; p. 38, Menghadap rebab dance (all pictures); p. 40, Minangkabau costume, *rebab* player; p. 41, Randai play and music; p. 42, Menora performer applying makeup; p. 43, Menora stage; pp.60–1, Mak Yong ritual theatre, clown; p. 79, modern Wayang Kulit musicians. **Cheong Lin Poo**, p. 49, Passage of South and Spring dances. **Chong Kah Leong**, p. 77, making of *sapeh*. **Crock, Robert**, p. 126, Hamlet. **Cultural Centre, Universiti Malaya**, p. 14, Dikir Barat; p. 20, *pantun* competition; p. 36, Orang Asli contemporary costumes; p. 41, Randai dancers; p. 45, Mangiluk dancers; p. 47, Asli dance, Tarian Payung, Kipas and Selendang; p. 82, Portuguese dancers; p. 83, Asli music singers; p. 86, sitar player, p. 98, Dabus dancers, *anak dabus* piercing; p. 100, Dikir Barat Kelantan, Nasyid; p. 104, contemporary Borea; p. 105, modern Borea skit; p. 108, Megat Terawis, Kerusi; p. 109, Syajar, Fitrah dan Takdir; p. 127, students of Mak Yong, student performances, rehearsals; p. 137, Randai performance. **Dama Orchestra**, pp. 106–7, Dama ensemble; p. 120, Dama Orchestra; p. 121, *liuqin* player. **Dewan Bahasa dan Pustaka**, p. 9, Raja Lawak; p. 108, Raja Lawak; p. 109, Yang Menjelma dan Menghilang, Tok Perak. **Dewan Filharmonik PETRONAS (DFP)**, p. 122, Datuk Ooi Chean See; pp. 122-3, Malaysian Philharmonic Orchestra. **EDM Archives**, p. 8, Bangsawan theatre; p. 10, shadow puppet; p. 12, Pak Dogol, Sang Yang Tunggal; p. 18, Bidayuh storytelling; p. 24, Balinese, Javanese and Thai shadow puppets; p. 25, Jayadrata and Seri Rama puppets; p. 26, early Wayang Kulit theatre; p. 45, Murut dancers; p. 46, Malay folk dance; pp. 52–3, Chinese opera; p. 58, female and clown characters; p. 59, 19th century Chinese opera costume; pp. 68–9, Orang Asli with musical instruments; p. 70, Orang Asli playing nose flute and stick zither, Orang Asli with fiddles; p. 71, bamboo plants, zither, flute, jaw's harp; p. 72, children playing *gendang silat*; p. 73, *rebani ubi*; p. 79, early Wayang Kulit musicians, Wayang Kulit puppet; pp. 88–9, Malay gamelan ensemble; p. 93, Terengganu Nobat players, Balai Nobat; p. 95, Cik Kemala; p. 96, Sepoy regiment; p. 105, Borea procession; p. 110, Penang Amateur Dramatic Society; p. 128, P. Ramlee. **Fallander, Mark**, p. 59, Chinese opera's stylized movements. **Five Arts Centre**, p. 111, Yap Ah Loy; p. 123, Rhythm in Bronze ensemble, Sunetra Fernando; p. 125, Teater Muda, Scorpion Orchid. **Fong, P. K.**, p. 74, Kayan woman chieftain; p. 75, Kayans singing; p. 76, Jaw's harp, Penan *engkerurai* player, man playing *sapeh*. **Gallery of Colour**, p. 6, Wayang Kulit; p. 7, Chinese opera; p. 22, Chinese puppet theatre; pp. 34–5, Chinese dancer; p. 44, Datun Julud dancer; p. 87, Bhangra performer; p. 99, Kuda Kepang performers. **George Chiew**, p. 45, Ngajat dancers. **Ghazali Basri**, p. 101, Berzanji. **Ghulam-Sarwar Yousof**, p. 7, Menora dancers; p. 8, Terinai dance master; p. 10, Mak Yong dancers, animism, Wayang Kulit and Mak Yong theatre; p. 11, Barongan, Hadrah theatre; p. 12, Mek Mulung opening ritual; p. 13, shaman, *angin* pictures (all pictures); p. 15, Awang Batil storyteller; p. 16, Awang Batil masks; p. 17, Tarik Selampit singer, Pak Mahmud, *batil*; p. 23, Monkey God shadow puppet, Wayang Kulit Gedek puppet; p. 24, *pohon beringin* puppet; p. 26, spirit offerings; p. 28, Hamzah Awang; p. 29, puppeteer; p. 30, *pohon beringin* puppet, Wayang Kulit Purwa and Gedek puppets; p. 31, puppet close-up, Wayang Kulit Melayu performance and ensemble; p. 34, Mak Yong dance theatre; p. 39, Mak Yong body language; p. 42, Menora theatre opening ritual, masked performer; p. 43, Penang style Menora; p. 50, Karagattam dance; p. 52, Jikey; p. 55, Jikey character and performance; p. 56, Alias Manan; pp. 60–1, initiating the rebab, ritual Mak Yong theatre, *balai tiang empat puluh*, offerings, Main Puteri; p. 61, Pak Yong; p. 62, Main Puteri healing and trance sessions; p. 63, Bagih healing ritual; p. 64, Mak Yong cleansing ritual and graduation, Khatijah Awang in ritual performance; p. 65, Cik Ning, Dewa Muda performance; p. 66, cleansing ritual; p. 67, Wayang Kulit Siam ritual; p. 68, shadow puppet theatre; p. 69, *gendang* drum; p. 73, *kertuk kelapa* ensemble; p. 80, Mak Yong ensemble, *jong dondang*; p. 81, Mek Mulung; p. 89, Mak Yong performer; p. 94, Seri Temenggung performance; p. 95, Khatijah Awang, Zainab binti Samad, Kumpulan Seri Temenggung performances; p. 96, Dikir Labah; p. 97, new Wayang Kulit puppets; p. 100, Mak Yong singers, Dabus performance; p. 101, Marhaban singers; p. 126, new Wayang Kulit forms. **Goh Seng Chong**, p. 11, Wayang Kulit Purwa puppets; p. 82, Ronggeng ensemble; p. 90, gamelan ensemble; p. 98, *gambus* player. **Gonzales, Joseph**, p. 9, contemporary dance; p. 114, AWAS!. **HBL Network Photo Agency (M) Sdn. Bhd.**, p. 9, vinyl records; p. 32, Chinese glove puppets; p. 33, glove puppet theatre; p. 85, young Ghazal troupe competition; p. 107, vinyl record; pp. 116–7, record labels and sleeves; p. 121, *huayue tuan* instruments. **Indah Klasik**, p. 129, P. Ramlee movie posters; p. 132, Sarimah; p. 133, P. Ramlee movie posters. **Istana Budaya**, p. 106, Ronggeng Rokiah; p. 124, National Theatre, Alang Rentak Seribu, Raja Tangkai Hati, Geeta

Gangsa poster; pp. 124–5, Mohram. **Jabatan Kebudayaan dan Kesenian Kedah**, p. 52, Bangsawan theatre; p. 54, Bangsawan death scene. **Jabatan Kebudayaan Perlis**, p. 47, Canggung. **Jabatan Ketua Menteri Melaka**, p. 82, traditional folk dance; p. 83, Dondang Sayang singers. **Jabatan Muzium dan Antikuiti Malaysia**, p. 31, Nik Abdul Rahman. **Jamil Sulong**, p. 131, Ranjau Sepanjang Jalan poster. **Johor Newsletter**, p. 84, S.A. Aishah. **Kee Thuan Chye**, p. 9, The Cord; p. 110, We Could **** You Mr Birch, The Battle of Coxinga, Antigone poster; p. 126, Narukami play. **Kelantan State Government**, p. 21, Dikir Barat; p. 72, Gendang silat ensemble; pp. 96–7, Dikir Barat. **Koh, Steven**, p. 48, Street Opera in Harvest. **Lee Sin Bee**, p. 66, offering for Sita Dewi; pp. 66–7, Wayang Kulit Siam performers. **Lee Swee Keong**, p. 114, A Cherry Bludgeoned, A Spirit Crushed. **Lim Joo**, pp. 14–5, storytelling in the longhouse; p. 18, giant; p. 19, legends of Nunuk Ragang and Nunuk Taragang; p. 33, Chinese puppets, Chinese puppet musical ensemble; pp. 36–7, Mah Meri dancers; p. 65, Dewa Muda story; p. 67, Wayang Kulit Siam musical instruments; p. 73, making of *rebab*; p. 78, Wayang Kulit Melayu ensemble; pp. 80–1, Jikey ensemble; p. 103, Zapin Melayu dance steps; pp. 120–1, Chinese orchestra. **Matusky, Patricia**, p. 18, Punan Bah singers; p. 21, Kenyah-Badang soloist; p. 73, Gendang tarinai; p. 74, wa solo singer. **Matusky, Patricia & Tan Sooi Beng**, p. 93, excerpt from 'Berlayar'. **Melaka Minggu Ini**, p. 82, Branyo dance. **Mew Chang Tsing**, p. 48, Chinese dance techniques (all pictures), Hang Li Po dance; p. 49, *selendang* dance; p. 114, Re: Lady White Snake. **Ministry of Information**, p. 90, Joget Gamelan. **Mohd Yunus Noor**, p. 24, Semar puppet. **Munan, Heidi**, p. 19, audience at storytelling. **Museum Orang Asli (Jabatan Hal Ehwal Orang Asli)**, p. 35, Orang Asli dancers; p. 70, proto-Malay ensemble; p. 71, women playing zithers, Orang Asli with stamping tubes, man playing nose flute. **New Straits Times Press (Malaysia) Berhad**, p. 84, Fadzil Ahmad, Ahmad Jusoh; p. 88, Terengganu royal orchestra; p. 91, Asyik dancers; p. 92, Terengganu Nobat drum; p. 95, Abdullah Supang; pp. 104–5, modern Borea; p. 117, P. Ramlee. **Ng Ken Liong**, p. 32, string puppets. **Nicholas, Colin**, p. 71, river scene. **Office of D. Y. M. M. Paduka Seri Sultan Perak**, p. 92, Nobat orchestra. **Penang Players**, p. 106, scene from The Miser; p. 111, Six Characters in Search of an Author. **Penang State Huayue Orchestra**, p. 120, Penang state *huayue tuan*. **Perbadanan Kemajuan Filem Nasional Malaysia**, p. 130, Selubung, Bukit Kepong. **Pesona Pictures**, p. 128, *Layar Lara*; p. 130, *Ringgit Kasorga*; p. 131, *Layar Lara* poster. **PETRONAS Art Collection**, p. 8, traditional theatre cartoon. **Picture Library Sdn. Bhd.**, p. 8, Tarian Lilin; p. 46, Joget; p. 47, Tarian Lilin; p. 70, Orang Asli boy with *rebana*, Temiar; p. 72, *kompang* group; p. 100, Qur'an recitation. **Planet Films Malaysia**, p. 127, Masters of Tradition video cassette cover. **Pos Malaysia Berhad**, p. 69, instrument stamps. **Positive Tone**, p. 118, Too Phat. **Prem K. Pasha**, p. 130, L. Krishnan; p. 131, Tun Tijah poster. **Professional Cultural Centre Orchestra**, p. 120, orchestra. **Pugh-Kitingan, Jacqueline**, p. 74, *tutubik* rattler; p. 75, Kadazdusun high priestess, *bobohizan* chanting ritual, *libabou* and *tantagas* ritual dancing; p. 76, *sompoton*, gong ensemble, hanging gongs, xylophone and gongs; p. 77, woman playing zither, man playing double-stringed lute. **Radin Mohd Noh Saleh**, p. 3, *pohon beringin* puppet; p. 68, sitar player. **Radio Television Malaysia (RTM)**, p. 122, RTM Orchestra; p. 135, Abdullah Zainol, PJ and Panggung RTM scenes. **Rahman B.**, p. 53, Bujangga poster; p. 54, Nooran Opera troupe; p. 56, Ainon Chick, Aman Belon, Rahman B.; pp. 56–7, Istana Iman poster; p. 57, Megat Teraweh scene; Bintang Timur chorus girls. **Raja Morgan**, p. 113, Vivekanandar, Manivasagar, Reh Shanmugam, Vijayasinggam, Suhan Panchatcharam, Reh Sha. Ananthan. **Ravi John Smith**, p. 11, *gambus* player; p. 35, Indian classical dancers; p. 40, *silat*; p. 116, gramophone. **Regis, Patricia**, p. 14, ritual chanting; p. 20, Runsay; p. 74, *mangahau-rumaha* ceremony; p. 75, women performing *menidong*. **Ringis, John**, p. 25, Thai mural. **Ronni Pinsler**, p. 140, Chinese opera. **Sarawak Museum**, p. 35, Sarawak traditional dancer; p. 44, Bidayuh ritual dance; p. 76, nose flute player; p. 77, man making *sapeh*. **Sarawak Tourism Board**, p. 77, Rainforest Music Festival. **Shafie bin Haji Hassan**, p. 78, *gendang* and *serunai* craftsmen. **Shekar, S. C.**, p. 24, Malaysia shadow puppet; p. 26, coloured shadow puppets; p. 27, Wayang Kulit orchestra; p. 28, perforating puppets; pp. 28–9, Wayang Kulit characters; p. 29, villager puppet; p. 34, Indian folk dance; p. 50, Indian folk dance, Bhangra; pp. 50–1, Swan Lake; p. 51, Bharata Natyam, Odissi dancers; p. 67, Betara Kala and damsel puppets; p. 79, Wayang Kulit Siam musical instruments (all); p. 87, Temple of Fine Arts orchestra. **Soon Choon Mee**, p. 112, Shall We Off...?, Chinese drama of the 1970s, Hang Li Po poster, Hui Niang Goes to School. **Sovereign Enterprise**, pp. 92–3, Selangor Nobat. **Star Publications (M) Bhd.**, p. 8, Ella; p. 14–5, Dondang Sayang singers; p. 21, Dikir Barat; p. 82–3, Dondang Sayang, female singers in *kebaya*; pp. 98–9, children performing Dikir Barat; p. 101, Hijjaz, Rabbani; p. 106, rock band; p.107, contemporary dance performer; p. 110, Edward Dorall, K. Das; p. 114, Lee Lee Lan, Mohammad Ghouse Nasuruddin, Oh Eng Sim, Frances Teoh; p. 115, Marion D'Cruz, Lari Leong; p. 118, Sheila Majid, Andre Goh, Siti Nurhaliza, Sharifah Aini, Francisca Peters, The Blues Gang, S. M. Salim, Sudirman; p. 119, Asiabeat, Lefthanded, Hang Mokhtar, M. Nasir, Manan Ngah, Zainal Abidin, Raihan; p. 123, Gus Steyn, Johari Salleh, Valerie Ross, Tan Su Lian; p. 135, Johan Jaafar. **Syed Alwi**, p. 110 Henry V scene. **Tan Chien Li**, p. 110, Lee Joo For. **Tan Hong Yew**, p. 12, Mak Yong dancers; p. 24, Southeast Asia map; p. 63, Main Puteri healing ritual; p. 122, Dewan Filharmonik Petronas. **Tan Lian Hock**, pp. 22–3, shadow puppet play. **Tan Sooi Beng**, p. 55, Bangsawan orchestra; p. 56, Minah Alias, Mahmud Jun, Mat Arab, Rahim B. & Rohani B.; p. 57, The Silver Mask poster. **Temple of Fine Arts**, p. 51, Kathakali, hand gestures; pp. 86–87, classical music ensemble, folk music ensemble, CD, *tavil* player; p. 90, Joget Gamelan movements; p. 125, Butterfly Lovers CD; p. 127, Umesh Shetty. **The Asian Centre, Penang**, p. 32, Chinese rod puppets; p. 33, children watching puppet play. **Tommy Chang Image Productions**, p. 21, Daling–daling dance; p. 44, Sumazau performers; p. 45, Sumayau Lotud; Cocos Islanders dance; p. 68, Lobou Murut at ritual ceremony; p. 74, Kadazandusun *bobilian*. **Trustees of the British Museum**, p. 28, Awang Lah. **Trustees of the Prince of Wales Museum of Western India**, p. 87, painting of drummer. **TV3 (Sistem Television Malaysia Bhd.)**, p. 128, sitcoms Cili Padi and Senario; p. 134, dramas Hilang and Rumah Kedai; p. 135, Antik, 2+1 and Jangan Ketawa, shooting of Senario. **Wong Kit Yaw**, p. 48, children's dance; p. 49, contemporary Chinese dance. **Yap Eng Huat**, p. 81, Mek Mulung instruments. **Yayasan Warisan Johor**, p. 6, Zapin dancer; p. 46, Zapin; p. 83, contemporary Keroncong; p. 84, handwritten Ghazal compositions, Ghazal Johor ensemble, Talib Ahmad; pp. 84–5, junior Ghazal groups; p. 85, CD cover; p. 96, Kuda Kepang; pp. 96–7, young Zapin dancers; p. 102, Zapin; pp. 102–3, Zapin performers; p. 103, children performing Zapin, CD cover. **Yeap Kok Chien**, p. 16, Tarik Selampit, Awang Batil and Selampit performers; p. 17, theatre opening ritual; p. 39, Mak Yong hand gestures; p. 55, opera tent; p. 59, Chinese opera hairdressing technique; p. 63, shaman with rattan leaves. **You Jae Ryuk/ TheimageAsia.com**, p. 11, Malay dancers; p. 28, man making shadow play puppet; p. 34, Malay and Indian dancers; p. 44, Ngajat dancer; p. 58, male and painted face characters; pp. 58–9, Chinese opera.

An adaptation of A Midsummer's Night Dream.